T0301602

The Foundations of Austrian Economics from Menger to Mises

Other books by the author

The Making of Marx's Critical Theory: a Bibliographical Analysis, 1983.

Marx's Critique of Political Economy: Intellectual Sources and Evolution, two volumes, 1984 and 1985.

Essays in Political Economics: Public Control in a Democratic Society, by Adolph Lowe, edited with an Introduction by Allen Oakley, 1987.

Schumpeter's Theory of Capitalist Motion: a Critical Exposition and Reassessment, 1990.

Classical Economic Man: Human Agency and Methodology in the Political Economy of Adam Smith and J.S. Mill, 1994.

The Foundations of Austrian Economics from Menger to Mises

A Critico-Historical Retrospective of Subjectivism

Allen Oakley

The University of Newcastle, Australia

Edward Elgar
Cheltenham, UK • Lyme, US

Published by
Edward Elgar Publishing Limited
8 Lansdown Place
Cheltenham
Glos GL50 2HU
UK

Edward Elgar Publishing, Inc.
1 Pinnacle Hill Road
Lyme
NH 03768
US

A catalogue record for this book
is available from the British Library

Library of Congress Cataloguing in Publication Data

Oakley, Allen.
    The foundations of Austrian economics from Menger to Mises : a
critico-historical retrospective of subjectivism / Allen Oakley.
    Includes bibliographical references and index.
    1. Austrian school of economists.   2. Menger, Carl, 1840–1921.
    3. Von Mises, Ludwig, 1881–1973.   4. Subjectivity.   I. Title.
    HB98.025 1997
    330.15'7—dc21   97–12120
                                                           CIP

ISBN 1 85898 308 8

Printed and bound in Great Britain by
Biddles Limited, Guildford and King's Lynn

For Renate

Contents

Preface

This study stems from my profound sense of dissatisfaction with the vision and methodology that are dominant in the orthodox and much of the heterodox economics literature. Common sense suggests that economics should be a science that gives priority to the origin of the things that it studies in the exigencies of human action. Paradoxically for outsiders, at least, a glance at any piece of economic analysis that meets the standards of scientistic formalism that is demanded in so much of the discipline reveals that there is precious little about human agents *qua* human beings. And yet when pressed, many authors of such pieces would agree with the self-evident observation that human agency is, as a matter of fact, the most essential element in the generation of the phenomena about which they have written. In spite of this, whatever else they may believe about their work, the immediate demands of being published lock these authors into methodological and epistemological preconditions that force them to side-step the intractabilities of human agency.

My decision to devote a period of critical research effort to Austrian subjectivism is a direct consequence of, and reflects precisely, the dissatisfaction expressed in the above preamble. I do not like very much the free-market, 'survival-of-the-fittest' ideology that has become identified with most Austrian economists and their literature. Indeed, I think it arguable that the very nature of their subjectivist and individualist principles, when fully understood, call for much more market intervention by governments in the interests of individual and social efficacy and equity than they would allow. In a modern capitalist economy, markets are for the most part not sufficiently competitive for their freedom to be justified on this criterion. And, more generally, whatever claims are made about their competitiveness, market failure is widespread to varying degrees. But such matters will be found to be not immediately relevant to what I have attempted to do in this study; at least it will be to readers who are prepared to see past these dimensions of the Austrian economic identity. My emphasis is on the fact that the Austrians and their modern Neo-Austrian followers have been among the only economics specialists who have adopted and pursued the working principle that economics is a human science. This is to their credit and warrants due recognition. What the founding Austrians did with this principle was, as I set out to show here, quite inadequate to address the deficiencies of the classical and neoclassical orthodoxies that emerged during their era. In particular, their subjectivist ontology did not go far enough to allow them fully to transcend the imposed constraints of *homo oeconomicus*.

The potential of the Austrian alternative, nonetheless, is bound up with its giving logical priority to establishing the subjectivist ontology of human agency before considering the consistent methodological requirements for theory development. This reverses the usual procedure that has come to dominate in all forms of instrumentalist economics. In the latter, enforced object simplification, including the way of representing human agents, is a condition of meeting the stringent demands of naturalist and formalist predilections. The reversal of the instrumentalist priority shifts our focus to the origins of economic phenomena as the products of human agency. Human agency, that is, as a balance of volition, contingency and containment in the deliberations and decisions of agents consequent upon their nature, nurture and situation. In this study, I set out to discover the extent to which the two key founders of Austrian subjectivism, Carl Menger and Ludwig von Mises, were able to realize the potential of their methodology in this sense. What is evident from my juxtaposed consideration of other subjectivist philosophers of the period is that both Austrians fell far short of realizing in economics the achievements of their contemporaries in the human sciences.

A significant part of the research for this study was carried out while I was on leave from The University of Newcastle, Australia during 1994–95. Much of this leave was spent in the Institut für Wirtschaftswissenschaften of the University of Vienna. I am grateful to Karl Milford and all members of the Institut, and to the staff of its fine Library, for their hospitality and assistance during my stay.

Allen Oakley,
Medowie, Australia

1. Introduction

1.1 Preamble

In the history of economic thought, the serious recognition and treatment of metatheoretical foundations emphasizing subjectivism and
individualism have come to be identified almost exclusively with the
work of Austrian economists. This is readily apparent in the now extensive secondary literature of the various strands of neo-Austrian
economics that claim adherence to the legacy of their Austrian founders.
Alex Shand's popular summary of Austrian methodology announces
that 'Austrians are subjectivists' and that subjectivism is seen in their
'prevailing attitude to all social phenomena' (1980, pp. 11, 12). That the
idea has been of profound significance for economics in general was
emphasized by Friedrich Hayek in his often-quoted claim that 'it is
probably no exaggeration to say that every important advance in economic theory during the last hundred years was a further step in the
consistent application of subjectivism' (1955, p. 31). Our attitudes
towards these references to subjectivism, as it is pursued by those
claiming an Austrian heritage, should depend crucially upon what we
believe constitutes the full scope of the idea and its proper application.
Comments such as Shand's to the effect that while 'no two Austrians
have ever completely agreed on methodology, there does seem to have
been broad agreement on the basic concept – subjectivism' do not help
much in this respect (1980, p. 13). It is especially challenging to reflect
upon what any particular meaning for subjectivism would lead us to
expect from its 'consistent application' to an understanding of economic
phenomena. Such reflection potentially drives a wedge between subjectivism as a generalized metatheoretical doctrine and the particulars of
its various neo-Austrian interpretations.

The issue thus posed, and that to be addressed at length in my
inquiries, concerns the extent to which these interpretations should be
taken to define the limits of the idea as it affects economics. My argument will be that any assessment of the treatment of subjectivism extant
in the works of Neo-Austrians should take account of the intellectual
foundations upon which they based their ideas. It will become apparent
from the exegetical evidence to be elicited in the present retrospective

study of these foundations that they cannot be taken as definitive
once the fullest extent of the status and meaning of subjectivism are
explicated. Indeed, some of the founding works reveal an effective
endeavour to side-step what were perceived to be the more extreme
and assumed destructive implications of the idea. The emergence of
subjectivism in economics and the accompanying fear of nihilistic outcomes has, according to Don Lavoie, 'provoked the Austrians into some
of their more dubious efforts to separate theory from history, and to
construct an objectivist, aprioristic, ahistorical foundation for economic
theory' (1991, p. 472). The critique that I document below indicates that
the founding subjectivist platforms of both Carl Menger (1840–1921)
and Ludwig von Mises (1881–1973), the main Austrians in focus here,
have suffered to some degree from the effects of an intellectual world
that expected all science to emulate the rigours of physics. As a result,
in their own different ways and degrees, 'even as they insisted that
the subject-matter of economics was subjective, [they] tried to make the
science of economics objective, and insulate it from that subjectivity'.
What is usually assumed to be the most blatant strategy of 'driving a
wedge between theory and history' in the attempt came in 'Mises's
aprioristic methodology [which] can be seen as an awkward move forced
by the need for a declaration of scientific objectivity' (Lavoie, 1991,
pp. 479, 480). These are strong words that later on I will find require
some qualification. This having been said, the sentiments expressed in
such an observation should be applied as much to the work of Menger
as to that of Mises.

Neo-Austrians make pervasive references to the merits of subjectivism as the essential grounding for substantive economic argument.
They have, in general as a result, taken a consistent stance against the
two most prominent methodological positions adopted in economics.
They have rejected the instrumentalist approach to theory construction
and assessment, with its emphasis on formalism of expression and predictive expectations. At the same time, they have not been prepared to
follow out the descriptive empiricism that is given primacy by insti-
tutionalists and others with similar roots in historicism. What is needed,
according to the Neo-Austrians, is a revision of economics so that it
is grounded in subjectivism and individualism, with emphasis on the
processes of human agency. Now it is readily apparent that these observations beg the question. There is no hint yet that subjectivism has
meant and means different things to different economists claiming membership of the group. Bruce Caldwell draws attention to the contention
that surrounds this core notion of 'Austrianness': 'A familiarity with the
old debates is crucial to an understanding of the development of Aus-

trian thought [and] knowledge about them is necessary if one is to make an informed judgement on the issues.' It may be apt, he continues, to argue that 'all Austrians are well described as subjectivists. But it does little to advance the very live debate within the Austrian camp as to what it *means* to be a subjectivist'. He concludes that 'until these matters are clarified, the claims and counter-claims of various Austrian subjectivists will be extremely difficult to adjudicate' (1991, p. 489; original emphasis).

The historical study of subjectivism that I pursue below comprises two perspectives that take up aspects of Caldwell's challenge. The first objective of my inquiries is to re-examine the endeavours of Carl Menger as the founding Austrian dedicated to the development of defensible subjectivist principles on which economic analyses could be grounded. My inquiries later shift to the most prominent inheritor of Menger's subjectivist legacy, Ludwig von Mises. Menger's immediate successors, Eugen von Böhm-Bawerk (1851–1914) and Friedrich von Wieser (1851–1926) found the mantle of subjectivism ill-fitting and, for the most part, preferred not to wear it. It was Mises who was mainly responsible for carrying Austrian subjectivist foundations into the twentieth century. And, it was his controversial ideas that formed the epicentre of the subsequent critical evolution of neo-Austrian subjectivism and the divergent strands of its revival in the 1970s and beyond. The second perspective pursued in my study is a re-assessment of the cognate subjectivist themes that existed in the broader context of the philosophies of history and the human sciences as these developed alongside, but largely independently of what Menger was doing. The comparative study of these chronologically juxtaposed intellectual developments will expose the origins of a number of particular characteristics and limitations that became lodged in the methodological position defended by Mises. Neo-Austrian subjectivist economists of all hues have had to wrestle with this complex Menger–Mises legacy and have variously endeavoured to mitigate its limitations or dialectically to build upon its strengths. The result has been the rise of a number of unsettled controversies about what it means to be a Neo-Austrian in economics. It is my preference to link such economics to the particular metatheory of subjectivism and ontological individualism that I will identify as having been present in a number of sources from Menger onwards. These sources can be shown to have had sufficient in common to have enabled Mises to represent subjectivism as a loosely defined set of *nascent* principles of human action primed for subsequent development.

My intention in pursuing this critico-retrospective inquiry is to reveal an image of subjectivism and individualism with all the human vitality that was originally associated with these ideas. Such vitality can be identified in the original contributions of Menger and ultimately in the legacy of Mises. It is intended to expose the very real contributions that early Austrian and German developments in subjectivist metatheory had the potential to make to an economics that is more obviously conscious of the irreducibly human dimensions of its substantive objects. And, for all their limitations and disagreements, Neo-Austrians who have been reacting to the work of Mises are among the few who explicitly treat economics as primarily a human science and are prepared to give due recognition to the resulting distinctive metatheoretical implications and demands. They have been prepared to argue that its methodology has quite different characteristics from those that can be encompassed within the naive positivism and instrumentalism of the physical sciences as these have been adopted by orthodox economics. And, they have correctly maintained the additional concern to preserve the ontological insight that all economic phenomena are the consequence of individual, but situationally conditioned and directed, subjective human actions. In doing so, they have mostly put realist ontological consistency of discursive representation before the demands of scientism and formalism. That their endeavours have been incomplete in these respects should not be allowed to detract from the fact that they have confronted and taken such awkward fundamental issues seriously.

1.2 Defining subjectivism and individualism

Whereas there can be no unique meaning given to the concept of subjectivism and to its complement individualism, I should indicate explicitly the general principles that will be guiding my present retrospective inquiries. In the efforts of dictionary writers to give some definition to the concept of subjectivism, two tenets pertinent to its use in economics are apparent (cf. Hutchison, 1994, p. 189). One is that the intended focus of subjectivism is on the mental and cognitive processes of the human subject that mediate in giving meaning to external objects. Perception and knowledge about, and value assessments of, the object world are thus limited by and relative to the human self. Real objects have a resulting dual existence for subjectivism: they have particular independent and existential qualities and quantitative dimensions, and they have a dependent and evaluated meaning for human beings who perceive them. This is the principle that underpins the familiar subjective theory of economic value adopted by Menger from some of his German and Austrian antecedents.

The other and consequent tenet of subjectivism is that such a perspective leads us to consider human subjects primarily as particular individuals with a certain given mental and cognitive constitution. Subjectivism, then, relates directly to human beings as *homo sapiens*, the only extant member of the species *homo* that has the capacity for wisdom implied by the appellation *sapiens*. But, human beings have also proved themselves as having an additional capacity of immediate concern to economists: that is the capacity *to act with self-interest and purpose* towards their environment in the light of their wisdom, as implied by their equally applicable identification as *homo agens* (cf. Mises, 1966, p. 14). This additional innate quality of human beings is significant in defining subjectivism in economics because it directs our attention to those particular actions that have deliberated and purposeful character and that originate in self-conscious, reasoned decisions and choices. All actions are not of this kind, but only actions of this character constitute the origin of phenomena of concern to economics.

In this sense, economic agents are envisaged by subjectivists as pursuing the satisfaction of their hierarchy of needs and wants by means of interacting with their environment. Where such needs and wants originate, in human biology and/or in human society, was a matter of debate. The resources available for achieving such satisfaction are scarce relative to demand for them in the case of human actions relevant to economics. Agents must deliberate and make choices on the basis of their interpretation and understanding of the environment that they confront. Whatever may be the limitations of this understanding that come from lack of information and/or shortcomings of the agents' cognitive capacities, their actions as individuals are to be understood as the result of the meaning *they* attribute to the environment and to the *telos* of the pursuit of *their* objectives.

The effect of such definitional essentials as just outlined is to give subjectivism the status of a general principle of human science and to separate it from the pseudo-subjectivism of the orthodox microeconomic analyses that rose to prominence after the 1870s. Such orthodoxy has the human being modelled as *homo oeconomicus*, a puppet-like being who mechanically responds to preferences and circumstances with logically rational conduct that is entailed by the premises and conditions established by assumptions (cf. Latsis, 1972). Positing different patterns of preferences and positing maximum utility as the singular human objective are not sufficient to render such conduct subjectivist. This pseudo-human character is less than a *homo sapiens* in not really

6

Except in theology, such ontologically oriented 'why' questions that ask for reasons have no place in the physical realm. The dimensions of cognition peculiar to the human sciences that follow from these observations are usually summarized under the objective of *Verstehen*. Inquiry about human phenomena, including those of economics, involves a process that leads to an *understanding* that has contingent characteristics stemming from exigencies of human nature that are not found in physical explanations. This is why subjectivists do not accept the immediate application of physical science methodology or its epistemological standards to investigations concerning human activity. All science has a place for observation in establishing what is *there* to be explained. And, the rules of logic and consistency of argument are fundamental to all scientific exposition. Nevertheless, in the case of the human sciences, the ontology of its phenomena is so distinctive as to require an independent effort to devise suitable methodological principles and realistic epistemological expectations. In this connection, there can be no avoiding the need for analysts to apply introspectively derived insight to the process of achieving *Verstehen*. As we are to see, the real challenge for subjectivists, including Menger and Mises, was to keep the role of introspection, and psychology more generally, in perspective by understanding their important functions and, at the same time, recognizing their limitations as means of eliciting knowledge about why particular human events occur. For the analyst as the observing subject of such events, extrapolations from self-knowledge to the object world cannot be avoided. In the human sciences, that is, analysts have an 'insider's view' of the formation of actions and their results that are not available to analysts observing nature. The temptation is to use this advantage in constituting knowledge.

A crucial concern here is the capacity of human beings to be creative, so that there will be no unique correspondence between any existential situation and a particular agent's action response to it. In a strict sense, then, it is an impossible task for the analyst to break into the mental constitution of another agent. But it is, nevertheless, the task that actually confronts human scientists bent on understanding what human agents do. Economists and others who intend to understand and explain human phenomena are required to make some defensible endeavour to resolve the problems thus posed. Indeed, the objective formalism imposed on economic action by the invention of *homo oeconomicus* may be seen as a way of avoiding the issue altogether. Another means of doing so is behaviourism that attributes understanding to observation of action alone. This may well give some purpose to the experimental study of human action, or its animal substitutes, but it inclines investigators to isolate their conclusions from the mental and cognitive processes that precede action. Subjectivism demands that analysts do better than this.

One alternative for actually confronting the objective of understanding human action is to treat it as the joint product of individual characteristics and the situational environment in which it takes place. The idea is to steer a middle course between the existential autonomy and contingent potential of human agency and the determinism that comes with extreme versions of functionalist and structuralist interpretations. The environment is envisaged as having multiple dimensions, but most importantly it has the overall quality of being shared by the agent with others. Particular problematic conditions may, as a consequence, be responded to by agents in a manner that has some delimited common and regularized pattern. This expectation is attributable to their need to utilize the facilities and recognize the constraints of the environment that they inherit and through which they are obligated to act. Otherwise contingent actions are thus directed and shaped into an essentially common form in accordance with the problem faced and the situational conditions within which it is resolved. Even the meaning agents ascribe to all the relevant outside things involved may have a common socio-cultural foundation for the majority of agents. This approach enables the subjectivist economist potentially to get beyond the relativism that may appear inevitable if the analysis requires the replication of other agents' mental processes. No more is needed than the reasonable psychological assumption that there is a core sense in which all human minds, those of the observer and the observed, function in a cognitively common manner. That this exists is certified by the fact that so much of what we do as individuals in our daily lives depends upon a mutually accepted interdependence with others. This can only operate successfully because we are able to understand and to depend upon the consistent operation of each other's psyches to some necessary extent.

1.3 The inquiries ahead

In the following chapter, I begin my inquiries with a brief survey of the extant Germanic philosophy of history and human science of the nineteenth century. The Historicists who founded the burgeoning Historical School brought knowledge of the past 'down to earth', as it were, by deviating from the idealist tradition that held dominance at the time. As far as they were concerned, any legitimate inquiry in the world of human phenomena had to give priority to empirical observation and accumulation of factual data. Some allowed a role for theoretical argument on the condition that it was grounded on the results of extensive empirical inquiry. Other Historicists, though, believed that in seeking historical understanding, generalized theory had to be avoided altogether. During this period of empirical historicism, Johann Droysen (1808–84) set out to give history a foundation that explicitly confronted the human ontology of its object phenomena. He argued that history should focus its epistemology on understanding of events as the intelligible and meaningful products of human action. His metahistory thus paved the way towards a subjectivist and individualist approach to the human sciences generally. Alongside these developments in the academic life of Germany itself, there arose in the Austria of the Habsburg Empire a distinctive orientation towards human inquiry that developed independently of and largely in isolation from German influences. There is evidence of a preference in Austrian academia for the scholastic tradition of Aristotelian realism that claimed to understand the reality of human phenomena as the inherently structured and coherent manifestations of relationships between identifiable elements. As I will show in Chapter 2, a number of such strands of philosophy contributed to the intellectual milieu in which subjectivism and individualism developed in the Germanic world. It was Droysen's focus on human action that we find carried through into the subjectivism of Wilhelm Dilthey (1833–1911) in Germany. The Southwest German (Baden) School of Neo-Kantians, especially Wilhelm Windelband (1848–1915) and his student Heinrich Rickert (1863–1936), reacted against Dilthey and their influence, albeit with a strongly dialectical outcome, was felt through the work of Max Weber (1864–1920). The foundations of Austrian subjectivism that are identified in the writings of Carl Menger working in the Austrian philosophical tradition may be linked to his background of German subjectivist and historicist ideas in economics. Later, in the work of Ludwig von Mises, what remained of Menger's subjectivism was passed into the temporarily obscured Austrian tradition in economics. Mises brought Austrian subjectivism to prominence again, but now in a context where the other juxtaposed German philosophical developments took on some importance as critical sources. In this connection, Chapter 2 concludes with some preliminary observations about their situation within these strands of philosophy and subjectivist economics that constituted their intellectual milieu.

Chapter 3 is concerned with Carl Menger. I argue there that endeavours to interpret Menger's epistemology and its methodological consequences that omit ontological inquiries concerning the sort of phenomena on which he focused cannot be considered complete. What such incomplete metatheoretical readings of his work fail to acknowledge in particular is the extent to which he was unable and/or unwilling to allow all of the tenets of subjectivism that he had actually identified, and explicitly made reference to, to enter into his formal analyses without fear or favour. The result, nonetheless, was a theoretical exposition which, for all its imprecisions and incompleteness, tried to capture the essential idea that subjectivist economics is about individual human agency and the *in situ* processes it generates. Menger's focus in his main writings was on the subjective nature and origin of all economic phenomena as the products of individual human decisions, choices and action. He was concerned to understand the *telos* of human agency as it involves the satisfaction of needs and wants and as it concerns the consequent subjective nature of the value of goods and services. He also adapted his subjectivist vision of economics to the problematic of goods production, including the valuation of inputs. Although he made few direct references to matters of ontology in these connections, the arrangement and tenor of his substantive arguments give us sufficient indication of his intentions. I go on to consider Menger's epistemological and methodological intentions as they developed in the construction of his revisionist ontology of economic theory. The mix of exact and realistic-empirical methodological principles he actually defended is outlined and argued to be an outcome demanded by his subjectivist and individualist understanding of economic phenomena. Finally, I propose some critical conclusions about the pertinent issues that remained without conclusive resolution in Menger's work and that his Austrian successors and later neo-Austrian followers were left to wrestle with.

In extending my exposition of the evolution of subjectivism, I turn next in Chapter 4 to the contributions of Menger's German contemporary Wilhelm Dilthey. He was arguably the most significant and original of the early subjectivist philosophers of the human sciences in general and was much influenced by the subjectivist historiography of Droysen. The orientation of his inquiries was very much like that of Droysen, except that he broadened and made more explicit the notion that the phenomena of the human sciences are the expressions, the objectifications, of the lived experiences and actions of individual human agents and can be understood only by rendering them discursively as such. His demand was that due recognition should thus be granted to all their subjective characteristics, along with the real ontological nature of the processes in which they engage and the phenomena they generate. The key experiential preconditioning of the mental processes of human agents come from their cumulative biographies and their situations, duly interpreted. There can be no relevant subjectivism that does not depict the conduct of human agents as bounded and contained by a variety of internal limitations and external situational conditions. Dilthey's concern was to ensure that human scientists are challenged to understand the origins of human phenomena as expressions of the lived experiences manifested in the meaningful, but situationally delimited actions of agents. The objective of *Verstehen* for Dilthey was to be transformed from the focus of historiography into the methodological foundation for inquiries concerned with the theory of human phenomena in general.

My main purpose in Chapter 4, then, is to elicit an ontological foundation for understanding the generation of human phenomena as it was understood by Dilthey. In doing so, he undertook to provide a descriptive psychology of individuals to replace the pseudo-scientific explanatory psychology he encountered in the literature. His idea was to 'get behind' the evidence of observed conduct and its empirico-phenomenal consequences in an effort more fully to understand their mental and cognitive origins. Actors' conduct interests and concerns human science most when it is purposeful and directed at particular objectives. Such actions as result, and the expressions that they generate, involve actors in engaging their situational environments. They transform their inherited conditions in the pursuit of life-world satisfactions. By focusing on their expressions of life, and on the situationally conditioned conduct of agents that generates them, Dilthey was led to shift away from his directly psychological inquiries towards a metatheory directed at understanding expressions. That is, he pursued the objective of *Verstehen* and his work took on an hermeneutical orientation as a consequence. We are, then, ultimately brought face to face with Dilthey's less than fully successful attempt to formulate an ontologically legitimated subjectivist foundation for the discursive representation of human agency. It was his awareness of this shortfall that led to a profound tension and insecurity in his work, which saw him complete so little of its massive bulk for publication. His search for an immanent foundation for human sciences in the human psyche and its claimed unity with existence also generated a deal of controversy over his published writings. The most important reaction was from the Baden NeoKantians, who set out explicitly to refute what Dilthey had presented. They are the subjects of the next chapter of my study.

During the period of Dilthey's philosophical activity in Germany, some philosophers were developing a very different approach to the human sciences which they, too, took to be the product of a generalized historical perspective on the real-world of human events. In their work, as it had been so for Droysen and Dilthey, the primary intellectual attack was on the intrusion into history of the positivist epistemology and methodology of the natural sciences. Two of the main contributors to these critical developments were Windelband and Rickert, the key figures in the Southwest German (Baden) School of NeoKantians that is the focus of Chapter 5. Their historicism emphasized the historical character and understanding of the human life-world and all its phenomena, and their neo-idealism was aimed at reasserting the role of human consciousness in the historical process. But they intended to establish the distinctive metatheoretical nature of human sciences on objective grounds that did not depend on the deeply ontological arguments, with their psychologistic references, employed by Dilthey. His idea that the identifying criteria for separating the natural and the human sciences could be found in the different ontologies of their respective phenomenal objects, with the ontology of the latter linked back to the immanently structured psychology of agents, was decisively rejected by the Neo-Kantians. This was a reflection of their return to Kant in response to the post-Hegelian uncertainty in German philosophy in the second half of the nineteenth century.

Kant's philosophy attributed an unreachable intellectual independence to reality-in-itself, that could only be represented in the human psyche by means of an imposed categorial structure. The latter had its origins in experience, but was not constituted by experience in the manner of Dilthey's psychology. Indeed, the Neo-Kantians would have nothing to do with any ontological inquiry, for they were intent upon providing historical science with an objective foundation that could be defended through the exigencies of established cultural influences. Rickert chose to accept the absolute dualism of unique historical reality and its conceptual representation, but he tried to formalize the understanding of that reality by objectifying the abstraction process through which concepts are formed. In so doing, he claimed to be espousing the representation of the phenomena of reality in a way that captures all their essential and meaningful dimensions as these are dictated by the axiological concerns of the analyst. These concerns, it was argued, are a product of the extant objectively valid value system of the analysts' own environment. In the process, Rickert shifted the focus to what he termed cultural sciences (*Kulturwissenschaften*) as an alternative to the human (mental, spiritual) sciences (*Geisteswissenschaften*) conception used by Dilthey and others. Rickert did so to reinforce his rejection of ontology as providing the demarcation criteria between his focus and the natural sciences, and as a reflection of the cultural source of the objective values on which his version of the historical sciences depended. Ultimately, though, his defence of this mode of dealing with the demarcation issue and the definition of human science cannot be considered successful in any rigorous sense. It was influential, nevertheless, most especially through the critical endeavours of his colleague and friend Max Weber who is the subject of the next chapter.

Weber's primary concern was with understanding and accounting for empirical social and economic phenomena as the products of situated human agents. Explanations in both their form and substance had to be oriented to reflect this fact explicitly, whatever the methodology required and whatever the epistemological status of the resulting analyses. Consistently with this orientation, he referred to the fundamental subject matter of economics as human action, human action that is a product of both natural and historico-social conditions. In their economic actions, individual agents act with self-consciousness, for they are endowed with the capacity and the will to take a deliberated attitude towards their situational environment and its problems and to lend them significance in a subjective sense. As I will argue in Chapter 6, these essentially human foundations for socio-economic science led Weber to pursue its objective of *Verstehen*, that is, of making intelligible and thereby understanding the causes of events and phenomena generated by the social actions of individual subjective agents. His *verstehende Soziologie* was thus developed as a science that attempts the interpretive understanding of social action in order thereby to arrive at a causal explanation of its course and effects.

I begin Chapter 6 with some introductory background to Weber's work, especially its situation with respect to other intellectual developments around him. This leads me to consider Weber's notion that exact theoretical economics had adopted natural-scientistic methodological preconditions and that it was thereby induced to understate and misrepresent the complexity of human agents as merely *homo oeconomicus*. My main objective then will be to establish the alternative and deeper understanding of individual human agency that can be found in his writings. He was concerned that social economics should emphasize that its object phenomena originate in intentional, deliberated and meaningful human action. As agents in all their life-world processes, human beings are also contained within and constrained by the structured situational complex comprising their many and varied social connections with others. It is the containing and shaping influence of such social situations that comprise the next stage of my analysis of Weber's ontological insights. The issue becomes how Weber attempted to apply his understanding of situated human agency to the causally adequate explanation of social and economic objects by means of the concepts of agent rationality and the ideal type. In the end, though, as the concluding section of Chapter 6 reveals, the dependence on agent rationality as the fundamental methodological mediation raised a number of problems that Weber failed fully to address. Nevertheless, he left a legacy of well-directed subjectivist ontological and methodological insights that warranted more critical attention than most of his successors have chosen to give them.

Mises was one successor who took Weber's contributions seriously. It is unfortunate that Mises has acquired such a controversial status in the evolution of Austrian subjectivism because of his idiosyncratic presentation of its character and import for economic analyses. As I will argue fully in Chapter 7, he has been sorely under-read, misread and misrepresented in such controversies. Whatever may be thought of the idiosyncratic nature of his ideas and ideals, he can be seen selectively and critically to have absorbed much more of the subjectivist philosophy that surrounded him than is evident in much of the modern literature. And, it is not only his critics who have failed fully to elicit his contributions but also his hagiographical disciples have chosen to avoid clouding their narrow image with any details that may complicate their free-market, not to say anarchic, version of economics.

Much of Mises's thought on the foundations for subjectivist economics is a mixture of ontological claims about the nature of human action and the epistemological positions that may be adopted in the search for formal knowledge about such action and its phenomenal results. From an ontological perspective, Mises followed Weber in emphasizing situated and conditioned human agents as the active generators of the phenomena that constitute the objects of study. In his epistemological argument, he recognized that the status of claims to knowledge of the world of reality are dependent upon and shaped by the ontological nature of a science's objects. It is for this reason that claims to realist knowledge in the human sciences were apparently more difficult to defend than in the sciences of nature. The variable and contingent origins of human phenomena in individual actions give such phenomena an appearance of impermanence and disorder that defies scientific generalization. The temptation, all too obvious in so much of orthodox economics, is to impose the required permanence and order by assumption. Mises, as with all subjectivists, refused to take this naive escape route. Establishing the nature of the interface between epistemology and ontology, and the balance of antecedent influences that shaped the approach to them in the foundations for Mises's subjectivist economics, is no straightforward matter. However, as I intend to show, the pursuit is warranted. In particular, I will use his writings on these themes to elicit, and thereby to expose the limitations of, the insights into the essential problematic of subjectivism that this founder of Austrian economics left as his legacy.

In Chapter 7, I examine first a number of key alternative philosophical orientations that have been attributed to Mises in the secondary literature. Most important were the Aristotelian and Mengerian milieu of his education and his critical study of the NeoKantians and Max Weber. Each of these will be found to have left some traces of influence on his work. The next step is to elicit textual evidence for the philosophical ambivalence that Mises displayed in formulating his praxeology. It will be argued that there are clear indications of the Kantian and neo-Kantian epistemological roots and orientations evident in his writings. However, these are situated alongside passages in which he emphasized the ontology of Aristotelian realism and dealt with its epistemological implications. I then turn to pursue Mises's treatment of the nature of human action as it originates in the deliberated choices of situated human agents. He approached this core theme on two levels: one is the pure thesis of praxeology as an ontology of rational human action, and the other is the study and explanation of observed economic phenomena. I argue that this distinction enabled Mises ultimately to establish the meaning of the tenets of praxeology as necessarily manifested within the reality of observed economic phenomena. He realized, though, that the requirement of giving agent rationality an ontological *a priori* status is not readily defended once the contingent realities of human agency situated in time are examined. It will become evident that he was aware of these temporal realities, but he chose not to link them to the rationality thesis upon which his subjectivist economics depended. As I go on to show, although Mises developed his ideas of praxeology as an *a priori*, and purely general science of human action, its rationale and utility could only be in its application to the understanding and explanation of empirico-historical phenomena. The conclusion that I reach is that it was the immediately ontological interpretation of the axioms of human action, and the contingencies of such action thus exposed, that rendered indefensible the epistemological foundations for subjectivism that Mises was inclined to pursue. Contrary to what he expressly sought to do at a number of points in his writings, he was unable to provide rational action with a sustainable defence as an ontologically relevant axiom. As a consequence, he failed to give his praxeology a cogent realist grounding and left its appropriate links to observed human action unresolved.

The concluding Chapter 8 draws together the various themes and theses that I have shown to have developed in subjectivist and individualist human science during the period between the work of Menger and its elaborated continuation in the contributions of Mises. I will conclude that a number of crucial issues lacked complete attention, and a number of fundamental problems remained incompletely resolved, in the subjectivist legacy of the period. These were to become all too evident to the Neo-Austrians who took up the Mises heritage in the Austrian economics revival during the early 1970s.

2. Germanic foundations

2.1 Preamble

For the positivists of the nineteenth century, the purpose of all scientific inquiry was to discover laws of how the world of reality functioned. In this respect, the world of human phenomena was no exception and the 'facts' that it presented to observer-analysts could be investigated and accounted for by the same methodological principles as applied in relation to all other aspects of nature. The methodology of science developed in the context of physical and biological inquiry. But its hypothetico-deductive logic constituted the standard of discursive explanation by which claims to understand any dimension of the real world were to be assessed. Any notion that somehow events in the human world were distinct in a sense that required them to be accounted for differently did not occur to the positivists. Some modification of the procedures involved may be necessary, but the ultimate aim was to establish objective, nomological accounts of how human phenomena were causally generated. No reasons existed, they assumed, for a shift in the nature of conceptual forms or the logic of argument when dealing with such phenomena.

Historically, the push for positivism and naturalism in the human sciences remained largely dominant in metatheoretical works published in Britain and France. By contrast, in the German intellectual world of the nineteenth century, a definite rejection of this scientism was identifiable in some particular quarters. For the dissenting German philosophers, the observed real world could not be fully understood and accounted for by the principles and procedures of natural science. The redirection was in favour of a continuation of the search for a metatheory of knowledge in history and, as a consequence, in the human sciences generally, that avoided the burgeoning scientism and naturalism in this context. Two key beliefs motivated this alternative push, although they were not always seen as interdependent: first, that phenomena originating in the actions of human beings have inherent characteristics that set them apart from natural objects; and secondly, that the science of human phenomena should pursue objectives and apply a methodology that are different from those appropriate in natural science. In the former case, to apply scientism in the human realm represented an ontological mistake; in the latter case, it represented a logical mistake. Both of these positions will be found to have had some influence in the rise of separately identifiable human sciences. It was the former ontological distinction, however, that was carried forward as the rationale for the subjectivist and individualist approach to understanding and explaining human phenomena. Thus, whatever is distinctive about the 'facts', objectives and methodology of the human sciences, these should be defended on the grounds of the ontology of their object phenomena. What mattered, fundamentally, that is, was the irreducible fact that human phenomena are created by human actions, and that certain of these actions are deliberated, purposeful and meaningful responses by the agents involved to their existential circumstances.

The anti-positivist foundational developments in the human sciences that accompanied the rise of Austrian subjectivist economics had their origin in the early nineteenth century shift of Germanic historiography away from its Romanticist and Absolute Idealist traditions. Historians also sought to break with the idea of history as comprising little more than descriptive chronicles of events. Instead, the search was for 'down-to-earth' explanations that were consistent with the real-world nature of empirically observable events. This nature was recognized to be dependent primarily upon the generation of these events by the creative actions of human agents. Historians began to ask questions about the causes of observed event sequences; that is, they tried to understand the reasons for the appearance of historical events, reasons that could only be sought in the experiences, values and conduct of the relevant human agent or group active at the time (Lachmann, 1970, pp. 19ff; Schnädelbach, 1984, pp. 33ff). Their recognition that the events with which they were concerned had a different sort of origin and existential status from those in focus in the natural and physical sciences, in that they were not the mere consequence of the concatenation of particular and permanent natural forces, began a long controversy about the metatheoretical principles pertinent to the science of history. The full comprehension of historical events required inquiries that go beyond the physicalist realm of innate human nature and its natural context to consider the subjectively influenced, mentally originated dimensions of history as a human product. But more than philosophical speculation was required to give history a scientific basis.

In the Germanic philosophy of history and human science during the nineteenth century, there were three strands of critical reaction against positivism that are of concern in the present context. Each can only be sketched in as background here. First, there arose the idea that the only means of access to historical knowledge was through empirical observation of facts and their subsequent rationalization as descriptions of varying degrees of abstraction. For the Historicists who founded the Historical School, legitimate inquiry in the human realm had to give primacy to empirical observation and accumulation of factual data. If theoretical accounts of historical events were to have any status, they must be derived from and reflect immediate consistency with empirical data. Some allowed theory a role on the condition that it could be established as the inductive product of extensive empirical inquiry. Others, however, went so far as to assert that in seeking historical understanding, generalized theory had to be avoided altogether. Secondly, there was the endeavour by Johann Droysen to give history a foundation that reflected the human ontology of its object phenomena. He argued that historical inquiry should pursue an understanding of events that involved rendering them as the intelligible and meaningful products of human action. In this respect, his metahistory pointed the way for a subjectivist and individualist approach to the human sciences generally. Thirdly, there existed a bifurcation of philosophy in the Germanic world between the themes that dominated in Germany itself and those that rose to prominence in Austria. To a significant extent, Austrian philosophy of the period developed independently of German influence, especially as this latter involved the legacies of Kant and Hegel. There is evidence of a preference in Vienna for the scholastic tradition of Aristotelian realism that sought understanding by exposing the coherence inherent in the immediate elements and structures of contemporary reality.

These three philosophical strands comprise the philosophical milieu within which subjectivism developed in Germany and Austria. These three strands are outlined in turn in the first three sections of this chapter. And, as a preliminary inquiry that relates to the backgrounds of Menger and Mises in particular, in the final two sections I consider their situations within these strands of philosophy and subjectivist economics that constituted their intellectual milieu.

2.2 The rise of the Historical School

During the period of this redirection of historiography, there emerged in Germany an historically oriented school of economics. It was represented especially by Wilhelm Roscher (1817–94) and Gustav von Schmoller (1838–1917), and carried forward the concern for explaining 'the facts' of real-world history. The metahistorical basis of their work is to be found in some particular, mostly implicit, epistemological principles concerning the theory of concepts and causality in human inquiry. The emphases given to these principles varied over time and rendered somewhat different the detailed methodological approaches of the various 'older' and 'younger' members of the School (Bostaph, 1976, 1978). Schmoller, the leader of the 'younger' Historicists, saw historical inquiry as inherently involving some balance of two opposing principles: those of rationalism and those of empiricism. These two principles, he believed, 'always face each other, take each other's place, and correct each other – although the sensible empiricist will never fail to admit that all experience is only the result of his thinking, and the rationalist, as a rule, does not deny that the stuff of his thoughts is made available to him by the world of the senses'. Nonetheless, he continued, 'it is from the different combinations of these elements that the different schools of thought spring, schools which are in conflict with each other . . .' (1952, p. 364).

In this endeavour, the Historicists followed the transitional post-Hegelian ideas of Leopold von Ranke (1795–1886). In Ranke's vision of history, the transcendental idealism of a collective *Volksgeist* provided the essential context and meaning of human historical development. But, this vision was maintained alongside the baldest Baconian version of inductivism and empiricism (Milford, 1992a, pp. 164f). It was Ranke who contributed much to the German rejection of philosophy and theory as the means of comprehending reality. Theory comprised of conceptual argument stemming from reflection, reason and abstraction could not give access to knowledge of complex historical events. The only way to such knowledge of facts was to find out 'how things actually happened'. In Schmoller's assessment, 'Roscher could rightly apply to himself the proud and modest word of the historian Ranke: he wanted only to show how things really are. Is it not a tremendous matter to know how things really are?' (1952, p. 375).

Ranke's general objections to theoretically expressed knowledge of human events led the Historicists to a critique of the rationalist and universalist economic theories of the Adam Smith and his classical successors. In Schmoller's reading, there emerged during the period from the work of the Physiocrats in the mid-eighteenth century onwards, an increasing emphasis on rationalist modes of thought and argument at the expense of empiricism. This tendency culminated in the work of David Ricardo: in sum, 'in this manner, intellectual rot was the outcome of a rationalism entirely divorced from experience' (1952, p. 365). The Historicists were concerned with the abstractly grounded and excessively formalized logico-deductive argument that comprised the classical theories. It was Schmoller's view that the Classicals had exaggerated the scientific progress that economics had made and prematurely adopted a deductive methodology. His interpretation was that they had oversimplified the nature of economic phenomena and thus been able to apply to it the methodology of the more exact sciences such as astronomy. In this respect, it appeared to be Schmoller's expectation that such scientistic emulation should be the goal of economic analysis. But, he pointed out, this 'highest state of perfection' of economic science had not yet been reached because of its evident incapacity to deal with more complex phenomena. To him it was 'obvious that only the very simplest phenomena open themselves up easily and swiftly to complete knowledge . . .'. He granted, nevertheless, that 'it surely was a great step ahead to explain market phenomena on the basis of the desire for gain and of the mechanics of production cost'. But, he went on, it was important to realize that in order to explain more complex economic phenomena, 'this requires first their scientific description' (1952, p. 374). For the Classicals to claim that their theories expressed absolute laws of the economy with an extent and permanence that made them relevant across nations and eras was a gross misrepresentation of what was possible at that stage in the human sciences. Much more accumulation of pertinent empirical data would be required before 'fact finding' could be converted into 'explanation of the facts' in the complex cases. Only then could Historicists apply the 'rare art of distilling the most important, the typical, the general, and of tracing a picture on the basis of inexhaustible, thousand-fold detail' (1952, p. 374).

Included in the Historicists' concerns about classical claims was the exclusive representation of complex human agents as the narrowly conceived *a priori* and ultra-rationalism of *homo oeconomicus*. Historicists could not accept as complete any account of human events that gave undue emphasis to the isolated individual, to the 'atoms' of economy and society, least of all to one with so limited a repertoire of characteristics as *homo oeconomicus*. They were holists and relativists in the sense that human involvement in observed phenomena was argued to be the result of individual containment, including the pursuit of self-interest, within the dominating spirit and structures of a particular nation and an age. Human conduct in all its interdependent dimensions was depicted as imbedded in and shaped by a totality of national and temporal existence. To study economic phenomena meant understanding human agents as operating collectively within the moral, political and social totality. On this basis, the Historicists favoured the direct search for whatever nomological regularities may be found in the cumulative evidence of historical and social experience at the collective level. However, Roscher in particular appreciated that the ontological nature of phenomena generated by human agency is distinct from that which characterizes the natural world. Consequently, direct inductive procedures could not be applied to elicit generalizations about the ever changing and uniquely occurring phenomena of contemporary economy and society. These phenomena simply lack the universality and constancy that is associated with the repetitions of the natural environment. When individual agents and their activities in the short term were acknowledged, as they had to be because of Roscher's espousal of a subjectively inclined economics, their conduct was taken to be subsumed and understood within the contemporary institutional dynamics of their situations. In sum, 'according to Roscher nations, peoples, and economic systems really exist and are not simply theoretical constructions built upon the basis of individual actions'. Such entities are historically evolved ' "wholes" which form the preconditions such that individuals may act or even exist' (Milford, 1990, p. 216). Therefore, 'analyzing the laws of their historical development will give us a true notion of their essence. Only after having explained their essence are we able to understand the historical situation in which individuals act' (Milford, 1990, pp. 216f; cf. 1992a, pp. 166f).

The national totality itself was considered to have a cumulative organic origin and carried its historical evolution into the present. Understanding its present meant, therefore, understanding its past, which gave historical inquiry the ultimate imperative as the foundation for contemporary human science, including economics. It was Roscher's conviction in particular that sufficient observation and data gathering in the processes of 'comparative and holistic studies of the historical development of different nations, peoples, or economies' could reveal nomological regularities within social orders and their dynamics over the longer-term (Milford, 1990, pp. 215f). This process was analogous, Roscher believed, to the practices of comparative anatomy and physiology and constituted what has been called an 'historical–physiological method' (Schmoller, 1952, p. 376). Studying the past of a nation, then, and comparing its evolution with other nations was expected by Roscher to expose immanent, generalized laws of national development that had an absolutist quality. Such laws would include an economic dimension, with economics envisaged as necessarily founded upon a study of the history of the economy.

Empiricist and holist metatheoretical principles formed the keys to the study of human phenomena of all types for the Historicists and became the hallmark of economics as it was presented in the subsequent work of Schmoller and others of the 'younger' Historical School. He referred to 'the foundation of German philology and German historical science [as] the truly scientific and scholarly movement that again, and for good, filled the veins of the consumptive body of economics with blood and life. Rationalistic anaemia was to be cured with the help of a strong dose of empirical–historical knowledge of the world' (1952, p. 366). Thus Schmoller emphasized the crucial importance of historical and statistical description as the bases upon which any theory possible in economics must be founded. He deviated from the 'older' Roscher in the extent of his dependence upon such description, for he was much less prepared to allow apriorism and rationalism to intrude into his search for theory (Schmoller, 1952, pp. 376f). There was a need, Schmoller believed, for theory to be comprehensive in its treatment of the complex origins of human phenomena. That is, to recognize the full scope of human nature exposed in contemporary psychology and to encompass fully the human situation within contemporary culture and society in any understanding of economic life. Rather than attempt the extremes of abstraction and simplification characteristic of the Classicals' deductive analyses, any abstraction required must be consistent with the empirical nature of the object of inquiry. Schmoller continued to espouse holism rather than atomism and isolation as the means of understanding human involvement in economic activity.

The Historicists' devotion to empiricist and holist methodology reflected some particular epistemological principles that remained largely implicit in their writings (Bostaph, 1976, pp. 82f, 87ff; 1978). Most fundamentally at issue was the age-old problem of how the minds of observers imbibe and represent coherently the complex sensory inflow from the real things upon which they choose to focus in the world around them. Arguing this process requires a theory of the nature and origin of conceptual forms in the first instance. Included in this theory must be some presumption about the laws of human thought: do the concepts employed give a structured form to an otherwise chaotic sensory input, or do they capture the essentials of a structural order already present as a consequence of the ontology of the object? A consequence of answering this question will be some claim about the nature of causality in the generation of phenomena.

For the most part, the Historicists were essentialist and emanationist in their belief that unfolding historical reality, as made evident by the accumulation of historical data, embodied its own immanent order. Concepts were such as to express this inherent order in more or less detail, with the Historicists favouring the most comprehensive possible reach of conceptual coverage as the only means of properly representing the nature of phenomena in discursive argument. Included in this position was a notion of causality and nomological relationships as already present in the descriptive accounts of the regularities of phenomena in their temporal setting and in their exposed connections with other phenomena. That is, the theory of causality should rely upon the empirical revelations of observation and the extrapolations of an associationist form of logic to express the inner connections between things. As a result of their belief in this intimate connection between the cognitive grasp of reality and the contemporary ontological form of that reality, the Historicists were reluctant to assign universality and permanence to any of the theories or laws they formulated. Roscher's claims about the long-term laws of development of nations stand out as an exception here.

2.3 Droysen's subjectivist philosophy of history

It was Johann Droysen whose work really set the stage for the transition from a realist philosophy of history to the subjectivist human sciences. His endeavours to formulate a metatheory for history and the historical sciences provided some vital insights that were taken over by subjectivist philosophers almost without change as far as they went. In his writings, he stressed the need for grounding historical inquiry on the principle of maintaining the consistency of the resulting discursive argument with the ontological nature of their phenomena. He read the object phenomena of history as comprising the expression of human psychic and psychophysical activity. For Droysen, then, if history was to have any scientific status, it would have to be as a science of conscious and purposeful human action.

The consequent human subjectivity confronted by such inquiries demanded that the observer penetrate to the 'inside', as it were, of the event's generation process. That is, to pose questions about why it occurred in terms of 'for what humanly attributable reasons?'. Human action is grounded in agents' reasoning about their interpreted situations and any understanding of the resulting phenomena must, therefore, focus on the reasons for the individual or collective actions generating them. These reasons comprise a complex of motives, intentions, purposes and plans of individuals who apply them within their relevant situations. The actions taken by situated agents have a meaning for them by virtue of this grounding in self-conscious reasoning. It is, then, through interpretive insight into the reasons for and the meaning of actions, along with an understanding of the situational influences that contained them at the time, that an observer can claim to comprehend the origins of an historical event. In Droysen's opinion, nothing could be achieved towards understanding such phenomena by means of the application of natural scientistic principles to historical inquiry. This view was dealt with at some length in his 1852 critique of H.T. Buckle's *The History of Civilization in England* in which Buckle had applied and defended these principles. The review carried the indicative title 'The elevation of history to the rank of a science' (Droysen, 1967, pp. 61ff).[1] It is to be noted that my concern here is not with the legitimacy or otherwise of Droysen's critique, but rather with what he saw as the meaning and significance of his reading for the future course of historiography and historical studies.

Droysen's focus in this paper was on the trend towards the notion that there could be only one test of scientificity for a field of inquiry as a consequence of the remarkable success of the physical sciences. This was to be that its phenomena can be treated as if they were physical in nature and thus obey the equivalent of natural laws. The question he addressed concerning non-natural inquiries was thus: 'Should the other realms of human discovery be obliged to recognize themselves as of a scientific nature only in so far as they are in a condition to transfer vital phenomena to the class of physical phenomena?' (1967, p. 62). The most immediate case in point at that time was the treatment of historical phenomena. History appeared to need some more consistent and objective metamethodological foundation around which to structure its inquiries, but the issue was the extent to which this need could be fulfilled by scientific methodology. Droysen was in no doubt about the very real achievements of the natural sciences. And, he was also prepared to grant that 'in the departments with which the "science of History" has to do, there is much that is level and accessible to natural scientific method . . .' (1967, p. 69). But neither of these observations negated the need to reflect critically upon Buckle's attitude of self-evidence towards the design of historical methodology as a replication of the existing sciences. 'Are there not', Droysen asked, 'various other forms of knowledge, other methods, competent, perhaps, in virtue of their nature to treat precisely the realities which the forms and methods of natural science decline and decline as a logical consequence of their point of view, and which the historical also either decline or treat inadequately?' (1967, p. 87).

In a passage from Buckle's work, quoted by Droysen, the presumed state of history was readily apparent: 'as regards all higher tendencies of human thinking, History still lies in deplorable incompleteness and presents so confused and anarchical an appearance as were [sic] to be expected only in the case of a subject with unknown laws or destitute as yet even of a foundation' (1967, p. 63, cf. p. 75). Droysen was in no doubt that as a consequence of this parlous state of historical inquiry that Buckle intended to rework its methodology to show that its phenomena could be accounted for by laws of human activity. More specifically, Droysen read Buckle as having found in history the dominant determination of events by a dual effect that involves 'the working of outer phenomena upon our nature and the working of our nature upon outer phenomena' (1967, p. 63). Buckle is then cited as claiming that by means of inductive fact gathering he could identify 'the standard and important ones' and thereby find 'the higher expression that unites them'; that is, to find their laws of appearance. In this context, 'generalizations then are the laws which Buckle seeks' (1967, p. 75). Now Droysen was prepared to accept that 'induction sums up particulars into the general fact . . . by combining particulars in that which is really common to them' (1967, p. 75f). The problem was that instead of positing this as the definitive end of the methodology, Buckle should have gone on to defend it explicitly as an 'analytical procedure' and a 'logic of . . . investigation' that has legitimacy when applied to historical inquiry. It was clear to Droysen that Buckle did not think that this was necessary (1967, pp. 75). Beyond his inductive efforts, Buckle proceeded 'deductively in showing how the historical development of civilization is explained by these laws [exposed by induction] . . .' (1967, p. 64). The pertinent question put by Droysen was: 'Is he [Buckle] the Bacon of the historical sciences and his work the Organon to teach us to think historically?' (1967, p. 66). What follows in the paper amounts to a decisively negative answer.

Droysen's essential premiss was that methodology is something that must be attuned to the nature of the object phenomena of a field of inquiry. 'Do not . . . methods [of inquiry] incessantly vary according to their objects . . .?', he asked (1967, p. 68) and went on to defend a definitely positive response. In particular, 'if there is to be a science of History, this must have its own method of discovery and relate to its own department of knowledge' (1967, p. 76). It was certainly inappropriate that existing scientific methodology should be adopted without question:

> The method of study belonging to natural science is in a different position . . . in respect to the point of view under which it apprehends phenomena. . . . Vital phenomena interest it only in so far as they repeat themselves, either periodically or morphologically. In the individual being it sees and seeks only the idea of the species or the medium of material change. (1967, p. 86)

It was apparent to Droysen that the phenomenal conditions of the natural world could not be readily found among the phenomena of historical science. For, as even Buckle was able half-heartedly to acknowledge, the ontological nature of all such phenomena was to be found in their generation by the actions of human agents (1967, pp. 72ff). These actions 'all fulfil themselves in that illimitably manifold interplay of interests, conflicts, businesses, of motives, passions, forces and restrictions, the sum of which has been well named the moral world' (1967, p. 72). Such phenomena are unique in themselves, unlikely ever to be repeated in exactly the same form and resist uniform and consistent inclusion within any classification akin to a species.

Droysen concluded that the misleading nature of Buckle's treatment of history was due to his failure fully to accept the true ontological foundations of observed phenomena that are only to be found in the processes of situated human agency. Thus, because Buckle 'neglected to examine and sound the nature of the subjects with which he undertook to deal, he proceeds with them as if they did not have any nature or character of their own at all and so did not need a method of their own . . .' (1967, p. 80). In his later work on metahistory, Droysen continued his focus on the methodological needs of historical sciences as driven by the special ontology of their objects that distinguished them from those of nature.

The major work of relevance here is his *Grundriss der Historik* that was circulated from 1858 onwards and published formally in 1867 (third edition 1881). It was translated into English as *Outline of the Principles of History* (1967). The work opened with the crucial observation that 'Nature and History are the widest conceptions under which the human mind apprehends the world of phenomena' (1967, p. 9). The crucial distinction between these phenomena concerned for Droysen the fact that history manifests continuous change through time that originates in the world of human being: 'only what pertains to man appears to partake of this constant upward and onward motion, and of this, such motion appears to be the essence and the business. The *ensemble* of this restless progress is the moral world'. Thus, 'it is only the traces which *man* has left, only what man's hand and man's mind has touched, formed, [and] stamped, that . . . lights up before us afresh' (1967, pp. 10, 12, original emphasis). Perceived most generally, 'History is humanity becoming and being conscious of itself' and 'History is humanity's knowledge of itself, its certainty about itself' (1967, pp. 48, 49).

Within this distinction is to be found the deeper ontological characteristic that historical phenomena are the mode of expression and realization of human existence. 'As he goes on fixing imprints and creating form and order, in every such utterance the human being brings into existence an expression of his individual nature, of his "I"' (1967, p. 12). It is the cumulative effect of an agent's biographical experiences that 'causes the mere creature man, by discovering in the sweat of his brow what he is designed to be, to realize this design and to discover it by realizing it. Out of the mere *genus homo* it thus makes the historical man, which means the moral man' (1967, p. 35). Moreover, it is because of this human ontological status that the historian can gain an immediate insight into such phenomena that is denied to the natural scientist. 'Whatever residue of . . . human expressions and imprints is anywise, anywhere, present to us, that speaks to us and we can understand it.' Droysen amplified his defence of this claim by noting 'the kinship of our nature with that of the utterances lying before us as historical material. . . . On being perceived, the utterance, by projecting itself into the inner experience of the percipient, calls forth the same inner process'. So it is that 'with human beings, . . . with human utterances and creations, we have and feel that we have an essential kinship and reciprocity of nature: every "I" enclosed in itself, yet each in its utterances disclosing itself to every other'. For the historian, 'the individual utterance is understood as a simple speaking forth of the inner nature, involving [the] possibility of inference backward to that inner nature' (1967, pp. 12f).

Most importantly, then, for his role as one of the founders of a separate identity for the human sciences, Droysen realized that it was the ontologically distinct nature of the phenomena addressed by these sciences that forced their methodology to diverge from that of the physical sciences and gave that methodology its special character. 'The method of historical investigation is determined by the morphological character of its material. The essence of historical method is *understanding* by means of *investigation*' (1967, p. 12; original emphasis). Understanding is made possible by interpreting the existential objects about which historical sciences inquire as the external expressions of the cognitive processes of human agents. The challenge for historical scientists was to work back from these empirically observed expressions to their generative origins. By this means, which cannot be applied to natural scientific inquiry because of the alien nature of its objects, discursive understandings of these phenomena could be achieved. While natural sciences can explain how things occur, historical sciences can understand why things occur in terms of processes linked to human creativity and reason.

Droysen hinted at an appreciation of what we call the 'hermeneutical circle' in his aphoristic quip that 'the individual is understood in the total, and the total from the individual'. He went on to elaborate the first part of the idea by noting that individual agents exist only in situations, including sets of social and moral relations with others. 'Every human being is a moral subject; only thus is he a human being' (1967, p. 43). What this means is that the 'human being is, in essential nature, a totality in himself, but he realizes this character only in understanding others and [in] being understood by them, in the moral partnerships of family, people, state, religion, etc.', so that 'the individual is only rela-tively a totality' (1967, p. 14, cf. p. 37). The other part of the quip inferred an ontologically individualistic understanding of human phenomena: 'All changes and formations in the moral world [of human history] are wrought by acts of will.... Acts of will are the efficients even where we say that the State, the People, the Church, etc., do this and that' (1967, p. 43). He noted that 'every so-called historical fact' is the consequence of 'a complex of acts of will' situated in relation to 'the connections, conditions and purposes which were active at the same time'. Historical investigations, then, are expected substantively 'to determine what relation the material ... before us bears to the acts of will whereof it testifies' (1967, pp. 21f).

Droysen asserted consequently that 'the life pulse of historical move-ment is freedom' (1967, p. 44) with the qualification that as it refers to the activities of the human agents who make history, the concept must be interpreted with care. Agents have a freedom to participate in the facets of the life-world that they choose. In doing so, they confront limitations to any complete flexibility of action by virtue of the necessity to operate through pre-existing 'moral spheres' of action. These make certain demands on the form of agents' conduct and on their limited total capacity to participate in a range of desired activities: 'In the collision of duties, in the constantly painful performance of these, and in the often crushing result, finite human nature sinks beneath the postulate of freedom.' Thus, Droysen reasoned, 'the problem of the life of History is not to be sought in the false alternative between freedom and necessity' (1967, pp. 44, 45). His astute insight here led him to point out that for interpreting human agency, the opposite of necessity is 'arbitrariness, accident, aimlessness' and not freedom *per se.* So, even though agents must act through 'moral spheres' and are, as a matter of principle and practice, contained and constrained by conditions not of their own choice, freedom as Droysen envisaged it still remains. In his words, 'being free is the opposite of suffering compulsion, of being dead of will, destitute of "I"; the moral is the willing of the good and is not subject to compulsion' (1967, p. 45). That is, the agents involved in the generation of any historical event are always 'morally' situated.

The interpretation of their actions must extend to take account of how their wills *volitionally and freely* interact with and are thus affected by the multiple dimensions of the 'moral' conditions under which they act.

More broadly considered, the situational dimensions of the 'moral' world include the obvious physical, spatial and other environmental conditions. For example, 'as man studies and comprehends *nature*, rules and transforms nature to serve human ends, the work of History lifts nature up into the moral sphere . . .' (1967, p. 35; original emphasis). But they also include a complex of other systems of human origin that are no less consequential in influencing agents' conduct: systems of social relations with others, systems of ideas and the ethical systems. Into all of these situational conditions agents are born and carry on their life-world actions. Thus, 'historical investigation presupposes the reflection that even the content of our "I" is a mediated content, one that has been developed, that is, is an historical result' (1967, p. 17). Or, more elaborately put:

> Born into an already existent moral world . . . [and] thus born to be conscious, free and responsible, each man for himself [exists] in . . . moral partnerships and using them as helps, builds his own little world, the bee-cell of his 'I'. Each of these cells is conditioned and supported by its neighbor, and in turn conditions and supports [others]. (1967, pp. 33f)

Ultimately, then, for Droysen, understanding human phenomena requires interpretation of the situated agents' actions that comprise their origin. Interpretation has a key psychological element that 'seeks in the given fact, the acts of will which produced it. Such interpretation may take cognizance of the subject who willed, and of the energy of his volition so far as this influenced the course of events under survey, and of his intellectual force so far as this determined his will' (1967, pp. 28f). However, as he was quick to point out, this process of interpretation as the basis of historical knowledge has one critical impediment: the problem of access to 'other minds'. First of all, the expression of the individual psyche in observed events is never a complete reflection of its total content: 'the subject of the volition [did not] fully exhaust himself in this one turn of things . . . [and] it is neither the pure nor the entire expression of his personality'. But also the content of the psyche *per se* is, as a matter of fact, not directly accessible to the observer: 'Human being understands human being, but only in an external way; each perceives the other's act, . . . yet always only this one deed or feature, this single element.' It is the individual's conscience that ultimately comprises 'the truth of his existence', but 'into this sanctuary the ken of investigation does not pass'. The conclusion about interpretation as a literal method of inquiry could only be as Droysen stated it: 'Prove that I understand my fellow rightly or entirely I cannot' (1967, p. 29). Such a comment is indicative of the incomplete subjectivist legacy that he left for his successors to contemplate.

2.4 Austrian philosophy

For the purposes of the inquiries that are to follow, it is important to give due attention to the idea that the philosophical developments outlined above were most directly influential in the German national intellectual context. The parallel philosophical origins, concerns and trends in Austria were rather different in character, a fact that Barry Smith has cogently emphasized in his several erudite contributions on the issue (1990a, 1990b, 1990c, 1994). I will make frequent reference to the work of Smith below because he is really the only scholar who has endeavoured fully to establish the nature of the interface between philosophy and economics as it was emerging in Austria during the formative period of the latter half of the nineteenth century.

There are some indications that a proper recognition of the distinctive philosophical environment in which the Austrian economists worked can be important for a complete understanding of the direction in which their subjectivism developed. In particular, two features of Austrian intellectual life, and its reflections in social and political life, are potentially pertinent here. One is the lack of any dominance by philosophical concerns *per se* analogous to those in Germany flowing from the likes of Kant and Hegel and from post-Hegelian developments generally. The other is that where philosophy was influential, it remained, most importantly for our purposes, in the peculiar form of pre-Kantian Aristotelian and Scholastic realism, with an ontological emphasis on 'down-to-earth' problems of the life world of individual people. The grandiose themes of transcendental Spirit, Reason and Idealism, and the subsequent intellectual shocks of reactions against such ideas, contributed little to the Austrians' psyche. In short, Austrian philosophy remained largely isolated from German formative influences for much of the nineteenth century and its adherence to its own peculiar ideas had a noticeable effect on the way the human sciences, especially economics, evolved.[2]

Barry Smith (1990a, pp. 266ff; 1990c, pp. 214ff) elicits a number of characteristics that can be identified as peculiar to the Aristotelian orientations of Austrian philosophy during the second half of the nineteenth century. Most importantly, he concludes that each of the characteristics that he lists played no role in the German traditions of the same period. The most significant of these characteristics for our purposes were the following, although there is opportunity for only a brief sketch here. First, Austrian philosophical inquiry was most immediately concerned with observed objects and problems of reality. The relevant mode of primary inquiry was thus empirical, and such inquiry proceeded on the *a priori* premiss that the real world in all its dimensions exists and is inherently meaningful and/or intelligible independently of any subjective and cognitive ordering of its elements by observers. Observers of all sorts, scientific and lay, can know what this world is like and can do so without any subjective prejudices. What observers cannot claim is that their knowledge is in any respect infallible. However exactly we may present our claimed knowledge of an object, we must always accept the possibility that our cognitive experiences and predilections have led us astray relative to *what is really there*. Secondly, there are present in the composition of real phenomena essences or elements, together with laws, structures or connections, which constitute their presence and that have a pre-structured and universal status. The consequence is that empirical reality as it is perceived will comprise an essential and general dimension imbedded in an individual dimension. Smith summarizes this 'immanent realist' position as one in which 'what is general does not exist in isolation from what is individual', so that 'the essences and laws manifested in *this* world, [and] not in any separate realm of incorporeal Ideal Forms such as is embraced by philosophers of a Platonistic sort', are the objects of scientific inquiry (1990a, p. 267; original emphasis). This view of reality links back to the first item listed in that it gives us an indication of how empirical objects and problems were thought about at the time. It is important to realize in this respect that ontologically devised exact theoretical argument that captures the essentials of a part of reality could not have been expected to provide accurate predictions. The laws established at the essential level cannot operate in a 'pure' form untainted by the modifying forces of contingent and ever changing individual conditions. Thirdly, the philosophers were realists who rejected the Kantian bifurcation of the phenomenal and the noumenal in relation to objects of inquiry. They gave primacy to ontological questions about the real world, with purely epistemological questions about the status of our knowledge of it being of secondary importance. Their realism was Aristotelian in its origins and entailed a commitment to discursive representations of reality that could claim existential and ontological descriptive adequacy. Such realism was 'understood both in an ontological sense (the world exists, more or less as we find it) and in an epistemological sense (knowledge of the world is possible and we are already in possession of substantial portions of such knowledge)' (Smith, 1990c, p. 214). Fourthly, in their relationship to the external objects of the real world, human agents adopt positions that are mediated by subjective considerations. In particular, agents form values of all kinds as functions of their individual mental makeups. This led the Austrians to a fifth philosophical characteristic: they interpreted all human phenomena as originating in the actions of individual agents. That is, they espoused an ontological individualism that underpinned their well-known methodological individualism. In so doing, though, they avoided any taint of reductionism by ensuring that the individuals were always depicted as acting interdependently with their social and situational environment.

At this point it is important to recognize that the philosophical position just outlined had its focus firmly on ontology. That is, in Smith's summary, 'it tells us what the world is like and what its objects, states and processes are like, including those capacities, states and processes we call knowledge and science. More generally, it tells us what sort of relations obtain between the various different segments of reality' (1990a, p. 275). At issue also in the Austrian philosophy of the period was the notion of *a priori acquisition* of knowledge about the ontology of the real world. In understanding this aspect of the philosophy, an epistemological distinction between two possible renderings of the *a priori* idea of access and claims to knowledge is required (Smith, 1990a, pp. 275f). First, the *impositionist* view involves the claim that knowledge can only be a manifestation of a mentally created and imposed conceptual framework with exclusively analytical status. Such knowledge will be about a part of perceived reality, but its conceptual form is the creation of the knowing subject. Access to a knowledge of reality-in-itself is denied along Kantian lines, with the necessary implication that this view avoids any immediate ontological associations. Secondly, in the *reflectionist* view, the *a priori* appears as a manifestation of the essential elements, relations and structures of the object reality that exist independently of any human perception. Here access to a knowledge of reality-in-itself is the identifying claim and the demand is for ontological veracity of discursive argument. The epistemology in this case is that of immanent ontological realism, for the *a priori* is argued to be imbedded in the real world.

Now it was this second perception of the *a priori* that came to be identified with Aristotelian realist ontology in Austria. It was Aristotle's well-known belief, expressed in his *Nicomachaean Ethics*, that as concerns its epistemology and methodology, 'our discussion will be adequate if it has as much clearness as the subject-matter admits of'. So, in progressing from ontology to methodology, the Aristotelian position was that it must be the former that dictates the form of the latter. In Smith's view, the associated idea of a human science was that its methodology sought to be such as to expose 'the qualitative essences or natures of and relations between . . . categories', what amounted to a 'categorial ontology', of some specific segment of human reality (1990a, p. 277). For Franz Brentano, psychology was in focus,[3] for Menger, it was economics. The puzzle that such an approach to the constitution of knowledge in any field must confront is how can there exist an inherently ordered and structured essential composition of the relevant human phenomena when they have their origins in the subjective, creative and contingent mental and physical actions of autonomous human agents? Smith uses the analogy of language to illustrate the evident potential for such order to be created by collective action and cumulative experience. It is a reasonable assumption that 'there are structures in (linguistic) reality which are universal to all languages. Such structures are at least tacitly familiar to everyone who has dealings with the objects concerned (i.e. to every speaker of a language)' (1990a, pp. 278f). This leads him to refer to the potential for an 'ontological grammar of economic reality' (1990a, p. 279).

It may well be, then, as Smith claims, that in the case of economics as an instance, 'economic reality is such as to manifest certain simple intelligible structures in and of itself. Economic reality is built up in intelligible ways out of structures involving human thought and action. It is for this reason that we are able, by appropriate efforts, to read off these structures in and of themselves' (1990a, p. 278). It may be, too, that the essences of economic phenomena are akin to the universals of linguistics that are 'not created by the linguist . . . [but] are discovered, through painstaking theoretical efforts' (1990a, p. 279). However, the sorts of claims made here beg many more questions than they answer. They *assert* the presence of a structured ontology of economic phenomena without explication as to how individualistic actions by isolated agents result in such an ontology. Just what is the nature of the 'human thought and action' that goes into building up an ordered and intelligible economic reality? Moreover, the notion of 'appropriate' and 'painstaking' theoretical efforts infers the need for a methodology that facilitates the required insight by analysts into the essences imbedded in actual phenomena. What is missing is an account of what that methodology might comprise in practice. That is, how the analyst confronts a mass of empirically generated information with a view to revealing its essential 'categorial ontology'. Smith grants the potential difficulties involved and recognizes that claims about reflectionist *a priori* orders and structures in economics 'does not mean – any more than in the case of linguistic universals – that economic theory must be free of empirical components. Indeed, it is a difficult matter to sort out precisely what the appropriate role for empirical investigations in economics (and in related disciplines) ought to be' (1990a, p. 279).

2.5 Germanic subjectivist economics

By the middle of the nineteenth century, the study of economics in German and Austrian universities was widespread and had a definite subjectivist orientation (Alter, 1990a, pp. 151ff; Milford, 1990, 1992a, 1995a, 1995b; Streissler, 1990c, 1990d). There already existed what Erich Streissler has aptly called a *protoneoclassical* tradition (1990c, pp. 154ff; 1990d, p. 32), characterized by some key ideas that would later become integral to the 'revolution' in economic thought of the 1870s. These included a rejection of the classical theory that value of produced goods is essentially an input cost determined phenomenon in favour of a unified demand oriented theory of value that could include both com- modities and the factors of production. Gone was the classical notion that income distribution is the outcome of a class struggle consequent upon the organization of the capitalist socio-economic structure in com- bination with the scarcity of productive resources. Crucial to the tenor of this revision of the theory of value was, Streissler observes, a general 'subjectivist outlook on the purpose of the economy and subjectivist definitions of many central economic concepts, centering around utility or "value in use"' (1990c, p. 154).

The themes dealt with in some of the major works of the period were those that are now familiar to us through Menger's writings, including analyses of the interactions between human needs and wants and the definition and value of what constitutes a *good* for economic purposes. As early as 1807 it was clear to Gottlieb Hufeland that 'all goods are only goods by virtue of the mind-picture which one man or several men make themselves of them' (quoted by Streissler, 1990d, p. 42). In 1852, Eberhard Friedländer wrote that 'value is usefulness [*das Nützliche*] in its special relationship to our needs, the expression of an essentially changeable relationship. Use value is the relationship of the needs of men to external things in their immediate application to the satisfaction of human needs' (quoted by Alter, 1990a, p. 156; my translation). Eco- nomics thus came to comprise all those activities of individual human agents that are directed towards the satisfaction of needs and wants through the acquisition of goods (cf. Alter, 1990a, p. 154). Even Wilhelm Roscher the Historicist was able to recognize that 'by economy we understand the well-planned activity of man in order to satisfy his needs for external goods' (quoted by Streissler, 1990d, p. 43). This gave economics a teleological basis that was widely recognized in the Germanic literature. Alter informs us that in the period, 'virtually all of the authors talk about the *Zweck*, the purpose, the aim, the *telos* of economic activity; for instance [Karl Heinrich] Rau, but not only Rau, for whom an explanation of value is only possible within the realm of human purposes' (1990a, p. 153). The mediation in all such processes is the subjective appraisal of a good as useful for this purpose. It was Alfred Schäffle who argued in this vein in 1867 that 'value [is] a relationship between all goods in human consciousness . . . [it is] predominantly of a *subjective* nature. It exists in a consciousness of purpose in matters economic [*wirtshaftlichen Zweckbewusstsein*]' (quoted by Streissler, 1990d, p. 43; Schäffle's emphasis).

A similar approach was extended to the valuation of the factors of production. This was done by means of the idea of an imputed use value that could be attributed to them because of their capacity to contribute to the production of useful goods. In 1832, the German Friedrich Hermann argued in the case of labour services that 'the entrepreneur does not buy labor for consumption purposes, but for the purpose of resale of its product; he acts only as an agent of the consumers of the product. Only what the consumers give for the product, constitutes the true remuneration of the service of the worker . . . (quoted by Streissler, 1990d, p. 45, n. 55). So it was that subjective value in use, 'utility', manifested as demand became the crucial force in the determination of value in exchange. To quote Friedländer again: 'exchange value is only a form of use value; it originates from the same principle and falls with use value' (quoted by Alter, 1990a, p. 156; my translation). In this context, too, demand was recognized as relevant in an economic sense only in the face of scarcity of supply. It was apparent at the time that 'free' goods, where continuous natural supply exceeds demand, will not command any market value no matter how useful they may be.

The valuation process for Germanic economists of this period already involved the interaction of supply and demand. It was clear to several of them that value and demand are inversely related in what constitutes a continuous function that we know as a downward sloping demand function. Behind this relationship was the idea of diminishing marginal utility. As expressed by Bruno Hilderbrand in 1848, the relationship meant that 'the more the quantity of a useful commodity is increased the more does the utility of each individual piece of the commodity diminish if the need is unchanged' (quoted by Streissler, 1990c, p. 157). And, as far as the marginal product valuation of factors of production was concerned, it was made clear by Roscher in the case of labour services that 'in each producing establishment (and also in the economy as a whole!) the additional product which the worker, who is last employed, produces is of decisive importance for the level of wages of his equals' (quoted by Streissler, 1990d, p. 46). Finally, what must be one of the most highly charged summaries of the era was written as early as 1832 by Hermann:

> [F]or those goods that are that are brought regularly and in any desired quantity to market the price is not at all determined by cost alone.... Much rather the first and most important factor determining prices is in all cases demand, the main roots of which are the value in use of the good and the ability to pay of the purchaser. Demand and the amount which those desiring a good are willing to bid for it determine what quantity of goods they are willing to forego for the sake of the desired good and this determines the costs to which the least productive sources of its production may amount to. (Quoted by Streissler, 1990c, p. 157)

This is a piece that covers much familiar micro-economic ground in a few lines. Its conciseness reinforces the idea that these ideas were well established by the time Hermann wrote.

2.6 Situating Menger and Mises

It is now generally recognized in the historical literature, albeit not without remaining controversy, that the founder of Austrian school of economics as it is characterized in the present day was Carl Menger (cf., for example, Vaughn, 1978, 1990). Streissler posits Menger in this role because of his 'wealth of seminal ideas and even more ... [because of his] original and unique *vision* of the economy ...'. He continues: 'Menger – given, of course, the personality that he was – had *the status, the institutional position to enforce at least initial concurrence with his opinions* and thus became the pivot on whom the school turned' (1972, pp. 427f; original emphasis). As Israel Kirzner testifies in this respect, 'in the course of the rebuilding of Austrian economics ..., Mengerian subjectivism was again and again to be the lodestar'. Underscoring the theme of my present inquiries, he goes on to write that 'it is in the gradual deepening and maturing of Mengerian subjectivism that the history of the Austrian School finds its unity and its *raison d'être'*. More specifically put, 'the Austrian position ... actually reveals a unique perspective on the nature of economic causation and on what can be known concerning that causation. That perspective stemmed from a Mengerian subjectivist understanding of the manner in which economic phenomena express human preferences and decisions' (Kirzner, 1994a, pp. xxiv, xxvii). Tempering voices on this matter are there to be heard, too. Max Alter, for example, gives due emphasis to the idea that the second generation of Austrians who came after Menger, led by Böhm-Bawerk and Wieser, began to deviate quite significantly from the complex, ambiguous and incomplete foundations that their mentor had laid (Alter, 1990a, pp. 8f, 221ff). The result was the really significant subjectivist and individualist insights of Menger were left behind. What were the truly Austrian dimensions became increasingly obscured by the blending of burgeoning neoclassical simplifications, especially as these affected the representation of human agency in understanding the generation of economic phenomena. It was only through the efforts of Mises that in the 1920s and 1930s and beyond, some serious pursuit of the subjectivist and individualist metatheory was maintained. His contributions remained in the wings with those of Menger and were brought back to centre-stage only when the revival of the Neo-Austrians took hold in the 1970s (see Vaughn, 1994).

Most importantly, sufficient recognition of Menger's foundations has been revived to facilitate a debunking of the myth that he was but one of the trinity of marginal theorists, including Léon Walras and W.S. Jevons, who reoriented economics towards modern neoclassical ortho-doxy. It is now generally accepted that Menger was the odd man out for a number of reasons. For example, Streissler has observed, with some justice as we are to see in the next chapter, that in his main theoretical exposition Menger incorporated '*practically all the ideas which make the application of the marginal calculus difficult and hazy*; and by his express refusal to recognize a unique and determinate market price he even discarded the main prop that supports marginalism' (1972, p. 438, original emphasis; cf. Jaffé, 1976). Menger's achievement was much more than his contribution to marginalist thought and his vision of the economy, founded on an extended ontology of subjectivist and individualist human agency, cannot be confined within mechanistic neo-classical principles. (cf. Kirzner, 1992, pp. 73, 83).

Menger's deep-seated subjectivism and emphasis on individual human processes, in particular, were just too profound in their implications for the methodology and substance of economics to be readily set in any formalized expression. He had, nonetheless, an ostensible desire to develop a universal and exactly argued body of theory. But we are soon to see how this was never to be possible, nor was it intended to be so, in any Walrasian-like sense. The prominence he gave to subjective value theory was but the first step in a much broader appreciation of the implications of subjectivism in economics. Menger was apparently unable to complete his intended project, and much of the rich legacy that he did leave is in a form that must be teased out from its often convoluted presentation.

All of the philosophical ideas examined in this chapter were present in the intellectual milieu that surrounded Menger. Even though he was immersed in the Austrian intellectual tradition, there can be little doubt that he was also quite familiar with German philosophical trends and was to some important extent influenced by them in formulating certain parts of his metatheory. His reaction to the German philosophical position on history and the human sciences comprised a critical backdrop for Menger in building up his epistemological and methodological principles (Alter, 1990a, pp. 23ff, 79ff, 89ff, 112ff). For example, it is apparent that although Menger admired Roscher and dedicated his first main work[4] to him, there developed a general disparity between the approach to economic analysis in Austria and Germany. A number of the Germans' metatheoretical principles, theoretical ideals and substantive ideas were in concert with Menger's own. Indeed, he apparently thought of his work as a continuation of the best that was being done in Germany by the 'older' Historicists rather than as opposed to it. He thought he was carrying on aspects of the work begun by Historicists in breaking away from the influences of classical economics. But he did not take such a definite position against the legitimacy of exact theory as they did, and he tried to preserve it in the context of an apparent acceptance of Aristotelian realism. The reason for this more immediate acceptance of such theory can be traced to Menger's quite different epistemological beliefs from those of the 'younger' Historicists.

As we have seen, Schmoller evidently thought of exact theory as a goal for economic science. But he thought of it as requiring much more fact gathering before the time would be right for endeavours to devise and substantiate such representations of the types of phenomena concerned. Such 'younger' Historicists were read by Menger as losing the qualities of historicism that he could accept, with their ever more dominant empiricist methodology and misplaced hostility to exact theory in economics. It was in a later work[5] that Menger made public his position against the Historicists' developments. At that time, he apparently intended to bridge the burgeoning gap between Austrian and German economics by giving a more reasoned account of the contrasts that had emerged. But the response from the Historicists to his metatheoretical criticisms of their work and to his own theoretical contributions was one of hostility and the *Methodenstreit* was the result. Although its origins are to be found in the disparate philosophical emphases of the two countries, this dispute manifested itself ultimately as an exchange between Menger and Schmoller over methodology that appeared in the literature of the early 1880s. But, as will be apparent from the metatheoretical positions outlined above, an argument about methodology in this context had a deeper source in their backgrounds of different beliefs about the epistemological nature of economic science. From their respective approaches to each other in the controversy, however, it is evident that neither really grasped what was at issue between them and thus there was little hope of ever reaching a settlement (Bostaph, 1976, 1978). The issues remained unresolved in what degenerated into a matching of personal and intellectual insults.

The precise nature of Schmoller's criticisms of Menger, or of Menger's attempts at a rebuttal in his later polemical writings, are not pertinent here (see Bostaph, 1976, pp. 70ff). The Austrian's position in the development of subjectivist economics is able to be assessed with little further reference to the particulars of this dispute. What remains important in the present context is the idea that Menger's stance originated from his adoption of metatheoretical principles that he believed were consistent with the *ontological* nature of the phenomena with which economics chose to deal. As has already been indicated, the core beliefs involved here were those of subjectivism and individualism.

As we saw in the previous section, Menger's subjectivism in economics, and many related economic ideas, continued an established Germanic intellectual tradition that began in the early years of the nineteenth century. It was from the extant Germanic economics literature that Menger drew what has become the enduring insight that economics is a science that has necessarily subjectivist foundations. There is no denying, then, that his thought in this direction was not completely original, for German economic philosophy included contributions in which many of the concepts and analyses that he pursued were present in various stages of development (cf. Alter, 1990a, pp. 152, 158). Be this as it may, the fact remains it was Menger's version of subjectivism and individualism that was transmitted to the Neo-Austrians by way of Mises. The imperative for this was reinforced by the fact that these aspects of German economics were suppressed towards the end of the nineteenth century. They were replaced at that time by the empiricism and holistic historicism of the 'younger' Historical School led by Schmoller (Streissler, 1990c, p. 159).

Whatever we may make of this German influence, Barry Smith and others before him have qualified the links by emphasizing that Menger as the founder of the Austrian school of economics can only be correctly interpreted when he is firmly situated in his relation to the peculiarities of contemporary Austrian philosophy. We have seen that the Austrian intellectual milieu was heavily influenced by an Aristotelian realism. As a consequence, it was a fundamental belief of Menger's that an essential order is immanent to the ontological structure of all reality and that this order has a nomologically form that can legitimately be represented by exact theory (Hutchison, 1973; Smith, 1990a, cf. Kauder, 1957; Alter, 1990a, pp. 112ff). He was an immediate realist in the sense that he claimed to identify essences in real phenomenal types on the basis of singular observations. The revealed essences define the necessary and sufficient conditions for the existence of a type of phenomenon, so it made no sense to pursue any extensive empirical inquiry in order to discover, reinforce and confirm its presence in reality as the Historicists had done. All that such inquiry could do was to enable the analyst to describe observable forms of the essentials previously established, for those essentials were not claimed to have any pure manifestation. Menger's distinctive methodology also reflected his ontological and methodological individualism. He was, that is, inclined to give priority in identifying the essentials of a phenomenon to those characteristics that link it back to the conduct of individual human agents. Causality in accounting for a type of phenomenon was similarly devised on the basis of individual relationships between the essential elements inherent in the structures that are likewise necessary and sufficient to define it. This causality could be exact if abstraction were sufficient, or it could retain realistic-empirical content where the scope of elements and relationships included were more extensive and conditional. In both these senses, causality is inherent in the identifying essentials of a phenomenal type and the laws of causality are laws imbedded in the essences and structures of the real type, with or without any empirical extensions. The fact that the representation of an exact essential causality was in a deductive logical format did not imply for Menger any retreat from realism. He believed that the logic was discovered and not imposed and that the 'laws of thought' are reflective of the 'laws of things'. And, moreover, such laws could only be relevant for relationships that involve individuals rather than collectives. For Menger, no collective could have a typical and hence an essential existence separate from its individual constituents.

Consistently with these Aristotelian ideas, it has been claimed that Menger sought to discover an 'ontological grammar of economic reality'

that could provide 'a pre-empirical qualitative framework' for understanding and explanation (Smith, 1990a, p. 279). He appeared, in this
respect, to be following out the implications of a type of methodology
grounded on an *a priori* rather than an empiricist epistemological vision
(Smith, 1990b, pp. 1f). However, judgements about Menger and any
apriorism argued to be evident in his treatment of economic phenomena
must be tempered by a proper understanding of the nature of the *a
priori* itself. For to be consistent, Menger had to sustain the idea of
realism at the same time (Smith, 1990a, 1990b, 1990c). It is the vision
of a reflectionist synthetic *a priori* that is asserted by Smith to be an
Austro-Aristotelian notion that was clearly and exclusively pursued by
Menger (1990b, *passim.*; 1990c, pp. 220ff, 230). The assertion thus made
is that 'the Austrian economist of whatever hue works against the
background of an assumption to the effect that the universals of economic reality are not created or imposed in any sense, but are discovered
through our theoretical efforts' (Smith, 1990b, p. 2). These universals
are assumed objectively to exist, but only imbedded within and as wholly
dependent upon the particular and unique empirically observable forms
of their instantiation. In this respect, Menger can be referred to as an
immanent realist concerning the existence of universals and to have
eschewed any view that they can only have a transcendentalist or nomin-
alist status (cf. Hutchison, 1973, pp. 17–18; Mäki, 1990, p. 295).

The Aristotelian reading of Menger's endeavour requires the epistemological legitimation of his belief in the essential order *as the product
of the actions of individual subjective human agents.* Any understanding
and explanation of the real-world existence of this order can only begin
from this ontological premiss. That is, from the most fundamental and
irreducible principle of the subjectivist and individualist vision applied
to the essentialist level of inquiry. The challenge then is to identify and
explicate the processes of such agency that can be shown by reasoned
argument to result in the creation of an essential order of events. And,
ultimately, these processes must be traced back to the purposeful actions
of individual agents, even though the actual form of the processes may
not be wholly explicable by conscious individual intentions alone. It
must be accepted that the subjectivist corollary of ontological individualism includes the potential for unintended individual and collective
consequences of agents' actions. More than this, too, in that if there are
to be laws of human agency and they are to have a universal and
timeless validity, the order must be shown somehow to have a real
and logical self-sufficiency that is ever present and independent of the
particulars of human agency that have resulted in the immediate, and
presumably unique and non-repeatable, empirical appearance of the

phenomenon concerned. Claims by analysts that such an essential order is simply 'there' as a matter of its common-sense intelligibility do not constitute a sufficient understanding of its generation to enable us genuinely to account for its existence. For Menger, Smith argues, 'the knowing subject and the objects of knowledge are ... in some sense and to some degree *pre-tuned* to each other' and that this view 'implies precisely that economic reality is such as to manifest intelligible structures in and of itself. It is because economic reality is built up in intelligible ways out of structures involving human thought and action that we are able, by appropriate efforts, to read off these structures in and of themselves' (1990a, p. 275, original emphasis; 1990b, p. 2). It is the nature of the 'appropriate efforts' that enable us as analysts 'to read off' the discursively representable immanent economic order that should be the object of further inquiry, even if we presume to believe the order to exist independently of our thoughts, *qua* analysts, about it. The origin of this belief, however, then needs to be defended in and of itself by establishing just how, *operationally conceived*, 'economic reality is built up in intelligible ways out of structures involving human thought and action', along with some insight into the ontological (existential) nature of this 'reality'. That is, as Smith emphasizes at one point, the espousal of a reflectionist apriorism in economics cannot mean a divorce from concerns with empirical reality, whatever means of mental access to the relevant essential categories are assumed (1990a, p. 279).

Menger's immediate successors in developing Austrian economics, Eugen von Böhm-Bawerk and Friedrich von Wieser, revealed little interest in addressing the metatheoretical issues that he left unresolved. They were preoccupied with matters of substantive economics and gave little attention to the import of subjectivism *per se* for methodology and epistemology (Alter, 1990b, pp. 221ff; Streissler, 1990c). Indeed, it is an unfortunate fact that what were some of Menger's most original and powerful insights were simply sidelined. The significant contributions of these successors, by which substantive Austrian economics became known to the world at large, involved some improvements in Menger's formulation of value theory (including Wieser's conception of diminishing marginal utility), but they comprised especially the more formal representation of the supply side in a theory of production (with an emphasis on the role of capital, albeit in its constricted Austrian guise) and an increasingly sophisticated treatment of marginalist distribution theory. Each explored methodological issues at some stage (Böhm-Bawerk, 1994; Wieser, 1994a, 1994b), but these were digressions that served largely to prioritize and reinforce Menger's defence of the status of abstract, universal theories in economics. Each maintained, at a formalistic level, Menger's subjectivism of preferences as the foundation for understanding exchange values, with little concern for any deeper roots and broader implications of the subjectivist idea. They allowed objectivist and instrumentalist intrusions, even into value and price theory, without much thought about how these could be made consistent with the more fundamental demands of subjectivism. But, most significantly, for neither of them was subjectivism an ontological foundation for understanding economic phenomena, and it did not suggest a teleological mode of explanation for such phenomena based on human deliberations, choices and actions.

In Böhm-Bawerk's methodological testament, he opened with the declaration that 'I am a defender of the method called by Menger "exact"', one which he renamed 'the "isolating" method' (1994, pp. 111, 127n. 2). However, at the same time, he seemed inclined to want to smooth out some of the differences with the Germans of the Historical School by adopting an eclectic approach founded on a quite superficial comparison. In doing so, his intention was to show that this 'isolating' methodology was *per se* empirical and that what the Historicists had been doing in practice all along amounted to the very same thing (1994, pp. 119ff). He thereby conflated the unresolved dualism that Menger had allowed for between 'empirical' and 'exact' theory. There was also in Böhm-Bawerk's argument a hint of Aristotelian realism carried forward from Menger. For instance, he espoused the practice of devising exact theory by 'the intellectual exploitation of the treasures of experience by all the methods which our mental constitution allows, and among them by the method of abstract-deductive "distillation"' (1994, p. 119). In a similar vein he went on to reiterate that 'the abstract-deductive method . . . is in its very essence a genuinely empirical method' which has 'no fancy *a priori* axioms as a basis for its inferences . . .' (1994, p. 122). Moreover, he compounded his eclecticism when he saw that the psychological foundation for economics called for by Schmoller was already present in the contributions of Menger and Wieser. On this basis, in referring to 'the so-called abstract-deductive school', he went on to assert that 'it would not at all surprise me if in the future this school should come to be called the "psychological school of political economy"' (1994, p. 123).

Of the two Menger successors, though, it was Wieser who was the more philosophically sensitive. His recommended methodology was very similar to that outlined by Böhm-Bawerk in its reference to Austrians as 'experientialists' whose methodology 'idealizes' in the sense that 'it does not copy nature, but gives us a simplified representation of it, which is no misrepresentation, but such as sharpens our vision in view of the complexities of reality . . .' (1994a, p. 237). In this claim, there is again the continuation of the Aristotelianism that was found in Menger's arguments. Wieser preserved some interest in the subjectivist roots of market conduct (1994a, pp. 246f) and also gave economics a psychologistic inclination that has been much disputed ever since. He can be seen to have struggled with the idea of economics as an essentially human science, but without a proper grasp of the subjectivist ontology that this idea entailed. Although he repudiated any resort to scientific or theoretical psychology in economics, he did allow that 'our subject matter is the consciousness of a person engaging in economic activity' (1994b, p. 289). And, the psychological penetration sought was delimited, for 'we wish to remain on the surface of consciousness, never to go into its remoter depths . . .' (1994b, p. 299). Wieser's 'psychological' methodology was nevertheless one that he attempted to defend on the basis of its reliance on introspective extrapolations by claiming that economic facts should be observed 'above all from inside one's consciousness'. From this perspective, psychological economists can 'observe incomparably more and in more depth than from outside' (1994b, p. 290). In doing so, 'they each put the crucial questions to themselves and answer them according to their inner experience . . .'. Such experience was sufficient, he claimed, to give economists insight into relevant laws: 'we obtain from the testimony of inner experience knowledge of a law which we know we can effectively take for granted in all circumstances' (1994b, p. 299).

All this seemed to be aimed at keeping economic inquiry in touch with its fundamentally human dimensions, but it really posed more questions than it answered by reference to self-evident, intuitively substantiable 'laws' and assumptions. At one point, though, Wieser revealed an important and enduring insight into what was at issue in pursuing the subjectivist alternative. Using an early work of Joseph Schumpeter as a case in point, he rejected the notion that methodology was to be imposed and prior to the exposition of economic understanding and explanation.[6] By contrast, he followed the arguably more apt Aristotelian procedure of putting consistency with the ontology of the object phenomena before the demands of methodology. Thus he wrote: 'Blinded by the success of the exact natural sciences, he [Schumpeter] takes their way of thinking as a model *even where it in no way suits our material* and thus constructs an artificial method . . .; here his view of the nature of theoretical economics prevents him from fully portraying its substance' (1994b, p. 287, emphasis added). At another point in the same context, Wieser saw, as Böhm-Bawerk had done, the need for idealized abstractions in constructing discursive argument about complex human phenomena. As Wieser put it, in idealized representations 'we elevate the empirical case in thoughts to the level of the highest possible perfection. For example, we assume the existence of a model person engaging in economic activity such as has never actually existed and never can...' (1994b, p. 295). There was in this a touch of Aristotelian realism that he reinforced with the qualifying observation that 'even such idealising assumptions in no way render our theory unempirical, for they ... are always only made in order to understand reality, and therefore they are only temporary assumptions which in the end have to be corrected' (1994b, p. 295). Unfortunately, the limited potential of Wieser's methodological insights were never fully worked out and he is largely remembered now for his attempt to give economics a 'psychologically' grounded rigour (cf. Hutchison, 1981, pp. 205ff).

These truncated methodological statements by Böhm-Bawerk and Wieser, in which they failed to pursue subjectivism as an ontological doctrine, signalled the beginning of the post-Mengerian decline of a uniquely Austrian economics. Indeed, it was especially through the dominant success of Böhm-Bawerk's *substantive* ideas, that the methodological and epistemological concerns resulting from an emphasis on the human exigencies of economics as they had been confronted by Menger, and to a lesser extent by Wieser, faded in importance. Menger's and Wieser's intuition that economics as a human science required its own ontologically driven methodology was not viewed as an imperative for 'doing' economics. Austrian contributions began to appear increasingly like the scientistic and formalist doctrine that was to dominate orthodox economics into the early decades of the twentieth century and beyond. It was by then already widely accepted as being a theoretical, axiomatic-deductive discipline. The blending of the Austrian dimension into British economics was reinforced through the influence of Lionel Robbins's widely read book *The Nature and Significance of Economic Science* (1932). Robbins took a very restricted view of the role of subjectivism as it appeared in Menger's and others' works available to him at the time. He did not recognize any need to follow out its broader and more intractable implications for understanding and formally representing explanations of economic phenomena. What Robbins revealed was a distinctive Austrian message, but it was one with little subjectivist penetration (cf. Addleson, 1984). It was ultimately the Austrian economics of the post-war variety, that arose in Vienna of the 1920s and 1930s, which came to identify the substance of the school. And, as it was extant at the time, with its links to Böhm-Bawerk and Wieser more obvious than those to the deeper subjectivist insights of Menger, the school had sufficient similarity to the essentials of the Marshallian and

Walrasian analyses for that separate identity gradually to be lost from sight (Kirzner, 1994a, pp. xviff).

By the time Mises began his main metatheoretical inquiries in the late 1920s, the more extensive ideas, implications and problematics concerning the place of subjectivism in the human sciences generally were well established and readily accessible in the philosophical literature. For Mises, inquiries oriented towards an extended subjectivism remained of immediate, if not exclusive concern. In some of his main works we find what amounted to a 'rediscovery of Mengerian themes'. It was Mises's collected essays on these issues published in 1933, together with his numerous later works, that were to set in place much of the foundation for subsequent developments in Austrian subjectivism.[7] To an extent, the return to Menger's subjectivist vision pursued in these works was a result of the socialist calculation controversy of the period in which Mises was the key protagonist (see Kirzner (ed.), 1994, volume III; Kirzner, 1994a, pp. xxff; 1994c, pp. xivff). His rejection of centralized calculation as a viable substitute for what markets do required him to write explicitly about the autonomous operation of the 'invisible hand'. That is, about those processes that mediate in the coordination of the collective outcome of individual choices confronted by scarce resources. The ensuing debate 'forced Mises ... to come to grips with aspects of the economic process which called for precisely those radically subjectivist insights which had been implicit, at the very least, in Menger's broad vision' (Kirzner, 1994a, p. xiii).

However, what my reading is intended to expose, in particular, is the extent to which Menger's seminal contributions, and much of Mises's development of them in his substantive economics, remained nevertheless removed from the more penetrating and extensive, existentially grounded subjectivist theses available in contemporary works of the philosophy of the human sciences. This alternative line of subjectivist ideas emerged largely alongside Menger's work, but there is little evidence that his ideas were affected by it. From its inception, though, the evolving alternative was more concerned with dynamic effects of active human minds and was more sensitive to the difficulties of understanding and accounting discursively for the resulting object phenomena. Menger, and later Mises, may have been aware that the import of subjectivism transcended the problem of economic value and the stationary equilibrium context, and they may also have begun to see human perception and action as the keys to understanding market processes. But, as I shall argue in detail in the next chapter, whatever may be rediscovered in Menger, a reading of his works against the background of the contemporary intellectual milieu suggests that his was a constricted view of subjectivism. It reveals that in forming his understanding of human agency, he chose to reach into the accumulated knowledge of the philosophy of the human sciences only to a limited and selective extent. Menger evidently had a less than complete appreciation of the true scope of this broader subjectivist perspective and how it reacted back on the totality of economics. Mises, by contrast, chose to pursue the accumulated philosophical literature at least in a desultory manner. His limited contact with and critique of the key writings of the interim period did enable him to reassert the place of subjectivism and individualism in economics. His was an idiosyncratic version of subjectivist economics, but one that was richer in insights than that devised by Menger. Nonetheless, it, too, remained less than complete in its coverage of the relevant philosophical arguments upon which he might have drawn. In the end, the limitations and ambiguity of the Menger–Mises legacy left much scope for clarification and development of subjectivism as the metatheoretical foundation for the understanding and discursive representation of substantive economic phenomena. As a consequence, it has been the attitude of neo-Austrian writers towards working out the nature and implications of subjectivism that has been a main contributing cause of the controversy and division among them that has become apparent since the 1970s.

Notes

1. Droysen (1967) contains both the review article on Buckle just cited as well as two other historiographical papers and the monograph *Outline of the Principles of History* (*Grundriss der Historik*) first edition 1867, third edition 1881).
2. The most significant writer of the era in Austria was Franz Brentano (1838–1917), an exact contemporary of Menger in the academic life of Vienna. He was a southern German Catholic, but his philosophical ideas and their intellectual influences were predominantly and characteristically Austrian. For most of his long life he lived in Vienna and his popular lectures at the University were attended by a wide range of intellectuals in different fields. By this means, and through his extensive writings, he had a wide-ranging and lasting impact on *fin-de-siècle* Austrian thought. The orientation of Brentano's philosophy, in his many works published (and left unpublished) over the period from 1862 onwards, was dominated by his life-long interest in the ontology, epistemology and psychology of Aristotle. This interest was congenial to the Austrians and provided the basis for Brentano's popular recognition. It was an Aristotelian realism that permeated especially into the 'descriptive psychology' for which he became most widely known (Brentano, 1973).
3. See note 2 above.
4. The *Grundsätze der Volkswirthschafslehre* of 1871 (1950, 1981).
5. The *Untersuchungen über die Methode der Socialwissenschaften, und der politischen Oekonomie insbesondere* of 1883 (1963).

6. Wieser published his critical review of Schumpeter's *Das Wesen und der Hauptinhalt der theoretischen Nationalökonomie* (1910) in 1911 (1994b).
7. The essays appeared as the *Grundprobleme der Nationalökonomie* (translated as *Epistemological Problems of Economics*, 1960) and his later main works included his magnum opus *Human Action* published in 1949 (1966).

3. Carl Menger's seminal subjectivist legacy

3.1 Preamble

The metatheoretical foundations of Menger's economics have two crucial characteristics. On the one hand, he intended to preserve the potential for theoretical rigour and precision that he associated with the epistemology of the physical sciences. On the other hand, he was a self-conscious subjectivist and individualist in his understanding of empirical economic phenomena, and he intended to maintain a theoretical orientation that was consistent with this ontology (cf. Howey, 1960, pp. 24ff; Alter, 1982, 1990a, 1990b; Streissler, 1990c, 1990d; Vaughn, 1990; Milford, 1995a; cf. Kirzner, 1994a, pp. xivff).

Menger's physical scientistic predilection in epistemology demanded that economic phenomena be understood as essentially nomological and be represented by universal and exact theoretical explanations. His ontological consciousness interacted with this scientistic prepossession in forcing him explicitly to confront the problematic of formally representing individual, subjective human agents as the generators of all phenomena of the human sciences. He well knew that individual human agency has chronically contingent dimensions to be contended with in formulating any exact understanding and explanation of economic phenomena. These contingencies had to be shown to be dispensable, or at least able legitimately to be held in abeyance, if valid theories were to be constructed according to the demands of formal, deductive logic and in a fashion that emulated the apparent qualities of physical science theories. The result would have to be a representation of the human agent as a consistently reasoning individual who responds to stimuli in a regular and reliable manner. At first sight, this requirement of scientistically precise theory demands an objective, so-called rational representation of the human agent. Menger focused on some specific non-contingent facets of agents' conduct in response to particular economic circumstances, but in the end, as we shall see, the temptation was to impose these by analytical fiat, as the Classicals had done with their *homo oeconomicus*, rather than by reasoned analysis. The apparent void that remained between the subjectivist and objectivist-scientistic levels of his methodological and substantive endeavours was thus never closed by any ontologically defensible argument, even though he identified just those elements of subjectivism and individualism that were responsible for it.

The seminal metatheoretical foundations and substance of an economics in which subjectivist and individualist insights into the generation of phenomena dominate were set out by Menger in his *Grundsätze der Volkswirthschafslehre* in 1871 (1950, 1981). His later contributions in the *Untersuchungen über die Methode der Socialwissenschaften, und der politischen Oekonomie insbesondere* of 1883 (1963), and in the papers that followed it, were then evidently intended to elaborate upon, but to remain consistent with, the metatheoretical principles already implicit in the 1871 work. His main writings are, that is, of a piece and the only appropriate reading is a 'synthetic' one that draws ideas from them all (Alter, 1990b, *passim*). Menger's immediate concern in the *Grundsätze*, and throughout his later writings, was to establish the independent validity of his new microeconomics, in both its methodology and substance, and to communicate it to others in the Germanic world. His clear intention was to reform the way economics had been developing in the Germanic literature, with its ever more dominant historicist and inductivist methodology. There was in this development an increasing trend away from theory altogether to contend with. While he was unhappy with the pure objectivism of the Classicals, theory had a place in economics that he saw as needing correction rather than negation. It was in the *Untersuchungen* that he set out on the basis of what he felt he had achieved in the *Grundsätze* expressly to convince the Historicists to mend their errant metatheoretical ways.

Menger's later writings, including the *Untersuchungen* and beyond, concentrated on a critique of the claims to exclusive relevance and validity of empirico-inductive inquiry of this sort in economics (1884, 1887, 1889). He implicitly thereby stood the metatheory of the human sciences on its head, as it were, by reversing the priority the Historicists attributed to the independent spirit of social wholes. Instead, he reiterated the primacy he had given to the active and subjective nature of individual agents in the *Grundsätze* of 1871. Menger's vision was of social wholes as the combined intended and unintended collective consequence of individual agents' deliberations and actions. His depiction of agents was as actively engaging their inherited dynamic situations through ongoing deliberation and problem-solving. At the same time,

they act collectively in a conscious or unconscious manner effectively
to change these situations over the longer period.

Menger was intent on differentiating his rendering of the science
from the predominantly empirico-historical and practical descriptive
treatments of economic issues that he found in much of the Germanic
literature. These were quite one-sided in their emphasis on the historical
branches of inquiry, tending to underestimate and/or misdirect morphological and theoretical work, and to be ineffective in their application
of economics to policy formulation. These characteristics were especially
evident in Germany and had a secure foothold among the Viennese
professors, too. A glance at the late nineteenth century economics
subjects on offer in the University of Vienna, and the credentials of the
professors teaching them, does not reveal any overwhelming concern
for theoretical inquiry, even though Menger's influence there increased
during the 1870s and 1880s (Howey, 1960, pp. 173ff; Hayek, 1981,
pp. 21ff; cf. Philippovich, 1912). But, during this same period, the hostility towards his sort of abstract and allegedly useless theory in
Germany was also increasing, very largely as a consequence of the
widespread and growing influence of the unbalanced historico-empiri-
cist economic thought espoused by Schmoller. It was these trends to
which Menger, evidently by around the mid-1870s, began to attribute
the poor reception of the first edition of his *Grundsätze*. His subjectivist
theoretical contributions, with their formally argued presentation and
their methodological individualist setting, had failed to gain what he
thought to be due recognition as the proper foundation and complement
for the other branches of economics. The *Untersuchungen* was explicitly
intended to improve mutual understanding with the Historicists along
these lines.

Two effects on Menger's work became evident at around this time,
both of which are important for our proper understanding of his ideas.
First, his attitude towards the Historicists themselves as contributors to
economics took on a negative and critical orientation. But, at the same
time, he maintained his view that there was value in their work as
representative of the historical branches of the science. Secondly, he
diverted most of his intellectual energies towards the primacy of methodological reform as the basis for the substantive revision of economics
as a whole. The intention was to establish an appropriate place for his
ontologically founded essentialist theory. Menger considered that he
had developed economics substantively as a formalized theoretical
science that was consistent with his subjectivist and individualist principles, while at the same time maintaining as far as appropriate the
standards of epistemology and methodology set in the natural-physical

sciences. At the same time, he emphasized that as a representative of Austrian economics, his differences with the Historical School should not be too sharply drawn. For example, merely labelling him a deductivist and them as inductivists was misleading. In a passage that tells us much about Menger's metatheoretical intentions, he stressed rather that:

> the true contrast between these schools is not even remotely characterized as that between an empirical and a rationalist approach or an inductive and deductive one. Both recognize that the necessary basis for the study of real phenomena and their laws is that of experience. Both recognize ... that induction and deduction are closely related, mutually supporting, and complementary means to knowledge. (1894, p. 279, quoted by Hutchison, 1973, p. 35)

Throughout his work, too, we find a devotion to reforming economics as a well balanced set of complementary branches, each of which had its legitimate methodology and substantive purpose and coverage. As late as 1898, for example, in his last published methodological piece, he rendered economics as comprising four branches of inquiry: the historical (statistics and history proper), the morphological (descriptive and structural classification), the theoretical and the applied (1960, p. 15).

My reading of Menger will highlight what I believe were his primary concerns with subjectivist and individualist ontology, an orientation also given some attention by Max Alter (1990a). By contrast, some scholars, Karl Milford (1989, 1990, 1992b) and Jack Birner (1990) most especially, have oriented their critical inquiries towards Menger's focus on the immediate puzzles of epistemology and methodology that he believed obstructed communication with German economists at large. Thus, claims Milford, Menger 'primarily focused on problems such as the aim and the task of the theoretical social sciences, the structure of their explanations, issues concerning induction, and a sound epistemological justification of the social sciences *qua* theoretical sciences' (1990, p. 219). My argument will be that even though Menger explicitly gave primary attention to such issues, he knew that they required the established ontological foundations of economics in order to explicate their nature and significance and to legitimate their resolution. Most of what Menger wrote about these issues, and most of the difficulties he encountered in doing so, whether he was conscious of them or not, were always an integral extension of and dependent upon his subjectivist and individualist ontological position. His claims to have formulated any theoretical representation of an economic phenomenon can be legitimated or otherwise by showing the degree to which the arguments are consistent with the ontological essentials of situated human agency. Moreover, endeavours to interpret Menger's epistemology and its methodological consequences that omit ontological inquiries concerning the sort of phenomena on which he focused cannot be considered complete. What such incomplete ontological readings of Menger fail to acknowledge in particular is the extent to which he was unable and/or unwilling to allow all of the tenets of subjectivism that he had actually identified, and explicitly made reference to, to enter into his formal analyses without fear or favour. It will be shown below that this was a result of his scientistic epistemological predilections and the consequent dualistic methodology that he adopted and so staunchly defended.

Menger's ontology concerned itself primarily with phenomena that are generated by the deliberations, plans and actions of individual agents in that most fundamental of human preoccupations, the endeavour to satisfy material and other essential life needs and wants. He depicted agents as most immediately engaging in activities dedicated to maximizing this objective within the bounds of their inherited resources, their given environment and situation, and their individual capacities and limitations. The relevant operations of production, exchange and distribution in which agents participate are all geared to this objective one way or another, and it is these operations, carried out as processes set in time, that constitute the vitalist vision of the economy perceived by Menger. Agents are bound to act to satisfy their needs and wants within a given resource structure, but in doing so they exhibit all the characteristics that render their conduct contingent with respect to any given problem and situation. They act according to various combinations of their innate characteristics and free will, together with their desires, beliefs, preferences, values, knowledge, information and expectations. Their deliberations and plans relate to the future and are thus always replete with uncertainty, in spite of which agents must act economically. In doing so, agents expose the limits of their capacity to apply reason to their circumstances and their resulting fallibility. They endeavour to mitigate their uncertainty and raise their rationality as far as possible through obtaining knowledge and information, but they are often forced to act on incomplete states of both. In the process, they also reveal their limitations as calculators and they are likely to make errors of judgement (cf. Jaffé, 1976, p. 521).

The result of these insights for Menger was a theoretical exposition which, for all its imprecisions and incompleteness, tried to capture the essential idea that subjectivist economics is about individual human agency and the *in situ* processes it comprises. It is not about states because it deals with systems in time and in constant flux, so that it is an inherently dynamic rather than a static inquiry. Menger was no systematically equilibrium economist and although his writings included references to the potential for individual and partial equilibria to exist, the essential thrust of his vision was towards non-equilibrating processes. Indeed, it is Menger's devotion to this broad subjectivist and individualist dynamic insight to which we must attribute most of the very limitations that can be exposed with the benefit of our hindsight. His consciousness of time in human affairs simply took him beyond what he could cope with in his attempts at formulating precise discursive representations of economic phenomena. Streissler's summary statement approximates the tenor of my own conclusions about Menger that will emerge in this chapter.

> He wrote a completely subjective theory; and that meant that he eschewed deriving concrete results. He was content to show all the manifold dimensions of causation in the economic field. In his view the final outcome of all these forces at work could not be fully described. And that is the basic failure of his theory: he ended in doubt and not in positive theorems. (1972, pp. 440f)

Although this nascently nihilistic reading of Menger is unacceptable to some, it is readily established to be a defensible one. Such an interpretation has also emerged from Alter's detailed research (1982, 1990a, 1990b). And yet, even these radical implications of his subjectivism left a wider sense in which it was 'incomplete'. This incompleteness took the form of his ultimate failure to draw together and fully to explicate the significance of his own multitude of subjectivist insights. It will be emphasized in my inquiries to follow that he was well aware of virtually all of the dimensions of human agency that should be included in a subjectivist and individualist ontology, and that he sensed the analytical intractability that resulted. Certainly, a more challenging legacy was left for his followers than merely his claimed failure to deal with needs and wants consistently within this perspective or his failure fully to appreciate the significance of entrepreneurial activities (cf. Lachmann, 1978a, *passim*; Kirzner, 1992, pp. 74ff).[1]

Section 3.2 below begins my main argument by examining the subjective nature and individual human origin of economic phenomena as these were exposited in the *Grundsätze* and the *Untersuchungen*. In this context, the essentials of Menger's ontology and his consequent concern to render all economic phenomena as the products of individual human action will become apparent. Although he made few direct references to matters of ontology, the arrangement and tenor of his substantive arguments in these works give us sufficient indication of his intentions. The particular themes of this section are first, the *telos* of human agency as it involves the pursuit of satisfaction of needs and wants and as it concerns the subjective nature of the value of goods; and secondly, the problematic of goods production, including the valuation of inputs. In section 3.3 below, I consider Menger's epistemological and methodological intentions as they developed in the construction of his revisionist approach to economic theory on the foundations of a subjectivist and individualist ontology. The mix of exact and realistic-empirical methodological principles he actually defended is outlined and argued to be a specific outcome of this ontology. Finally, in section 3.4 below, I draw together the metatheoretical issues that Menger pursued in his writings. I propose some critical conclusions about the pertinent issues that he left without conclusive resolution and that his Austrian successors and neo-Austrian followers were driven to wrestle with.

3.2 A subjectivist ontology of economic phenomena

In the preface of his *Grundsätze*,[2] Menger focused immediately on the existential nature of the phenomena with which he was to deal and the discursive representational challenges that confronted him as a consequence. His stated intention was to rework 'the fundamentals of our science' (p. 46) and thereby to restore some of the lost faith in economics that he claimed had become widespread among those who needed to apply its principles. Menger's ostensible emphasis was on the presentation of economics as a science with an epistemological status that emulated the natural sciences. In particular, he believed that he should seek 'to demonstrate successfully that the phenomena of economic life, like those of nature, are ordered strictly in accordance with definite laws' (p. 48). 'In what follows', he wrote, 'I have endeavoured to reduce the complex phenomena of human economic activity to the simplest elements that can still be subjected to accurate observation . . . [and] to investigate the manner in which the more complex economic phenomena evolve from their elements according to definite principles' (pp. 46f).

In these passages, Menger's vision of economic phenomena is that, in their constituent elements, they are immanently ordered in and of themselves. Here we have a purely ontological assertion that makes an explicit claim about the nature of the reality with which economic argument must deal. And, his use of the words 'reduce' and 'evolve' in the second piece, with their suggestions of imbeddedness and operational generation respectively, are similarly ontological. These are Aristotelian like presumptions that suggest his adherence to a non-Kantian reflectionist *a priori* view of mental access to reality (cf. Smith, 1990b, 1990c). Menger's insight was such in the present context, though, as to allow him at least to sense, rather than clearly to see, the important differences in the application of the scientistic methodology that flow from the distinct ontological nature of the object phenomena in economics. He was explicitly critical of claims that the methodology could be directly transferred between sciences. Thus, the Aristotelian argument that 'every method of investigation acquires its own specific character from the nature of the field of knowledge to which it is applied' (p. 47) renders methodology effectively posterior to the establishment of the ontology of the object phenomenon. Moreover, it reflects his realist epistemology in that it presses for methodology to be devised in a manner consistent with the object's essential and accurate, if simplified representation.

3.2.1 The *telos* of human agency and subjective value

Menger's pre-analytical vision is of a system in which goods (including services) are produced and exchanged. In this respect, he approached his theoretical inquiries in two stages. Some goods were presumed to be available as stocks and primarily designed to meet final consumers' demand directly. These were the focus of the valuation and exchange processes and immediately involved in the satisfaction of needs and wants. Other goods of an intermediate nature may be produced for use as means of production in the future production of consumer goods. These sorts of goods can meet needs and wants only indirectly. A production process in which they are used is at root a means of physically transforming input goods into output goods of a different form, generally incrementally closer to final consumption. But for Menger, the vision of the process had to be presented as a subjectivist complex if the material dimensions involved were to have an *economic* form. Individual human agents were just as much involved in production as they were in the *telos* of exchange. What Menger began to recognize in the second stage of his analyses was that the subjective dimensions of production were rather more intractable than those concerned with valuing and exchanging given final goods.

In this total economic complex, the needs and wants (*Bedürfnisse*), and the activities of human agents directed at their satisfaction, directly or indirectly, were brought to the fore. Consequently, at its ontological roots, an economy's existence in this vision is constituted by, and its empirical phenomena are the manifestation of, the many subjective facets of satisfying human needs and wants that give rise to the teleology of human action. Thus, Menger argued, 'needs arise from our drives and the drives are imbedded in our nature', and 'the attempt to provide for the satisfaction of our needs is synonymous with the attempt to provide for our lives and well-being'. But more than this is involved, for Menger added the powerful insight that the pursuit of needs satisfaction 'is the most important of all human endeavours, since it is the prerequisite and foundation of all others'. It is this notion that makes production the most essential of the economic processes in which agents engage: 'In practice, the concern of men for the satisfaction of their needs is expressed as an attempt to attain command of all the things on which the satisfaction of their needs depends' (p. 77). The reference to 'things' here emphasized that there exists a mediation between needs and their satisfaction that Menger posited as the physical form of the good. Most significantly, though, to reiterate the subjectivity involved, 'man, with his needs and his command of the means to satisfy them, is himself the point at which human economic life both begins and ends' (p. 108). In the *Untersuchungen* this most fundamental idea was further emphasized when he recognized economic aims, and hence economics itself as meaning most essentially that 'only the premeditative activity of humans aimed at the indirect or direct satisfaction of their material needs is to be considered as economic...' (1963, p. 193n, cf. p. 217). The use of the term 'premeditative' reflects Menger's subjectivist premisses in that it defines scientifically relevant human activity as self-conscious, purposeful and deliberative.

The fundamental status of needs and wants in Menger's study of economics was reinforced by the fact that when working on the planned second edition of the *Grundsätze*, he chose to give more explicit and detailed emphasis to the theory of *Bedürfnisse* in a new chapter.[3] Most especially, this additional attention was indicative of the crucial ontological importance he attributed to the satisfaction of needs and wants as the driving and directing force of economic action. In the new chapter, he opened with a quite clearly stated set of ontological foundations for what was to follow.

> The point of departure for all theoretical investigations in economics is the nature of humanity that is in its needs and wants [*bedürftige Menschennatur*]. Without needs and wants there could be no economy, no economic system, and no science of them. Needs and wants are the ultimate origin of, their satisfaction is the meaning and ultimate measure of, and their protection is the ultimate objective of human economic activity. The theory of needs and wants (the knowledge and understanding of their essential nature) is of

fundamental importance for economic science. Similarly it is the bridge
which leads from the natural sciences, especially biology, to the human
sciences in general and to economic science in particular. (Menger, 1923,
p. 1, quoted in Alter, 1990a, p. 124; my translation)

Menger emphasized that the ontological origin of all economic activity
is to be found in the fact that human agents have needs and wants
imbedded in their nature. These give a *telos*, comprising an objective
and direction, to the resulting economic activity by agents at its most
fundamental level. So it is that the needs and wants are the final cause
of economic activity and their imbedded ontological status means that
the explanation of economic activity must be teleological in that its
purposes are its essence (cf. Alter, 1990a, p. 127). It is the form taken
by the pursuit of the satisfaction of these needs that constitutes an
economic system and generates the phenomena that comprise the
economy. These phenomena are the objects of the inquiries and of
the consequent theories that comprise the foundations of economic
science. Menger also posited economics as among the human sciences,
which because they deal with the pursuit of purposes of subjective
agents, must ultimately reach beyond the limits of anything that the
natural sciences can have to say about the human realm. The natural
and human worlds of science are linked only by the fact that the
natural dimensions of human existence, the imbedded needs and wants,
are reflected in, but in no way determine absolutely, the *subjectively
devised* actions of agents to satisfy them.

Material goods mediate in the satisfaction of needs and wants, but
the idea of a *good* itself was subjectively defined by reference to four
simultaneously essential causal conditions for the existence of such a
potentially useful thing. Each of these causal roots had an irreducible
human connection: a human need to be met; the capacity of the thing
to cause the need to be satisfied; individual knowledge that this causality
exists; sufficient command over the thing for it to be directed by the
individual to the satisfaction of the need (p. 52). For Menger it followed
necessarily that the value of goods[4] could not be identified on the basis
of any characteristic or status of a good itself, for value 'is a judgement
economizing men make' and it cannot 'exist outside the consciousness
of men' (p. 121). Value is tied directly back to the confrontation between
the existential state of the agents who generate it and the capacity of the
relevant good to change that state in a way desired by the agent. As
we have seen, the state to be changed is one of need or want and the
change itself is the satisfaction of that need or want. 'The value of goods
is therefore nothing arbitrary, but always the necessary consequence of

human knowledge that the maintenance of life, of well-being, ... depends upon control of a good or a quantity of goods' (p. 120, cf. pp. 51f, 147f). As well as espousing the subjective *nature* of value, Menger also emphasized that its *measure* is similarly subjective in that the degree of satisfaction delivered by a particular quantity of a particular good will vary from one individual to another. Thus: 'Goods always have value *to* certain economizing individuals and this value is also *determined* only by these individuals' (p. 146).[5]

Human needs and wants were, according to Menger, among the 'most original factors of human economy'. These comprise 'the needs, the goods offered directly to humans by nature (both the consumption goods and the means of production concerned), and the desire for the most complete satisfaction of needs possible (for the most complete covering of material needs possible)'. His essential premiss was that all these factors 'are ultimately given by the particular situation, independent of human choice' so that the 'starting point and the goal of all economy ... are ultimately given to the economic human, strictly determined in respect to their nature and their measure' (1963, p. 63, cf. pp. 216f). But care is needed in interpreting the 'given' and 'determined' status of needs and wants implied here. Menger said quite explicitly in the *Untersuchungen* that extant needs and wants are those determined for each economic subject '*by his individual nature and previous development (by his individuality)*' (1963, p. 217; emphasis added). It is clear that while some part of the needs is genetically and biologically linked to sustaining human life itself, the import of 'previous development' and 'individuality' are that this innate basis of needs is modified by the agents' cumulative biographical and socializing experiences. Here Menger emphasized that needs and wants can change over time, presumably in their nature and ranking (cf. Rosner, 1990, p. 2). Included here are responses to changes in the physical nature and availability of goods, as well as changes in subjective factors alone, in particular changes in the patterns of human needs and '*changes in* the *knowledge* men have of the importance of goods for their lives and welfare' (p. 148). Thus there will be variations in the perceived optimum route to the satisfaction of needs and wants through the choice of goods and the relative values ascribed to them by agents. The crucial point to be made is that the satisfaction of needs and wants by goods cannot be entirely divorced from the physical–technical properties of the latter. And, if they are to be of proper use to agents, the agents must know fully what these properties are.

But, whatever may be the explanation for the perception and ranking of needs and wants that agents have at the beginning of any period of observation of their conduct, and whatever may be the origins of the inherited economic situation selectively confronted by agents, these things are to be taken as given only for the purpose of understanding of the subsequent pursuit of the satisfaction of the needs now immediately apparent to them. Menger emphasized in the *Untersuchungen* that '*the starting point and the goal of every concrete human economy are ultimately determined strictly by the economic situation of the moment*' (1963, p. 217). And, whatever their origin, the intensity of the drives experienced by agents to satisfy different types of needs and wants vary considerably with the agents' characters and conditions. Menger was astute enough to recognize, too, that the intensity of this drive varies inversely with the progressive degree of satisfaction of the total of a particular need or want until it disappears altogether (pp. 123ff, 131, 139). As is well known, this scaling of the intensities of drives to satisfy needs and wants, both as between different needs and wants and as between the progressive stages of degrees of satisfying any particular need or want, became the foundation of the marginalist notion of subjective value determination.

The intensely subjectivist nature of Menger's value theory was compounded by his explicit recognition that not all agents have equal capacities in their value calculations and that even the most able of agents may make errors of judgement in the process. 'Error is inseparable from all human knowledge' he wrote in this regard, and added that 'the determination of the value of particular goods is beset with manifold errors in economic life' (p. 148). In the *Untersuchungen*, he effectively amplified this subjectivity by noting that the satisfaction of needs is a *process of adjustment* in which judgements must be made by the agents concerned. 'What we can do to maintain our life and well being, what in this respect depends on our power and volition, is to travel the road from a strictly determined starting point to a just as strictly determined goal in as *suitable* a way as possible, i.e., in as *economic* a way as possible' (1963, p. 217). But he reinforced the strongly subjectivist orientation of this interpretation by adding that 'volition, error, and other influences can, on the contrary, and actually do, bring it about that human agents take different roads from a strictly set starting point to a just as strictly determined goal of their action' (1963, p. 217). But it remained the case that although 'in every concrete economy innumerable orientations of the action of the economic subjects are conceivable . . ., it is certain that only *one* orientation of economic conduct can be the most suitable, can be the *economic* one, if we disregard economically irrelevant differences' (1963, p. 218).

3.2.2 Goods production

Now all goods cannot meet needs directly; in Menger's language, not all goods are of the first order. To maintain the subjectivist focus of his work, all non-consumer goods, goods of higher orders, were argued to have the imputed quality of satisfying needs potentially and indirectly as the rationale for their production, use and value. Their existence as goods was then conditional on their being so situated as to be actually primed for transformation into final consumer goods through production. This meant that they had to be accompanied by all of the other complementary higher order goods physically required to produce some good of a lower order for their goods status to be sustained (pp. 61ff, 84ff). But the requirements for production, Menger realized, went beyond these stocks of goods *per se* over which agents exercised command. For production to proceed effectively in most cases, a range of other influences had to be present and could affect the outcome without being under the agents' control (pp. 70f). Menger gave few indications that there is actually a complete world of preconditioning *physical–technical* processes underlying his extensive discussion of the subjectivist dimensions of goods and their production. He did write suggestively that the periods of production may differ considerably 'according to the nature of the case' and went on to give some physical examples of why this may be so (pp. 68–9). And, he referred to the 'greater or less[er] degree of . . . [agents'] knowledge of the elements of the causal process of production, and . . . the greater or less[er] degree of control they can exercise over these elements' (p. 71), which also suggests some physical links, albeit here mediated by agents' knowledge. It is nonetheless readily apparent that throughout his analysis, the *necessary* condition for the existence of goods of higher orders was that they have the appropriate qualitative and quantitative physical–technical relationship to their complements in the current technology of production in use. That this is not a sufficient condition for them to be economic goods is clear, but it is a dimension of the world that underpins the economy as Menger thought of it.[6]

A stock of all orders of goods will exist in any one period, together with the prospect that more can be produced for the future. Decisions about the production of goods taken in the current period relate to the satisfaction of needs and wants in future periods. This raised the spectre of the dealing explicitly with the problematics of *time* in a subjectivist context in two connected senses: one relating to the fact that production itself takes time and the other relating to the fact that the objective of production is to satisfy needs and wants expected to arise in the future.

Menger faced up squarely to the analytical puzzles thus posed and provided some crucial seminal insights that he was unable or unwilling to pursue to their logical and more far reaching conclusions.

Apropos the former time problematic, he recognized that the relation of causality that links the stages of the production process 'is inseparable from the idea of time'. Production is 'a process of change [that] involves a beginning and a becoming, and these are only conceivable as processes in time. Hence it is certain that we can never fully understand the causal interconnections of the various occurrences in a process, or the process itself, unless we view it in time and apply the measure of time to it' (p. 67). The most immediate subjective impact of this period of production is that it introduces a degree of quantitative and qualitative uncertainty into the future availability of each particular good, an uncertainty that has physical–technical roots (pp. 68–70). However, an additional degree of subjectivism was introduced by the complication that the mediating agents can affect the degree of uncertainty by the state of their knowledge and understanding concerning the technical nature of the production process (p. 71, cf. p. 74). At this point Menger emphasized that the uncertainty generated by the existence of the period of production 'is one of the most important factors in the economic uncertainty of men, and . . . [it] is of the greatest practical significance in human economy' (p. 71).

Such uncertainty is compounded by the second facet of the time problematic cited above, namely the fact that production is directed at meeting *expected future needs and wants* within some planning horizon (pp. 78–9). So, not only is the actual physical outcome of production tinged with uncertainty, but also the actual objective that it is supposed to meet is similarly uncertain. The latter depends on the foresight that can be exercised by agents with respect to their anticipated pattern of needs and wants up to their planning horizon, given their knowledge concerning the processes by which the required flow of goods may be produced (p. 80). However, Menger stressed that in spite of the uncertainties involved, human agents must necessarily engage in these planning activities if a constant supply of goods is to be available to them. He signalled his intention to follow through a sequence of inquiries related to this difficult subjectivist economic problematic, a sequence that really set the stage for the remainder of the work. In particular: how agents establish their future requirements for first and higher order goods, how they estimate the flow of goods that will actually be available and how agents 'endeavour to direct the quantities of goods (consumption goods and means of production) at their disposal to the most effective satisfaction of their needs' (p. 80). This represented a challenging analytical task, to say the least, and we should consider briefly the manner in which Menger went about it. My intention here is not to provide an outline of his substantive arguments, but rather to elicit the ongoing dominant impact that the subjectivist and individualist ontology had upon the nature and direction of his inquiries into these temporally conditioned activities of human agents. What will become clear is that this impact was manifested in the methodology he chose to adopt in formally representing his understanding and explanations of these activities. We shall find that often his ontology was allowed to overrule his desire to emulate the exactitude of the physical sciences in the methodology adopted.

The uncertainty about future needs and wants, brought on by 'deficient foresight', as it involves first order consumption goods will vary with the nature of the need or want to be met, and may be of a qualitative and/or a quantitative sort in terms of the goods that will be required. Included here will be the prospects for any growth in the needs or wants of particular kinds (pp. 81ff). Agents will form their expectations about future needs and wants 'within feasible limits' of calculation and within the limits of their chosen planning horizon, 'to a degree of exactness that is sufficient for the practical success of their activity' (p. 84). Menger was clearly aware that in this most readily calculable case of expectations affecting economic conduct, the outcomes for individual agents would always be contingent to some degree. But such contingency afflicts calculations with respect to higher order, means of production goods to a significantly greater extent, as he went on to recognize (pp. 84ff). It is to be recalled that these goods are only required as the means to obtain additional consumer goods, in the present circumstances where these latter are expected to be required in quantities in the future to an extent beyond the current potential to carry forward existing stocks. For modern readers, the sorts of complications for human decision-making based on expectations that that planning for future needs involves here are readily apparent. Menger's analysis was limited in its scope, as would be expected, but he made some points of importance.

For the given technology, a future flow of additional consumer goods requires that the full complement of higher order goods of the appropriate qualities be on hand in the technically appropriate quantities when production must begin. Such a set of goods must also be produced and this fact introduces a network of interdependencies between sectors of production producing the goods and that producing the consumer good (p. 87). The network is compounded by the additional fact that each of the means of production themselves must be produced by other means of production, and so on. Menger did not explore this line of analysis and understated the complexity of the problematic that he had exposed. He was aware, at least, that included in the pattern of production interdependencies were variations in the periods of production and that these would need to be coordinated if the required goods flows were to be correctly timed. His limited reflections on the problem show a consciousness of the complications that this would mean for the decisions of agents (pp. 87ff). And, on top of all these essentially physical–technical dimensions, explicated by case examples in the *Grundsätze*, is imposed the mediation of human agents who must deliberate and make *ex ante* decisions about the processes concerned in order that they are activated.

It is unfortunate that Menger did not see the need to go on and give attention to the puzzles of agents' uncertainty, expectations formation and the ultimate contingencies of the outcomes that are raised by this extensive and intricate set of relationships and actions. He also failed to recognize that he had touched on inquiries that could only proceed if agents were properly *functionally* classified, for the deliberations and decisions now extended beyond those that could be undertaken by consumers directly. Rather, entrepreneurial agents would also be concerned and face uncertainties that are compounded by the fact that they must include among their expectations the expected future needs of other agents on whose behalf they are to produce goods. In touching on the role of such agents, Menger considered the problem of how the quantities of all categories of goods to be made available within any planning horizon are calculated and managed (pp. 89ff). Here he made reference to the mediating roles of government and merchants, both of whom communicate to producing agents information about stocks of goods in existence, including those comprising the public infrastructure. In all this, he often revealed an acute awareness of the problematical nature of ensuring an optimum flow of goods by means of individual agents' decision-making. However, this did not prevent him from drawing the naively sanguine conclusion that 'economic disturbances would appear that laymen usually consider completely abnormal, but which are, in reality, entirely in accordance with economic laws' (p. 87). At this point, Menger's subjectivist insight failed him and he drew a simplistic conclusion about the motion of market systems that belied his sometimes insightful seminal understanding of the matter.

In applying his ideas about value determination to goods of a higher order, the means of production, Menger faced some further difficult puzzles. The first principle of understanding had to remain that of subjectivism, with the value of such goods being no less dependent on the cognitive assessments of agents involved than was the case for first order goods. 'Our need for means of production', he wrote in the *Untersuchungen*, 'is limited . . . by our need for consumers' goods and the *ultimate* goal of all human economy is thus to cover our direct material needs, to assure satisfaction of our direct needs' (1963, p. 216). It follows that inputs to production that are economic goods are valued in accordance with reflexive imputations that assess their relative contributions to the values of their lower order products. This, too, is a subjective process that serves to put the valuation of all exchanged goods, including consumer goods, means of production and factors of production, on the same basis independently of their 'distance' from directly satisfying individuals' needs and wants. Menger was thus able to emphasize to his readers, albeit with a somewhat casual use of the concept of price rather than value, that:

> I have devoted special attention to the investigation of the causal connections between economic phenomena involving products and the corresponding agents of production . . . for the purpose of establishing a price theory based upon reality and placing all price phenomena (including interest, wages, ground rent, etc.) together under one unified point of view . . . (p. 49)

But which agents are pertinent in analysing decisions relating to production? Menger had already stressed that the consumers of the final products are not concerned with production characteristics when valuing goods. Only those actually responsible for production are so concerned. He realized immediately that producing agents cannot value the goods in their possession, or that they require, on the same criteria, for the use to which they will put the goods cannot directly satisfy needs or wants. The agents concerned engage in production in order ultimately to be able to command first order goods, but this final outcome is mediated by the condition that they produce goods that are valued by other agents in and of themselves (consumer goods or means of production for sale) and that they do so in advance of the manifestation of such value. The means of valuing the higher order goods comprise an assessment of the value to these other agents of the lower order goods to be produced. Such reflection of value can only be imputed and must be undertaken *ex ante* to production itself, as Menger was able to recognize (pp. 150ff). This made the imputed value highly subjective and very difficult to calculate. The reason for this, as he grasped it, is that the value has to be based on an 'expected', or 'prospective' value that is not yet a reality. The uncertainty introduced for the valuing agents went beyond the fact that the produced value is only to be realized in the future. What he did not make clear was that here, the valuing agents must base their notion of value on sheer speculation, tempered in practice by introspection and extrapolations of relevant past experience, about the future subjective states of mind of other agents. Menger did not pursue this matter any further and it represented yet another incomplete resolution of the extended subjectivist value idea.

Menger went on from here to reiterate the importance of *time* in the structuring of production processes and to inquire further about the implications of this for the agents responsible for undertaking them. Subjectively, beyond the uncertainty involved in entering into production as a means to satisfying needs and wants indirectly, there was also the period of delay between having command of resources and being able to realize them in a form that can be applied to final satisfactions. In short, producer agents must be prepared to wait for their subjectively calculated, expected returns. For Menger, this represented a penalty in the sense that these agents must have available sufficient resources in the present period to cover not only their current consumption needs but also to allocate to the prospect of being able to satisfy future needs and wants. Here he confronted the notion of capital. The productivity of stocks of goods applied to production as capital with the intention of satisfying expected future needs and wants represented 'one of the most important truths of our science' (p. 156). But assertion was not a substitute for understanding and the problem remained to account for how and in what sense capital could be productive for the agents who possess and apply it. Such anticipated productivity comprises an integral part of their subjective and imputative valuation process of the goods involved. Menger simply claimed that the *possession itself* is an economic good under conditions of scarcity and thus has a value: 'command of quantities of economic goods for a certain period of time is *for economizing individuals* a means to the better and more complete satisfaction of their needs, and therefore a *good* – or rather, an *economic good*, whenever the available quantities of capital services are smaller than the requirements for them' (p. 156, cf. p. 172). He went on to explicate the necessary condition for the realization of the rewards of capital possession as the intervention of human agents in activating the production process itself. The immediate consequence was to complicate the idea of capital and its value return by including the technical labour services of these entrepreneurial agents in the calculation. Indeed, he considered the potential to deliver these services to be one of the higher order goods at the agents' command (p. 160). On this theme he reasoned more fully that:

the aggregate present value of all the complementary quantities of goods of higher order (that is, all the raw materials, labour services, services of land, machines, tools, etc.) necessary for the production of a good of lower or first order is equal to the prospective value of the product. But it is necessary to include in the sum not only the goods of higher order technically required for its production but also the services of capital and the activity of the entrepreneur. (p. 161)

But more is involved than the technically skilled labour of entrepreneurs. For it is they who are called upon *to deliberate about and calculate the prospective results of applying capital* in the form of higher order goods to actual production for the time period required by the technology available. What is more, they can only base their *ex ante* decisions on the uncertain prospect of some expected value of the good to be produced. In these respects, Menger's understanding of the production problematic confronted by human agents was considerable. He listed four key functions of the entrepreneur that went beyond their purely technical participation in the physical production process. These agents are also required to gather appropriate information pertinent to the economic situation, make calculations about the organization of production and its prospective results (presumably both in physical and economic terms), and undertake the required supervision of the realization of production itself in the most efficacious manner. In addition, such agents must apply what Menger called 'the *act of will* by which goods . . . are assigned to a particular production process' (p. 160). Clearly, all of these functions have a strongly subjective dimension, for they demand of agents all sorts of open-ended judgements and speculative calculations about matters yet to be realized, matters that affect their personal economic well-being and future prosperity quite profoundly in most cases. He rejected outright the idea of risk bearing as an additional function on the ground that 'this "risk" is only incidental and the chance of loss is counterbalanced by the chance of profit' (p. 161). This simply begs the question by conflating the rewards of the entrepreneurs with the return on capital goods in their possession. With respect to the nature of their reward, his proposition was simply that entrepreneurial services 'must definitely be counted as a category of labour services' (p. 172).

Menger approached the final stage of his theory of value, that of attributing value to the services of factors of production, land, labour and capital, with an air of confidence that the matter would present few difficulties. He simply asserted that their values could be accounted for in the same way as those ascribed by their possessors to higher order goods. The principle of imputation from the value of their lower order products was to be applied and Menger rejected any extant theories that attempted to render such valuations in any way different from that of goods *per se* (pp. 165ff). The problems that this idea posed for him in the case of capital and entrepreneurial services have been considered above. His discussion of land services had little analytical content and he resorted largely to assertions in reaching conclusions, both concerning the fallacies of extant theories and the validity of his own theory. He rejected any claim that land has properties that rendered it distinct from produced higher order goods and finally concluded that 'the value of land . . . has no exceptional character' (p. 169).

There is some limited suggestion in Menger's treatment of the valuation of the services of labour that he realized their distinctive nature. His immediate inclination was to reject any notion that labour services values have anything to do with the supply side of their availability and to claim instead higher order goods status for them (pp. 169ff). To this he added the qualification that there exist negative perceptions of labour effort: 'some varieties of labour services have unpleasant associations for the laborer' and thus command some premium in return for their supply (p. 171). Menger left this matter in the air, too, and simply went on to conclude that most labour is enjoyable and amounts to an end in itself that workers would be prepared to engage in even without the pressure of the needs and wants satisfaction that it affords. Undertaking work for payment is merely a function of the availability of opportunities to do so (pp. 171f). Such simplistic and naive argument belied Menger's very real analytical talents and does not warrant any further critical comment here.

A similar reaction is appropriate to his tentative venture into the distributional morality of capitalism (pp. 173f). Here he opened with the idea that it is 'one of the strangest questions ever made the subject of scientific debate' to enquire about the morality of rent and interest payments. They are simply there, as it were, as a result of the systemic organization of economic activity. However, this observation did not give him quite enough comfort and he noted that for a 'lover of mankind' the distinct inequality of incomes and of the amount of human effort that goes into obtaining them could well be the cause for some concern. His response was to claim that 'the cause of this is not immoral, but simply that the satisfaction of more important human needs depends upon the services of the given amount of capital or piece of land than upon the services of the laborer' (p. 174). An increase in labour's share of the values produced would amount to paying labour above its value unless accompanied by qualitative changes to make labour more productive. And, for some reason Menger chose to designate this value as now 'the value of its [labour's] services *to society*' (p. 174; emphasis added). The concept of value has taken a new turn here, one that has no connection with the subjectivist and individualist theory and one that raised a host of potential problems of its own that Menger did not stop to consider. Finally he was content to leave the issue as only resolvable by means of 'a complete transformation of our social order' (p. 174).

3.3 Epistemological intentions and methodological realities

Menger recognized quite explicitly what problems would surface in his concern to set economics apart from the physical sciences while trying to retain the widespread appeal and credence that application of their dominant epistemology and methodology would bring. These sciences are most often characterized by formalized and universal discursive argument, the epistemology of which reflects the laws of the natural world that scientists claim to have discovered in their respective fields. But his defence of this scientism was never dogmatic for the reason that he was always sensitive to the existence of some absolutely crucial ontological differences between the respective phenomena of the physical and human worlds.

He went on to draw physical science analogies several times in the *Untersuchungen* (1963, pp. 52f, 58f, 85f, 214f). The thrust of his argument was that all scientific theory of an exact kind is constructed from abstracted representations of empirical elements that make up reality. The concepts that make up a pure theory in this sense are the discursive representations of elements that are never actually observed by the human senses. Rather, they are always bound up with impurities and in this sense are non-empirical. On this basis, Menger reasoned that the human sciences are no different from the natural sciences. Among the natural sciences are those accepted as inexact, but this does not reduce their usefulness. Meteorology and physiology are examples. However, the problems of exactitude go beyond these examples to include some of the most exact of the physical sciences. A purely exact representation of human agency as comprising only non-contingent dimensions of conduct was to be thought of as just as appropriate in economic theory as a pure element is in chemistry and a moving body without friction is in physics. None of these is ever observed as such but their existential potential is not doubted in the physical cases, so why should it be in the economics case?

There is an all too apparent complexity here that never confronts the theorists of physical phenomena. In principle, their world is 'there', as it were, and remains existentially independent and stable in a way that the life-world of human agents cannot be. Evolutionary and geological time-frames of change that affect the natural world are only of concern to particular sciences in themselves and most often not because of their general impact on the objects of contemporary inquiry. Geomorphology is a science of change, but the chemical elements and minerals that compose its objects are constant. Thus, the natural world is not subject to continuous, short-term change that renews its essentials from day to day in an ever adjusting empirical form as is the world confronted by the human scientist. Most especially, though, the elements that comprise the natural world are not conditioned by the potential contingency of free will and creativity that is present in the generation of those elements of concern to the human scientist. Human phenomena can have a truly original character that stems from sources in the mind of the agents that generate them. Such sources are beyond the capacities of observers to comprehend formally and to represent discursively with any guarantee of accuracy. In the natural environment, there is nothing really new under the sun in a contemporarily created sense, whereas in the human world, every day brings much that appears in its current form for the first time.

In the case of the human world, nevertheless, Menger the Aristotelian reasoned that actually imbedded in the contingent realities of observed human conduct is an essential core of constancy. This was one of his most basic ontological presumptions and the analyses in the *Grundsätze* established its pertinence to an understanding of some key economic phenomena. What he would not be able properly to defend, though, was the claim that the empirical deviations from this core, which result from agents' contingencies of conduct, are analogous to the sort of impurities that beset the phenomena of the physical world. In principle, the latter impurities themselves are physical, too, and have a uniformity, constancy and predictability that the deviations from regularized representation of human conduct can never have. This is for the reasons suggested above concerning the intractability of human contingency. In the *Untersuchungen* we find that Menger gave prominence to these very subjectivist contingencies, but chose to maintain his claim to have legitimated by ontological references a dualist theoretical strategy that demanded that they be abstracted from for some purposes.

Through the use of analogies with the physical sciences, Menger emphasized the primacy of universality and exactitude as desirable epistemological qualities of their theories. But, because of his historicist background, he was also a realist who valued empirical observation as a source of particular historically relative knowledge. At issue was the ontological nature of the empirical objects that human scientists, including economists, endeavour to understand and explain and how this nature was to be retained in scientifically constructed theories. In all cases, the penetration of observed phenomena required insights into how they are generated by human agency. The thrust of the problem for present purposes is that the contingent dimensions of human agency can only be avoided in the construction of generalized economic theory by two means: by an imposed construct that models agents as artificially mechanical and reliable, or by showing that agents have a sufficient degree of essential, immanently explicable, ontologically grounded containment and regularity for laws to be relevant to understanding and representing their conduct. Menger's dualist metatheory, with its two modes of theoretical inquiry: the non-universal, logically open-ended 'realistic-empirical', and the universal, logically closed 'exact', can be shown to be best understood as his way of confronting the ontologically rooted problem of representing human agency. It is here that there emerges one of the crucial conundrums that, in my view, remains unresolved in his work: can his subjectivist and individualist ontology of economic phenomena, so frankly exposed in all of its contingent dimensions in the *Grundsätze*, be shown to be consistent with the epistemological position he adopted and the dualist methodological strategy that he defended? The arguments of the *Untersuchungen* have a particular orientation towards communication with the Historicists, but within this context, the work contains a considerable amount of direct and amplified explication of ideas that were implicit in the *Grundsätze*.

We have seen that Menger was conscious of the distinction between the natural–physical sciences and the human sciences, even though economics, at least, he claimed, could emulate the former in the analytical formality and universal relevance of its theoretical arguments. Although its objects of knowledge are quite different from those of the physical sciences, he would not allow a proper understanding of the ontological nature of economic phenomena to be an impediment to their precise discursive representation as logically ordered concepts. In its totality, however, we have seen that he considered economics to be a science with multiple dimensions of inquiry. These dimensions enable different branches of the science to be identified, branches that should be kept separate because they have distinct substantive objectives and methodological requirements. But, one of these branches would always be that devoted to theoretical inquiry in the dual sense formulated by Menger.

The vision and approach of the Historicists, as it was understood and critically questioned by Menger in the *Untersuchungen*, ruled out any idea that the full richness and complexity of concrete reality could be represented by any form of abstraction that relied on human reason alone. Rather, if an imbedded nomological generality exists within this reality, it could only be exposed by cumulative inductive inquiries over an extended period. As Menger noted, some Historicists remained sceptical altogether about the existence of any laws of economic conduct, even inductively revealed ones, and some rejected the idea of economics as a separable dimension of the human life-world altogether (1963, pp. 24f).[7]

One thing about which Menger was quite convinced was that the properly constituted and universally valid theoretical knowledge that comprises any science cannot be obtained by the direct inductive means espoused by the Historicists, no matter how many consistent observations of real-world associations of phenomena are made (cf. Milford, 1990, pp. 227, 232ff). Their metahistorical work was a classic case in which an 'accurate feeling for the goals of research coming from the nature of the subject matter has been lost' and in which 'the progress of a science is blocked because erroneous methodological principles prevail' (p. 27, cf. p. 31). Not only were their principles of inquiry astray but also they emphasized one orientation of research in economics and excluded all others, which meant that their conception of economics was inevitably one-sided and incomplete (p. 55). Menger rejected this strategy as inadequate to ensure coverage of the range of inquiries that comprises the various branches of economics in its totality.

Now while it is possible for analysts to pursue scientific inquiry by applying theories to the cognition of concrete phenomena, especially for the historical and practical objectives of economics, the crucial orientation of inquiry for Menger was towards the demands of ontologically consistent theory construction (pp. 44ff). He was adamant about the due status of theory in this respect.

> The understanding of *concrete* facts, institutions, relationships, etc. . . . is to be strictly distinguished from the *scientific basis of this understanding* . . .; and the *theoretical understanding* of concrete economic phenomena is especially to be distinguished from the *theory of economy*. . . . For no matter how carefully and how comprehensively an individual strives for theoretical understanding of the *concrete* phenomena of the economy – for instance, on the basis of the prevailing theories! – this still does not make him a theorist in economy. *Only* the one is so to be considered who makes the *development and description of the theory itself* his task. (pp. 45f)

As far as Menger was concerned, the Historicists were prone to this confusion and could not be considered true theorists, whatever may be the merits of their work as historical accounts of the generation of economic phenomena (pp. 46ff). Theory construction as the 'goal of research in the field of theoretical economics', he claimed, 'has the task of investigating the *general nature* and the *general connection* of economic phenomena, not of analyzing economic *concepts* and of drawing the logical conclusions resulting from this analysis' (p. 37n. 4). Concepts *per se* were required as means of discursively *presenting* a theoretical argument once it had been constituted by means of proper inquiry.

Menger's expectation was that through the *Untersuchungen* he would establish himself in the eyes of others once and for all as a true subjectivist theorist in the above sense of explicating and defending more directly the metatheoretical essentials of his work. He stated his position with respect to this expectation very precisely.

> The goal of scholarly research is not only the *cognition*, but also the *understanding* of phenomena. We have *gained cognition* of a phenomenon when we have attained a mental image of it. We understand it when we have recognized the reason for its existence and for its characteristic quality (the reason for its *being* and for its *being as it is*). (p. 43)

Thus, 'the purpose of the theoretical sciences is understanding of the real world, knowledge of it extending beyond immediate experience, and control of it' (p. 55). There is in these statements a strong ontologically grounded methodological challenge that reflected Menger's approach to theory construction and assessment already present in the *Grundsätze*. Theorists are expected to have the cognitive insight required to represent to themselves the essential nature of a phenomenon and to go on to understand its generation in a coherently reasoned way on the basis of the relationships between the elements thus exposed. In the human sciences, including in economics, this means contending in this precise manner with phenomena that have their origin in the deliberated and teleological, but nonetheless contingent actions of human agents. An understanding of such phenomena cannot be expressed merely in terms of their observed physical and quantitative manifestations if it is to conform to the standards that Menger had set out here. The theorist must reach beneath the observable surface of economic events and grapple with the prior and obscured essentials of the processes of human agency through which they are generated.

It is in this regard that Menger's differences with Léon Walras become important. In their correspondence of 1883–84, Menger explained the fundamental vision of economic research that he espoused: 'I am concerned in my researches with tracing back the complicated phenomena of economics to their true origins, and to their constituent elements, and with the investigation of the laws according to which the complicated phenomena of economics are constructed from these elements' (Jaffé, 1965a, p. 768).[8] He reiterated this point in a later letter, emphasizing that whatever its appearances, economics is concerned with more than mere quantitative manifestations of phenomena. 'We do not simply study quantitative relationships but also the ESSENCE (*das WESEN*) of economic phenomena' (Jaffé, 1965b, p. 3). His consequent belief was that mathematics is a conceptual medium of expression of preconstituted theoretical ideas. It cannot be a means of actual research designed to expose the ontological origins of the elements of reality and their relationships that the theory is intended to represent. As Menger put it to Walras, 'I am of the opinion that the mathematical method is essentially one of *representation* and *demonstration* and not of research. Every economic law, . . . can be *clothed* in mathematical formulae, or *demonstrated* through graphical representations. These things are very useful for some problems of our science, however they do not touch on the essence of *research*' (Jaffé, 1965a, p. 768). In the research process, 'it is necessary that we go back to the simplest elements of the mostly very complicated phenomena that are at issue here. . . . The method we must apply in such investigations will . . . be the *analytical-synthetic*, or the *analytical-compositive*, not, however, the purely *mathematical*' (Jaffé, 1965b, p. 4).

Menger thus showed himself as ready to defend his metatheoretical position, including the priority he gave to the construction of ontologically grounded theory, as being consistent with what he considered to be the essential nature of the phenomena to be represented and understood by economic science. For him: 'Insight into the nature of the truths of . . . [economics] can only be the result of comprehensive and competent consideration of the realm of phenomena to be examined by us and of the special demands life makes on our science' (p. 26, cf. p. 30). Most generally stated, Menger's objective in the *Untersuchungen* was to reinforce and defend a much more precise version of the metatheoretical principles that were implicit in the subjectivist analyses of his *Grundsätze* where the ontological nature of the relevant phenomena had been outlined.

It was his distinction between the '*realistic-empirical orientation*' and the '*exact* orientation' of theoretical research that embodied Menger's recognition of two crucial problems in formulating a defensible theoretical economics. First, that of transcending the impotence of inductive inquiry to deliver theory directly; and secondly, that of providing precisely reasoned accounts of economic phenomena on subjectivist and individualist foundations (pp. 54ff). Theories constructed under the rubric of the realistic-empirical orientation are to express empirical understanding, even though their arguments are once removed, as it were, and may not always be immediately consistent with, the details of immediate observation. The *empirical laws* so formulated, comprising the relations between *real types*, to use Menger's own terms, are not necessarily without exception. But here he comforted his readers by noting that in the natural world scientific inquiry often only results in laws that have a similar lack of precision and reliability. These results may be 'formally imperfect', but they are well established as 'important and valuable ... for human knowledge and practical life'. The fact remains, though, that theories of this sort could, according to his own testament, 'give us only a deficient understanding of the phenomena, only an uncertain prediction of them, and by no means an assured control of them' (p. 59). As I shall explore further below, when contrasting this realistic-empirical orientation with the exact orientation in the case of economics, the deficiencies of the former approach pointed to by Menger were a genuine reflection of the subjectivist ontological nature of the object phenomena to be dealt with. And, as we will see, too, such deficiencies are present in exact theory with an even greater vengeance for this same reason. His claim that somehow exact theory delivered more understanding, prediction and control of economic events will soon be seen to be untenable.

Menger's idea of this dual orientation of theoretical inquiry was built around a number of ontological observations concerning human agents and agency. He reiterated his observation that 'it may be admitted ever so unreservedly that people are governed in economic things neither exclusively by a single definite propensity, in our case by their egoism, nor are uninfluenced by error, ignorance, and external compulsion' (p. 64). So it is that 'man's will is guided by innumerable motives in part really in contradiction with each other ... [and] a strict regularity of human actions in general and of economy in particular is *a priori* out of the question' (p. 83). He went on to elaborate, in the economic connection, that:

> people in their actions are guided, to judge by experience, neither in general nor in particular in their economic actions exclusively by a definite motive. For along with self-interest, which at most can be recognized as the main-spring of human economy, also public spirit, love of one's fellow men,

custom, feeling for justice, and other similar factors determine man's economic actions. (pp. 83–4)

Here, too, Menger added to these qualifications to the pursuit of self-interest when he drew attention to 'another factor . . . which surely can be separated still less from human action than custom, public spirit, feeling for justice, and love of one's fellow man can be separated from economy'. The reference he made was to the potential for human agents to be *in error* about their 'economic interest' and their 'economic state of affairs'. Thus he effectively rejected the dogmas of 'ever-constant self-interest' and of 'the "infallibility" and "omniscience" of humans in economic matters'. To this he added immediately a rejection of the dogma of *'complete freedom from external compulsion'*, along with 'others' not specified (pp. 84, 85). The matter had already troubled him in the *Grundsätze* where he asserted that he wished 'to contest the opinion of those who question the existence of laws of economic behavior by referring to human free will, since their argument would deny economics altogether the status of an exact science'. And, he continued:

> although reference to freedom of the human will may well be legitimate as an objection to the complete predictability of economic activity, it can never have force as a denial of the conformity to definite laws of phenomena that condition the outcome of the economic activity of men and are entirely independent of the human will. (1950, p. 48)

But, in spite of these realistic, ontologically grounded insights, it was also the case, he believed, that 'wherever we look, economic life confronts us with regularities both in the coexistence and in the succession of phenomena' (p. 64). It was quite apparent to Menger, it seems, that due recognition of these sorts of observed regularities in the results of human agency could provide at least the realistic-empirical theoretical inquiry with its object phenomena. An empirical law, as it was expected to be made available by this orientation of theory, 'states certain regularities in the succession and coexistence of phenomena which are by no means necessarily absolute. But . . . *it must agree with full empirical reality, from the consideration of which it was obtained'* (p. 70; emphasis added).

For observer-analysts, whatever may be their own introspectively devised extrapolations from experience as active agents, external human agency and its concrete phenomenal results comprise the given objects of scientific inquiry. 'We' the analysts are required to interpret and understand the deliberations and actions of other active agents who generate the concrete phenomena in our focus. The mental reduction of any observed phenomena to what Menger called their *empirical* forms is accomplished, as was suggested above, by means of the concept of the *real type*, an entity whose empirical existence is always imbedded in the particulars of observation and thus not 'immediately perceived'. The relevant, empirically derived typology is applied to the representation of operational elements and their relationships. We 'investigate the types and typical relations of phenomena as these present themselves to us in their "full empirical reality", *that is, in the totality and the whole complexity of their nature ...*' (p. 56). Leaving aside for the moment the question of which particular agents are concerned here, Menger showed a remarkable insight into the significance of the *type* category for human inquiry, deliberation and action:

> Without the knowledge of [typical] empirical forms we would not be able to comprehend the myriads of phenomena surrounding us, nor to classify them in our minds; it is the presupposition for a more comprehensive cognition of the real world. Without cognition of the typical relationships we would be deprived not only of a deeper understanding of the real world ..., but also, as may be easily seen, of all cognition extending beyond immediate observation, i.e., of any *prediction* and *control* of things. All human prediction and, indirectly, all arbitrary shaping of things is conditioned by that knowledge which we previously have called *general*. (p. 56)

This is a powerful statement, the implications of which reach deeply into our understanding of human agency. Primarily, he believed, 'the nature of theoretical economics can under all circumstances consist in nothing else than in the exposition of just ... types and typical relationships' (p. 51). However, while 'the fact that the laws of the succession and the coexistence of phenomena are not rigorous ones accordingly diminishes the certainty of the conclusions based on them', in no way could such a lack of strictness of the laws of the human world detract from the usefulness of theory for the purposes of 'the prediction and control of phenomena' (p. 52).

Nor was it the case, in Menger's view, that the pursuit of theory in economics should be deterred by 'the circumstance that theoretical research in the realm does, indeed, encounter difficulties that are foreign to natural-science research' or by 'the circumstance that for theoretical economics there are not always present problems of exactly the same kind as for the theoretical natural sciences' (p. 53). Just what these 'circumstances' consisted of, he did not say here, but it is apparent from his passing references to the issue that they have a very definite ontological connection with the peculiar subjective origins of human phenomena. But, be all this as it may, ultimately the requirement confronted by Menger was to show that theoretical inquiry could and should transcend the typified, merely empirical representation of economic phenomena. We are about to see how he tried to meet this demand through his notion of an exact approach to the methodology of theory construction.

It was Menger's view that economic theory has to sustain a very particular epistemological status. In accordance with his Aristotelian inclinations, he insisted that the phenomenal elements and their relationships that constitute the substance of a theory have a real existence that is independent of, but corresponds to, their conceptual representation in the argument. He wrote, therefore, that 'the analysis of concepts may in an individual case have a certain significance for the *presentation* of theoretical knowledge of economy, but the goal of research in the field of theoretical economics can only be the determination of the general nature and the general connection of economic *phenomena*' (p. 37n). As has already been suggested above, the first task that confronts the theorist is 'the determination of the empirical forms and of the laws, the types and typical relations of economic phenomena', in particular, 'the empirical forms recurring in the alternation of [concrete] economic phenomena, for example, the general nature of exchange, of price, of ground rent, of supply, of demand, and the typical relations between these phenomena...' (p. 42). But Menger's metatheory demanded more than this. It is the *generation* of value, price, exchange, and other phenomena as explicitly human products, the results of individual and collective, deliberate and purposeful, human action, that he had hoped to understand and represent in theoretical form in the *Grundsätze*.

Menger remained less than completely satisfied that the realistic-empirical orientation set limits for what is epistemologically possible in formulating theoretical economics as a science. He was convinced that whatever exactitude could be achieved in the natural sciences could be emulated in the human sciences, including economics. However, it was readily apparent to him that for ontological reasons '*empirical laws of absolute strictness* are out of the question in the realm of the phenomena of human activity' (p. 214). Some alternative approach to theory had to be employed if 'absolute strictness' and universality was to be shown to be potentially available in economics. It was the '*exact* orientation' of research that Menger considered to be a genuine metatheoretical option for the 'ethical world' of the human sciences, that is, for the 'realm of ethical phenomena' that includes economics (pp. 59ff). He asserted without further argument that this alternative reflected another orientation of the 'human mind' towards theoretical inquiry that is distinctive in 'both in its aims and in its approaches to cognition' (p. 59). The procedure for constructing theory at this essential level requires that 'we reduce human phenomena to their most original and simplest constitutive factors. We join to the latter the measure corresponding to their nature, and finally try to investigate the laws by which *more complicated* human phenomena are formed from those simplest elements, thought of in their isolation' (p. 62). He remained resolute, though, that somehow, however paradoxical such a claim may appear to be, while exact theory 'does not arrive at exact laws of the *real* ... phenomena of human economy ... it does arrive at exact laws of economic reality' (p. 218).

It especially made no sense, Menger repeatedly stressed, to attempt to 'test' the validity or usefulness of exact theories by comparisons with real world observations of any sort, or with the results of realistic-empirical inquiries (pp. 69ff). In particular, he stressed that in no respect does the deviation of exact theory from immediate identification with empirical reality render it epistemologically inferior to realistic-empirical theory. He followed Aristotle in the view that the essences and their relationships imbedded in reality cannot exist in isolation from their empirical manifestations. The presumption that because realistic-empirical theory deals with regularities more self-evident to observation it is somehow superior to exact theory, that it is 'the better guaranteed road to cognition', was firmly rejected by Menger (pp. 68f). He granted that 'it would be extremely desirable if we could gain *exact* knowledge that simultaneously agrees with full empirical reality.... Human cognition, the prediction and control of phenomena, would be essentially aided and simplified by this'. But this cannot be, 'given the actual relationships which the world of real phenomena regularly offers' (p. 70). Thus: 'Realism in theoretical research is not something higher than exact orientation, but something different ... [so that] the results of [a] realistic orientation stand in an essentially different relationship to the empirical method than do those of exact research' (p. 70). 'Rather, the function of each of them consists in making us understand the total realm of economic phenomena in *its* characteristic way.' And, as reiterated a little later, 'a science can never be called *one-sided* if it completely fulfills *its* task' (p. 79).

Once having made these claims about the necessary virtues of exact theory, Menger was confronted with the need to defend them as consistent with what he well knew to be the distinct ontological nature of the phenomena of economic reality. Some care is required in interpreting Menger here if his intention is to be accurately grasped. At least it remains unclear the extent to which he recognized the difficulties that were involved in the endeavour to move his analysis from a theoretical world of real types and empirical laws to one comprised of their respective essential and exact dimensions (cf. Milford, 1990, pp. 230ff). He wrote that an exact orientation has as its aim 'the determination of strict laws of phenomena'. These comprise, he went on, 'regularities in the succession of phenomena' and 'regularities of the coexistence of phenomena'. Then he added the following crucial rider that these regularities 'do not present themselves to us as absolute, but . . . in respect to the approaches to cognition by which we attain to them simply bear within themselves the guarantee of absoluteness' (p. 59). The implication here is that it is the methodology of the inquiry, the 'approach to cognition', rather than any ontological reasoning that facilitates the exactitude, the 'absoluteness', of the laws established.

The next step was to specify the required mode of cognition and this led Menger to one of his most cryptic metatheoretical assertions.

> There is one rule of cognition for the investigation of theoretical truths which as far as possible is verified beyond doubt not only by experience, but simply by our laws of thinking. This is the statement that *whatever was observed in even only one case must always put in an appearance again under exactly the same actual conditions*; or, what is in essence the same thing, that strictly typical phenomena of a definite kind must always, and, indeed in consideration of our laws of thinking, simply *of necessity*, be followed by strictly typical phenomena of just as definite and different a type. (p. 60)

The logical import of this 'rule of cognition' that follows from our 'laws of thinking' was claimed to be that if 'strictly typical' phenomena **A** and **B** are observed to be followed in only one case by the 'strictly typical' phenomenon **C**, then under exactly the same conditions **C** will always and without exception follow **A** and **B**. This piece of logic is quite inadequate to defend in a convincing manner the bona fides of the so-called 'rule of cognition'. And yet Menger intended to depend heavily on it in his attempt to legitimate exact theory. The logic claims that **A** and **B** are combined to account for the occurrence of **C**. This overlooks two alternative scenarios. First, it is possible that the instance of **C** in question may be associated with an unobserved **Z** as well as with the two phenomena actually referred to, so that their occurrence cannot alone logically entail the occurrence of **C**. Here **A** and **B** may be necessary to account for **C**, but they are not guaranteed to be sufficient on the evidence presented. Secondly, the fact that even if this causality is secured by the logical entailment of the argument, it cannot be ruled out that the occurrence of **C** could in actual fact be observed as a consequence of causes other than **A** and **B**, say **X** and **Y**, in accordance with a similarly secure logic. The former, then, may be sufficient to account for **C**, but there can be no guarantee that they are necessary on the basis of the logic presented. So, even at this logical level alone, the 'rule of cognition' could not provide Menger with an unambiguous means of grasping an exact law, even if he believed he had exposed the real essential elements that comprise its substance.

If we look beneath the logic of Menger's exact methodology, the ontologically oriented aspects of the argument are comprised by the key reference to '*under exactly the same conditions*' and by the key categorial quality of *strict typicality*. The precise meaning and the legitimacy of either notion cannot be taken as self-evident. Menger's view was that the quality of strict typicality, and the associated potential for 'exactly the same conditions' to have a repeatable existence, can be revealed as imbedded in existential reality by empirical inquiry that somehow transcends the fallacies of 'Bacon's empirical-realistic induction' (p. 60). The inquiry thus presupposes the ontological belief that the exact explanatory elements to be sought have an actual existence and that the task of the theorist is to form the apt discursive concepts to represent them (Milford, 1990, p. 229). The idea was that the theorist 'seeks to ascertain the *simplest elements* of everything real, elements that must be thought of as strictly typical just because they are the simplest'. It remained irrelevant that these elements may not be, and possibly could never be, 'present as *independent* phenomena . . . in their full purity' (p. 60). The exposure of elementary constituents and their relations, then, enables the theorist to 'arrive at laws of phenomena which are not only absolute, but according to our laws of thinking simply cannot be thought of in any other way but as absolute' and 'as such to be complete' (p. 61).

Thus, according to Menger's formulations, 'exact economics by nature has to make us aware of *the laws holding for an analytically or abstractly conceived economic world* . . .'. Strictly defined and absolutely contained 'phenomena of *abstract economic reality*' are thus required as the objects of exact research (pp. 72f, 218). The following observation is pertinent to our understanding that the abstraction involved has some ontological rationale: 'It is a peculiarity of the exact social sciences that exact research in the realm of the phenomena of human activity starts with the assumption of *a definite volitional orientation of the active subjects*' (p. 215n; emphasis added). Here the presumed volitional orientation is such that agents are depicted in isolation to be pursuing their economic goals, and to be motivated purely by the principle of maximizing the satisfaction of needs and wants, however measured. At one point,

Menger included among his examples of the purified categories relevant to exact theories the notion of 'a person pursuing only economic aims' (p. 61). In the context of exact theoretical research, such categories were presumably those that are further isolated by the theorist from the regularities of the realistic-empirical analyses. It was an integral part of this procedure that 'the results of exact research . . . are true only with certain presuppositions, with presuppositions which in reality do not always apply' (p. 69). This is a procedure that also, as Menger admitted quite candidly, is more readily seen to be realistic in the cases of simple rather than complex economic phenomena (pp. 68f).

The conclusion that we reach in this examination of Menger's endeavours to come to grips with the design and defence of exact theory in economics is that it failed. He may well have been correct in his notion that as a matter of principle, economic theories could be constructed so as to express the essentials imbedded in actual economic phenomena, essentials that can account for their generation as exact types in terms of exact laws. But there was no practical way evident for theorists intellectually to reach these essentials from empirical observations that could be defended as consistent with what those observations revealed about the ontology of agents' conduct. Menger's failure came about for two related reasons, one founded on the subjectivist ontology that he pursued and the other stemming from more general problems of epistemology and methodology that he confronted. The former has been argued from its immanent sources within Menger's own exposition, the latter has been made apparent in the philosophy of science and applied to his work most especially by Milford.[9] The relationship between the two sources of failure is simply that whatever unresolved methodological problems are identified as applying to the natural sciences and then carrying over to the human sciences, their impact in the latter is more profound and intractable by virtue of the exigencies of human agency that are the ontological source of its phenomena.

We are left after all this with what now appears to be the implicit existence of a vaguely defined methodological continuum along which relevant, real-world phenomena are represented by theory at one end and particular historical description at the other. At or towards one end, placed according to the empirical scope of its representations, there can be claimed to exist a legitimated position appropriate to realistic-empirical theory. Beyond this, in Menger's own argument, it was simply not made sufficiently clear what particular metatheoretical criteria are to be applied in drawing the borderline between exact and realistic-empirical theory or how theorists were actually to formulate the transition. Two alternatives appear to me to be possible here. One is the

Aristotelian claim that exact theory is a kind of more abstract realistic-empirical theory, the categories of which enjoy real ontological status at a deeply imbedded essentialist level of existence. Intuitive and introspective ingenuity appears to be the answer for theorists here. The other is that exact theoretical arguments can only be grounded on imposed abstract conceptual forms with no ontologically defensible foundations. In this case, theorists can simply draw on mechanistic-behaviourist representations of human agents. Most probably, Menger as an Aristotelian thinker intended to defend the former position involving effectively a realistically grounded exact theory, but in the end he failed to do so with any cogency.

3.4 Critical reflections and open questions

Menger's alternative treatment of economics as the science of subjectivism in the production, valuation and exchange of goods brought human agents as individuals into prominence as the consciously reasoning and active generators of a selected range of economic phenomena. This turn was, however, in its effect on the representation of economic agents in much of his theoretical argument, more ostensible than real. For his individualism was often confined to the conception of the human agent that he thought relevant for the very narrow set of substantive economic concerns upon which he focused formally. Where his analytical vision was of the market economy operating in accordance with universal and reliable laws, he chose to base it on the most elementary and least consequential subjective perceptions and calculations by very narrowly conceived agents (cf. Kirzner, 1992, pp. 74ff). This immediately mitigated against the inclusion of many of his deeper insights into the more contingent facets of situated human conduct that he had explicitly recognized. Menger's vision of economic agency emphasized valuation, exchange and consumption, in the processes of which the most passive and predictable characteristics of human agents are prominent and in which they act much in accordance with slowly changing habits and traditions. As most consumer decisions, individually and singularly considered, are of limited economic import, the inclination of and scope for agents to exercise their free will or caprice is minimal. Here the potential is for agents to appear as omniscient and as consistently and reliably rational in acting with full information and certainty. From this perspective, the deliberative demands made upon human agents in their decision-making is minimal. This must be taken to be the effect and import of the passage delimiting his vision:

'This is the very branch of our science . . . in which the events of economic life most distinctly appear to obey regular laws' (1950, p. 49).

Menger's choice of substantive emphasis was to be more on consumers, exchange and markets involving pre-existing final commodity stocks, with only some limited attention to the potential flow of future goods through production. This was not without its quite profound consequences for what happened to his seminal subjectivism, for its more penetrating elements were able to be cited only in passing and then left aside without disturbing his pursuit of theoretical precision. In the real-world economic context, it is agents other than consumers whose deliberations involve most personal initiative and creativity, demand the most detailed profiles of knowledge and information and require the greatest talent for complex calculations. It is these agents who are most concerned with the temporality of their decisions to act and with the effects of uncertainty and expectations, and for whom errors are most probable and most economically significant. Such agents are those who make decisions about the production of commodities and those who invest in new means of production, often embodying new technology. The latter are also most required to conjure up views of the future with imagination and creativity, to perceive and pursue interstices of economic opportunity and to make forecasts that have extended time horizons of effect. Most often, too, the subjectivism of the agency involved is complicated by the fact that these sorts of decisions are taken by hierarchical coalitions of individual, but situated, agents, in particular by those comprising enterprises with corporate structures. Understanding and discursively representing such coalitional decision-making presents its own special problems. In all this, then, Menger did not ever give himself the occasion to explore more fully the import of subjectivism and individualism for the really vital processes of economic agency in which the import of these principles becomes most crucial and most complex. His treatment of the more analytically intractable economic phenomena in their strictly temporal setting, especially exchange and distribution as market processes *per se*, together with the investment and production that are operationally and logically prior to them, was minimal. So, in spite of his awareness of a significant number of the deeper contingent elements afflicting human agency, such as the exercise of free will and caprice, uncertainty, expectations, calculation errors and lack of information, he was able simply to assume them away in his chosen formal context. However, whatever may have been the virtues of such a limited scope for ensuring the scientificity of economics, he was really not excused from defending ontologically the regular laws claimed to characterize the phenomena involved. They should have been shown to be consistent with the fact that they are the result of the individual deliberations and actions of independent but commonly situated categories of human agents.

Be all this as it may, I have shown above that Menger's expressed subjectivist concerns and insights went well beyond the role of individual agents' values in decision-making and problem-solving in the narrow context of the exchange of pre-existing stocks of relatively scarce consumer goods. He noted much that is of relevance to the broader vision of a producing and reproducing dynamic market economy operating under a range of influences, including the exercise of monopoly power by some agents. He appreciated the relevance of knowledge and information, together with the import of varying profiles of agents' abilities and ignorance, of institutional formations and of real time in the constituent processes of a capitalist system. He realized that agents had to contend with uncertainty because of the chronically temporal dimension of economic choices and actions, especially those to be undertaken by the entrepreneurs who put in a brief appearance in the context of his limited treatment of production. The problematics of time then combined with often imperfect information and knowledge to render fallible agents' expectations, deliberations and calculations, and their consequent decisions to act. Such problematics ensure that agents' best endeavours to carry out their premeditated intentions can rarely meet with individual success in full and that their collective consequences can become clear only *ex post*. And, in an ever changing environment, with the ever present need to cope with a perfidious future, the potential for agents effectively to learn from failure and thus to improve their decision-making is severely limited.

At the back of Menger's analyses, then, even at their most formal level, there existed conceptions of economic agents and their agency in which human vitalism actually transcended any omniscient image of an *homo oeconomicus* motivated by the simple pursuit of maximizing self-interest in the satisfaction of needs and wants. Menger simply left incompletely defended his decision not to allow the subjectivist detail of human agency that he was so clearly aware of to have full and consistent representation in the construction of his formal economic argument as far as he chose to take it.

What Menger had not fully carried through is a complete ontological defence of the idea that the selectively delimited situational conditions in and through which agents act, in particular with respect to the production, valuation and exchange of goods, are such as consistently to shape the essentials of their activities independently of their free will. The systemic assumptions that underpin the argument in the *Grundsätze* comprise those of free-market capitalism. Such a system is constituted for any period of economic activity by an inherited set of structures and relations with physical–technical and human dimensions. Individual agents intent upon some action have no option but to deliberate about how their objectives may be best served by working through the environment that for the moment confronts them as more or less a *fait accompli*. The majority of them may arguably be presumed to conform to the conditions and conditioning that the relevant market institutions and other influences impose upon them in this situational environment. Their constrained actions in response to particular categories of problems may thus be typified and rationalized. This presumption, when fully explicated, could mean that their actually typical economic conduct can be reliably represented in its essentials by formal theories. But such a serendipitous outcome could not have been taken for granted, even if Menger had recognized its potential.

In the process of my inquiries, I have posed some issues concerning Menger's subjectivism that suggest that his main legacy was to pose the terms of the problematic to be confronted rather than to have provided solutions. That is, he pursued the right issues and was conscious of the need for some philosophical investigations in order properly to ground economics as a definitely human science. But, in the end his inconclusive and truncated treatment of his ontological insights into the nature and role of subjectivism and individualism meant that these principles were left only as guideposts for those who were to follow him. At the same time, though, and incompletely recognized by Menger and his followers, other philosophers of the human sciences were working out with more consistency and articulation just the metatheoretical foundations that he implicitly sought.

But, in all that has been said in this chapter one thing has nevertheless become demonstrably clear. There are very good reasons for concluding with Kirzner that Menger's subjectivism 'fell short of exploiting its own full potential' (Kirzner, 1992, p. 70). The potential would only begin to be teased out later by Mises, the one Austrian successor prior to the 1970s who really endeavoured to carry forward his subjectivism and individualism. The complex situation that Menger confronted in his subjectivist endeavours was well captured by Lachmann in the following passage.

> Menger, a man between two worlds, an Aristotelian who had to live in an age of triumphant positivism, was a nineteenth century subjectivist who was unable to rid himself of his reliance on objective wants and his quest for 'exact laws'. But at the same time his work points beyond itself and beyond

his day to important issues with which we are today intensely concerned. (1978a, p. 59)

For us it is important to understand the limitations of the scope and analytical penetration of the subjectivism and individualism that Menger chose to accept. In the chapters to follow, I explore some alternative treatments of these ontological themes. These will prove to be much more penetrating in their understanding of the issues that should be of concern to subjectivists in economics. Mises had access to all the contributions that are to be examined, and what he was able to make of them will be taken up as the final stage of this retrospective inquiry.

Notes

1. As a dissenting voice against any fully subjectivist reading of Menger, Terence Hutchison has sometimes noted how difficult he and his Germanic contemporaries found it to break away from the exact rigour of the Classicals' *homo oeconomicus* and the effective assumption of '*Allwissenheit*', or complete knowledge, that went with it. In Hutchison's view, 'it is far from easy . . . to discover any *very* consistent application of subjectivism on the part of Menger and his Austrian followers . . .', especially where subjectivism includes as a necessary condition avoiding any representation of the human agent that does not recognize the failure of '*Allwissenheit*' (1994, p. 199, original emphasis). In Menger's case, the problem comes with his efforts to defend 'exact laws' of economics in which subjectivism could not be readily sustained as an ontological foundation. Hutchison's substantiating quotations from Menger do reveal the latter's consciousness that exactitude in economic theory requires a denial of some self-evident subjectivist realities of human agency (1994, p. 199). But, ill-founded though Menger's 'exact' theoretical endeavours may have been, it was much more to his credit that he worked fully conscious of the limitations of such an approach than Hutchison allows. More generally, there was a greater subjectivist awareness in his work than Hutchison captures in his briefer writings. Moreover, when he had the opportunity to examine Menger's philosophy more fully, although the theme of subjectivism hovered in the background, it was given little explicit recognition as the ontological foundation of the methodological ideas being critically examined (Hutchison, 1973).
2. Page numbers in parentheses throughout section 3.2 refer to Menger (1950) unless otherwise stated.
3. Evidently, Menger worked throughout much of his later life on this projected second edition of his main work. It remained unpublished until some two years after his death when it was finally edited from drafts by his son Karl (Carl Menger, 1923; see Hayek, 1981, pp. 27f, 32f). The account given by Alter of Menger's writings indicates that this rarely used edition was, according to its editor, largely unchanged in its organization or substance from the first. Changes were confined to an expansion and elaboration of arguments originally presented, even though its chapters were rearranged and even though it was nearly twice as long as the first. A new opening chapter dealt explicitly with the crucial theory of *Bedürfnisse*, that is, of human needs and wants, the satisfaction of which drive and give direction to all economic activity. Its main arguments were prepared for the first edition, but as a separate piece that was omitted at the time (Alter, 1990a, pp. 82ff, 122ff, 159ff).

4. The detail of Menger's theory of goods valuation is too well known to warrant any repeat exposition here (1950, pp. 114ff). A modern and critical exposition is contained in Alter (1990a), chapter III.
5. In all quotations from Menger's writings in this chapter, the emphases shown are in the original unless otherwise indicated.
6. Menger's disinclination to be explicit about the existence of this physical–technical dimension left open some issues that become significant if we tackle a more complete treatment of subjectivism in the market economy. For example, a change in the physical nature of some production can render void the status of particular things as goods and introduce into an economy the need for significant subjective adjustment responses by agents if the new technique is to be adopted and absorbed.
7. From here to the end of section 3.3, unless otherwise stated, the page numbers in parentheses refer to the *Untersuchungen*: Menger (1963).
8. The translations in the following quotations from Menger's correspondence with Walras are my own.
9. Milford (1990, 1992b) is critical of the methodological strategy employed by Menger in the effort to devise and defend theoretical foundations for economics that are consistent with the particular nature of its phenomena. Milford's critique focuses on the epistemological and logical problems of Menger's efforts and complements and reinforces the critical approach that I have followed above on ontological criteria. The foundation of Milford's critique is that Menger rejected direct induction as a means of establishing explanatory knowledge about the phenomena of the real world. As a consequence, Menger sought to establish the theoretical basis for economics as a science concerned with the real world by means that avoided naive induction. He attempted this through his dual methodology of realistic-empirical and exact inquiries. But, as Milford interprets the situation, the rejection of induction already confronted Menger with 'a most serious epistemological problem' as he proceeded to try to devise a theoretical methodology for economics that was consistent with the requirement of sound empirical science: it should comprise 'strictly universal theories exclusively decided by experience'. Induction claimed to allow such theories to be formed; but induction is invalid. Implicitly, Menger sought to override the problem of induction by pursuing non-empirical modes of establishing universality (Milford, 1992b, pp. 3ff, 34ff).
    The exact orientation alternative was, according to Milford, for Menger the only ultimately desirable standard for theory because it promised the universality that adhering to empiricism could not (1990, p. 228; 1992b, pp. 35f). It required Menger to extract theories of general relevance that are comprised of universal elements related together by exact laws. Once again, these can only be put together by the intervention of the theorist, who must for this purpose apply the allegedly innate 'rule of cognition' to establish a strictly logically argued explanation. Milford's response to this endeavour is to reject its validity on the grounds that Menger did not adequately justify the cognitive principle he adopted (1990, pp. 232ff). Nor could he have done so, Milford continues, because the process involved is still essentially inductive, relying as it does on applying 'an induction principle that is *a priori* valid' and that takes the form of identifying the simplest and thus strictly typical essences of real phenomena (1992b, p. 37). But Milford insists that no inductive inquiry can succeed in delivering universal and exact theory, whatever the form of intervention by theorists may be (1990, pp. 230, 232, 234). Claims to have formulated such theory automatically sever it from claims that it can be derived from, or justified by empirical experience.

4. Wilhelm Dilthey and subjectivism: the human sciences

4.1 Introduction: from natural to human science

Wilhelm Dilthey's philosophy of the human sciences included a version of subjectivism that gave explicit emphasis to the ontology of human agents as the generators of relevant object phenomena. In the subjectivism of Menger, the full scope of this human dimension had been allowed less than due attention and influence in theory construction. His inclination had been to confine subjectivism within imposed substantive economic bounds and within the limits permitted by exact theory. For Dilthey, the human sciences were to be grounded in the self-conscious purposes and expressions of human life in all its dimensions, always in contact with explicit historical, social and situational conditions. In contrast to Menger, he tried to preserve this rich ontological content in his search for a metatheory that he thought could grant universally valid status to the entire substance of these sciences.

Just as it had been for Menger, the immediate focus of Dilthey's critical inquiries[1] into the state of the human sciences was on the overwhelming intellectual dominance of the positivists' endeavours to bring history and the human life-world (*Lebenswelt*) generally within the grasp of natural scientific methodology and explanation. The critical and most fundamental problem with the positivists' approach that Dilthey pointed to was that, in order to meet this objective, they were forced '*to mutilate historical reality to accommodate it to the concepts and methods of the natural sciences*' (1988, p. 72; emphasis added; cf. Ermarth, 1978, pp. 68ff).[2] That is, the selective representation of reality is required to meet standards demanded by the exigencies of the imposed methodology, a direction of argument that Dilthey could see is opposite to that dictated by common sense. His view was that subjectivism in the human sciences demanded a methodology that enabled discursive explanations to maintain an ontological integrity as its primary criterion of acceptance.

The positivist approach had led to the human sciences adopting 'a superficial and sterile empiricism, and thus [an] increasing separation of life from knowledge', with evidence, also, of a 'widely admired present-day tendency in jurisprudence, [and] political economy wholly to exclude psychological foundations' (1977, pp. 29, 30). Such tendencies amounted to an exclusion of human life and expression as the essence of human sciences. He concluded that 'in contrast with [their] methods, which approach human sciences from the outside, we must meet the challenge to establish human sciences through epistemology, to justify and support their independent formation, and to do away definitively with subordinating their principles and their methods to those of the natural sciences' (1988, p. 142).

Again in a similar vein to Menger, at the same time Dilthey also wanted to prevent the human sciences from retreating to the more simplistic and inductivist aspects of contemporary German historicism. He considered himself to be a member of the Historical School in so far as it comprised the advocacy of unique metatheoretical foundations for historical science. However, some of the Historicists had fallen victim to the illusion that the laws of history could be pursued by fact gathering and purely inductive means: 'This superstition subjects the labors of historians to an arcane process to transform alchemistically the singular materials they discover into pure gold of abstraction and to force history to betray its ultimate secret' (1988, p. 131). Dilthey joined Menger in expressing his dissatisfaction with the one-sided, naive empiricism and resistance to theoretical representation of many members of the Historical School. Their approach to historical inquiry had 'not broken through the inner barriers which were bound to limit its theoretical development'. These barriers comprised a failure to realize the need to ground their inquiries on a properly formulated ontology of individual consciousness and expression, and of the human life-world in general, along with a failure to establish a 'sound connection with epistemology and psychology' which meant that they 'never achieved a method of explanation either' (1988, p. 72). In this latter respect, they had underrated the value of formalized abstract theory, and in company with Menger, Dilthey saw this as a profoundly restrictive aspect of their mode of inquiry. He, like Menger, was intent on reinforcing the merits of properly grounded and argued theory as essential for the progress of the human sciences in all their dimensions and objectives.

At the most general level, Dilthey considered himself to be a 'philosopher of life'. His concern was to emphasize the primacy of the consciousness of 'Life' (*das Leben*), 'Life Experiences' (*die Erlebnisse*) and 'Life Expressions' (*die Lebensäusserungen*) of human beings in understanding the phenomena of human science. His intention was to ensure that all human sciences began from a proper grasp of human beings as they are in the total reality of their complex of situated and purposeful activities. That is, as beings with profound mental capacities to interpret and volitionally to engage their natural and human environment, within the efflux of real time, for the purpose of satisfying their needs and desires. They achieve their ends with varying, but always reflexively monitored degrees of success. Human beings are, at the same time, chronically contingent and protean, but socially and historically conditioned creatures.

These insights meant rejecting all inquiries that began from artificial and delimited constructs that purported to represent human actors, such as *homo oeconomicus* and *homo sociologicus*. Thus, he rejected any constructivist approach that somehow claimed to begin from abstract elements *a priori*. Indeed, 'it was by rupturing this connection' between actors and their historical situations 'that disastrous errors have come about, which, as [in] abstract natural law, abstract political economy, have ruined the sciences and injured society' (1988, p. 144). He thus ruled out the notion of classical economic man and the approach of the classical economists as imposing a misleading logical precision on the complexities of the human life-world and as thus distorting the nature of human science inquiry. In particular, this approach failed to capture the richness and capriciousness of the economic life of situated individuals that Dilthey intended to highlight in his philosophy of the human sciences.

It is apparent that Dilthey saw historical and social reality as comprised of the actions and manifested expressions of subjectively conceived individual human beings. I will emphasize this orientation throughout my inquiries below, for it is simultaneously the source of Dilthey's profound contributions to the advance of the human sciences and of his equally profound difficulties with devising any conclusive metatheoretical foundations for them. More explicitly, what Dilthey confronted was 'the task of developing an *epistemological foundation of [the] human sciences* and of then using the instrument developed in that foundation to determine the inner connection between special human sciences, the limits [with]in which knowledge is possible in them' (1988, p. 146). He claimed that 'the basic conception of my philosophy is that up until now no one has put *whole, full, and unmutilated experience* at the basis of philosophizing, that is to say, the whole and full reality' (quoted by Ermarth, 1978, p. 24; Dilthey's emphasis). It was this immediacy of contact with the reality of the human life-world that he found to be the strength of the empiricist approach that he adhered to as an Historicist. Ermarth's interpretation of Dilthey here is indicative of my own emphasis below: 'Method in the useful and practical sense begins as reflection upon experience, not [as] a set of [meta-]theoretical prescriptions set down in advance. Indeed all theory of method must be on guard against the nearly incorrigible tendency to fix the terms of inquiry in a manner which narrowly predisposes the outcome' (1978, p. 168). Most importantly, he concludes as I will that Dilthey's 'adversary was not science but scientism, not reason but the kind of rationalism which restricts reason solely to the methods of physical science and then extends these methods to all forms and features of reality' (1978, p. 350). What is given due emphasis here is his adherence to the principle of attributing priority to faithful representations of the ontological realities of phenomena instead of to preconceived notions of what theory should look like.[3] As he put it himself, the human sciences 'have the right to determine their methods independently corresponding to their object' (1977, p. 27). In this adherence, then, he was intent upon ensuring that the objects of a science are not 'mutilated' for the sake of discursive methodological form.

It was through his explicit and self-conscious adoption of the *die Geisteswissenschaften* concept[4] that Dilthey gave some initial notice of his intention to explicate and defend the independent status of 'the entire range of sciences which deal with historico-social reality' for which 'there is no generally accepted designation' (1988, p. 78; cf. Plantinga, 1980, pp. 24ff). In separately distinguishing the *die Geisteswissenschaften* Dilthey maintained that 'the motivation behind the habit of seeing these sciences as a unity in contrast with those of nature derives from the depth and fullness of human self-consciousness'. An active individual 'finds in this self-consciousness a sovereignty of will, a responsibility for actions, a capacity for subordinating everything to thought and for resisting any foreign element in the citadel of freedom in his person: by these things he distinguishes himself from all of nature . . .' (1988, p. 79). He emphasized, then, that what sets the human sciences apart is their focus on the subjectivist ontology of human action that constitutes the source of their phenomena.

We will find Dilthey emphasizing a fundamental epistemological contrast: while nature is external and only given to individual observers, and must be explained on that basis if at all, the world of human phenomena can rather be *understood* by actors because other actors like them are its creators. The quite apparent reason for this was that 'nature is mute for us. . . . Nature is alien to us. After all, it is for us only an outer thing, not an inner one' (1988, p. 97). The human sciences are distinguished from the natural, therefore, 'in that the latter have for their objects facts which are presented to consciousness as from outside, as phenomena and given in isolation, while the objects of the former are given originaliter from within as real and as a living continuum' (1977, p. 27). At the same time, however, Dilthey referred to the 'inestimable advantage there is for ... [physical science] in the stability of its objects, the free recourse to experimentation, the measurability of the spatial world!' (1977, p. 26). By contrast, the 'uniformities we can establish in the sphere of society are far inferior in number, significance, and formal precision to laws we can determine about nature on the solid foundation of spatial relationships and characteristics of motion' (1988, p. 97). Compared to the precision and long time horizons of calculations possible in astronomy, for example, he concluded that the 'sciences of society cannot offer this sort of satisfaction to our understanding' (1988, p. 98). The phenomena of the human world are understood ontologically if they are understood at all, for it is the nature of human being and expression that constitutes their essence and the substance of their representation in the human sciences. '[M]an becomes the subject-matter of the human studies only when we relate experience, expression and understanding to each other. ... A discipline only belongs to the human studies when we can approach its subject-matter through the connection between life, expression and understanding' (1976, pp. 175f). As a result of the ontological differences between the objects of nature and society, for observer-analysts, any 'knowledge of [the] principles of the mental world remains in the sphere of the mental world, and the human sciences constitute a system which is independent in its own right' (1988, p. 73). So it is that while the natural sciences have 'become remote from our day-to-day contact with the external world ... in the human studies a connection between life and science is retained, so that thought arising from daily life remains the foundation of scholarly activity' (1976, p. 182).

Dilthey was intent on identifying the potential for the arguments of the human sciences to have legitimate, universally valid and formal existence. For this reason, he went on to claim that despite the obvious intractabilities of human actors' conduct and expressions as the phenomenal objects of science, as compared to the immanent order attributable by scientists to the world of nature, working with such objects had its own advantages. 'The human sciences have the advantage over the cognition of nature that their object is not mere appearance given in external sensation as the mere phenomenal reflex of something real but an immediate reality itself. And this reality, moreover, is given in the form of a coherence experienced from within' (quoted by Ermarth, 1978, p. 99). It follows, Dilthey argued, that if 'we explain nature, [while] we understand psychic life ..., the methods by means of which we study psychic life, history, and society are very different from those which have led to the knowledge of nature' (1977, pp. 27f). The distinction that Dilthey drew in this context was between the processes of *Verstehen*, the objective of understanding applicable only in the human sciences, and those of *Erklären*, the objective of explanation in the natural sciences (cf. 1977, p. 341, ed. n. 22). As the phenomena of the human sciences have their origins in actors' experiences, deliberations and decisions, whatever may be their empirical forms of expression, access to an understanding of them is from the 'inside', as it were. Observers are, therefore, required to extrapolate from their own experiences and introspective insights to the psychic states and cognitive processes of relevant other actors. In order to do so, according to Dilthey, they grasp the expressions of life as the means of understanding. But, as he was prepared explicitly to grant, 'the very manner in which reality is given in inner experience gives rise to great difficulties in apprehending it objectively' (quoted by Ermarth, 1978, p. 128). We shall find below that he never fully succeeded in overcoming these 'great difficulties'.

The purpose of the next three sections is to elicit an ontological foundation for understanding the generation of human phenomena as it was presented by Dilthey. He sought to focus on the subjective and situationally conditioned nature of human actors as the means to accounting for these phenomena. Section 4.2 examines the psychology of the individual actor at the most general level argued by Dilthey. He undertook to provide a descriptive psychology of individuals to replace the pseudo-scientific explanatory psychology he encountered in the literature. His idea was to 'get behind' the evidence of observed conduct and its empirico-phenomenal consequences in an effort to understand more fully their mental and cognitive origins. Actors' conduct interests and concerns human science most when it is purposeful and directed at particular objectives. Such teleological actions and the expressions that they generate involve actors in engaging their situational environments as *agents*. Actors thus become agents to the extent that their conduct is devoted to transforming inherited conditions in the pursuit of life-world satisfactions. The manifold nature of the situational conditions confronted by agents, and the way that these conditions facilitate and contain their conduct, are the subjects of section 4.3.

With respect to this more complex conception of individual actors as situated agents, it became apparent to Dilthey rather quickly that his initial inclination to rely on a purely introspective psychology could not fulfil his metatheoretical objectives. Most especially, it understated the role of the manifest expressions of psychic processes, which are the first point of contact between agents and the mediation for their understanding of each other. The emergence and significance of all forms of expression for agents' conduct and their relations with others are explored in section 4.4. Focusing on these expressions of life, and on the situationally conditioned conduct of agents that leads to them, led Dilthey to shift away from an emphasis on the psyches of individuals as the origin of observed phenomena. That is, to move away from his directly psychological inquiries towards a metatheory directed at understanding expressions, *Verstehen*, with its consequent hermeneutical orientation. He sought to defend the subjectivist insights that his psychology had provided while suggesting to analysts that they move to a depiction of agents and their expressions as types. Agents balance situational facilitation and containment against existential freedom in designing their deliberated and purposeful conduct. And the meaning of the resulting expressions to these agents can only be understood in relation to the situations in which they were generated. We are, then, ultimately brought face to face with Dilthey's less than fully successful attempt to formulate an ontologically legitimate foundation for the discursive representation of subjective human agency. The concluding section sums up the main threads and methodological implications of Dilthey's ontological efforts and points to some of the unresolved metatheoretical issues that subsequent human scientists were left to contend with.

4.2 A descriptive psychology of individuals

The most fundamental element underpinning the phenomena of concern to the human sciences was for Dilthey the self-conscious and purposeful individual human actor: 'In analyzing human society we [analysts] confront *man* himself as a living unity, and so *breaking up this living unity constitutes the basic problem* for analysis.' But, in his effort to avoid intellectualism and all depictions of actors as isolated minds, his focus was consistently on whole individuals as they really are in the *totality* of their life-world conditions and activities. So, 'if one tears away the gray web of abstract substantial entities, what remains is – *man*, that is men related variously to one another amid nature' (1988, pp. 302, 307; cf. Plantinga, 1980, p. 51). Dilthey pointed out that 'analysis finds in living unities ... the elements out of which society and history are constructed ... [These] unities which mutually interact in the marvelously intertwined whole of history and society are individuals, psychophysical wholes, each of which is different from every other, each of which is a world in itself' (1988, pp. 92f).

As a consequence of his subjectivist view of human phenomena, Dilthey's initial approach to the metatheoretical grounding of the human sciences was dominated by an attempt to redirect psychological inquiry. He rejected the notion that psychology could only be a natural science, applying only their methods and accepting only their epistemological standards.[5] This kind of psychology was inclined to deny the viability of explanations of behaviour that relied on separable and independent concepts of mind and consciousness (cf. Ermarth, 1978, pp. 76ff; Bulhof, 1980, pp. 132ff). The object of Dilthey's alternative descriptive psychology was human *being*, its situations and its manifest behavioural expressions of all sorts in their empirically existential forms. But as the origin of phenomena of interest to human science, human individuals' activities comprise more than what is usually understood by *behaviour*. Metals, gases and animals behave in terms of their perceived movements and changes as physical bodies. Of course, so do human beings. Dilthey's position here was that while physical observations may be sufficient to devise accounts of behaviour in the natural world, they certainly are not in the human world. In the latter case, they remain as necessary only (Rickman, 1988, p. 108).

Human beings, then, are much more than just very complex natural entities for the purposes of our efforts to understand and discursively to represent them through the human sciences. The phenomena of these sciences have their origin in what human beings feel and do as active, self-conscious actors: they are conscious of their bodily dimension, its functions and limitations; they are aware of their natural environment and they shape it to their purposes, as in the case of tool using and crop growing; they have emotions, feelings, motives and goals; they are creative and originating in the formation of ideas; they formulate and pursue purposes; they deliberate about available means; they plan for, and can imagine possible future scenarios *ex ante*; they make decisions on the basis of preconceived expected outcomes; they consciously study others around them and condition their own actions, where relevant, by what they expect them to do; they consciously interact and communicate with others; they participate in institutions, adopt conventions, and follow rules and traditions; and they make judgements and follow prejudices. Most of all, they self-consciously reflect on what they do and learn, change and adapt as a consequence. Now *none of these characteristics and problems can be attributed to the behaviours of objects in the physical sciences.*

The ever present problem for the human sciences, as we have seen it previously, is that an analyst faces the need to regularize the depiction of human individuals in order that they may be discursively represented by formal argument. In response, Dilthey postulated that the observed conduct of individual human beings that is of concern to the human sciences (other than those concerned with mental disorders) has its origins in the common elements that bring an essential uniformity of the qualitative makeup of their psychic profiles (cf. Ermarth, 1978, pp. 284f). In positing these claims about the essential qualities of human nature, he was quite definite:

> *Individualities are not distinguished* from one another by the presence of *qualitative* determinations or by certain modes of connection in one that would not be in the others. . . . The uniformity of human nature is manifested in the fact that the same qualitative determinations and forms of connection appear with all men (where no abnormal defects exist). But the *quantitative relationships* in which they are presented *are very different* from one another; these differences are *combined into ever new combinations on which depend . . . the differences of individualities.* From these quantitative differences and their relationships *arise those which appear as qualitative characteristics.* (1977, p. 109)

On the importance of the common dimensions of these qualitative profiles for human science inquiries, Dilthey was similarly decisive: 'A basic experience of what men have in common permeates the whole conception of the mind-constructed world; through it consciousness of a unitary self and similarity with others, identity of human nature and individuality are linked. This is the presupposition for understanding' (1976, p. 186).

It is also the case. Dilthey went on to claim, that the combinations of qualities are '*subject to certain rules which restrict the possibilities of the coexistence of quantitative differences*' (1977, p. 110). The qualities in the quantities in which they are present thus have a structured arrangement. Actors possess them innately, and acquire them through the cumulative experiences that comprise their biographies in the life-world, in different quantitative profiles. Dilthey posited the complex of influences to include race, gender, nationality, social class and education (1977, pp. 115f). But in this potential for difference, Dilthey identified an overriding characteristic that further delimits the possible arrangements that occur in individuals. Their survival and prosperity in the life-world depends on the quality of *purposiveness* in their conduct. This can only result from the appropriate quantitative structure of their psychic profiles: 'There is active, therefore, in individuality a *principle of unity which subordinates the forces to the teleological nexus*' (1977, p. 111, cf. p. 116).

To understand the goal directed actions of individuals, Dilthey realized, requires us to have some grip on the way they actually exercise their capacities and abilities. His theory of human action linked it to the psychic states of individuals. Actors confront the internal psychic and external situational conditions of their life-world as a complex comprising opportunities and facilities, as well as impediments and problems, concerning the satisfaction of their desires, needs and wants. At any point in time, the existential state that they experience and interpret opens the potential for actions that are expected to lead to a desired change in that current state. The change most often takes the form of the satisfaction of desires or needs made evident by experience. For Dilthey, 'it follows from the theory of the structural nexus of psychic life that the external conditions in which an individual finds himself, be they obstructive or beneficial, always evoke the desire to produce or maintain a state of fulfillment of our drives and of happiness' (1977, p. 95). So it is that the pursuit by actors of satisfactions of various kinds 'connects the play of our perceptions and thoughts with our voluntary acts into a structural nexus' (1977, p. 87). This 'volition emerges out of the global situation of our instinctual and emotional life', for it is 'an inner state or event [that] is a motive to the degree that it can become the factor of a voluntary decision'. The process of volition 'has as its intention the modifying of that situation', and the actor must reflect on what is to be done: 'Already during deliberation the idea of means is connected to the idea of the end' (1977, p. 71).

It was in this context that Dilthey gave his argument a distinctly subjectivist twist, very much in line with the ideas of Menger outlined in Chapter 3. Dilthey posited his version of the subjective nature of actors' consciousness of and pursuit of satisfaction most explicitly in the following passage.

> The purposiveness which rules over psychic life is . . . an intrinsic property of the nexus of [psychic] constituents. Therefore, far from this purposiveness being derived from the idea of a goal situated outside us, every concept of a purposiveness effective beyond psychic life is rather derived from this inner purposiveness. . . . The former is transferred from the latter. It is in our psychic structure. Only in virtue of a transference from it do we qualify as purposive any sort of system situated outside of psychic life. For goals are given to us only in this psychic structure. . . . This *purposiveness* of the psychic structure we designate as *subjective and immanent.* (1977, p. 96)

The structure of the psychic nexus of individuals situated in the mind-constructed world is such that it 'creates value and realizes *purposes*', and this constitutes 'the immanent teleological character of the mind's system of interaction' (1976, p. 197, cf. pp. 198f). So it is that 'the value we attribute to objects reflects our personal relationship to them' (1976, p. 242).

Individual actors selectively draw on their profiles of abilities and talents in order to cope with the problems of satisfying their life-world needs and requirements of all sorts under the conditions confronting them. Exercising these abilities and talents, and the formation of skills and habits, in this ongoing engagement with the life-world depend upon the actors having available to them the qualities required in the appropriate quantities, intensities and durations (1977, pp. 114ff). It was the nature and roles of free-will, experience, reason, purpose and actions of individual human actors as the fundamental generating forces of the empirically observable phenomena of the historical sciences which Dilthey developed most fully and formally as he could under the rubric of his descriptive and analytical psychology. Most specifically, as an actor:

> everything which man accomplishes in this historico-social world happens through the compression spring [*Sprungfeder*] of his will: it is purpose, however, which functions as the motive power in that will. It is his nature, it is the universally valid and the supraindividual in him, no matter what formula one uses to grasp it, on which the complex of purposes which permeates wills rests. In this complex of purposes the usual activity of men, which is concerned only with itself, nevertheless accomplishes what it must. (1988, p. 108)

Dilthey was aware, implicitly in the above arguments, that actors are situated in and experience a life-world that is forever moving within the continuous and irreversible efflux of real time. All experience, including deliberations and actions in response to perceived needs and wants, has a temporal, or diachronic dimension. However, the actual experience of time is subjective and means more to individuals than its mechanistic perception as a sequence of moments counted by clocks. As he realized, human action is set *in time* in the sense that its processes are thought of by actors as necessarily involving differentials and transmissions between past, present and expected future experiences. These temporal categories flow into one another and are integral to the dynamics of situated human experience (cf. Ermarth, 1978, pp. 115f, 172; Bulhof, 1980, pp. 120f, 153, 166, 168ff). It is, in fact, 'the experience of time in all its dimensions [that] determines the content of our lives', for 'life is always and everywhere spatially and temporally determined . . .' (1976, pp. 210, 232). This temporal dimension becomes an integral component of their experience and of their purposes, deliberations and actions in pursuit of satisfactions. 'The ship of our life is, as it were, carried forward on a constantly moving stream . . .' (1976, p. 209). But *individuals experience time as problematical*: 'The antinomies which thought discovers in the experience of time spring from its cognitive impenetrability' (1976, p. 210). Now be this as it may, it is an absolute imperative for actors to reflect on and somehow to cope with the exigencies of this diachronic dimension of their life-world, most especially its uncertain future orientation. They cannot opt out of the time experience. In coming to grips with time, there can be no doubt, stressed Dilthey, that 'time is there for us through the synthesizing unity of consciousness. Life, and the outer objects cropping up in it share the conditions of simultaneity, sequence, interval, duration and change' (1976, p. 209). These categories reflect the natural and mechanistic dimensions of time, which for actors provide a framework of temporal reference but cannot exhaust 'the experience of time through which the concept of time receives its ultimate meaning' (1976, p. 209).

Actors experience and deal with the exigencies of time in terms of the self-conscious unity comprising an existent present, the remembered past and the future yet to come that can only be imagined. 'Here time is experienced as the restless progression, in which the present constantly becomes the past and the future the present. The present is the filling of a moment of time with reality; it is experience, in contrast to memory or *ideas of the future occurring in wishes, expectations, hopes, fears and strivings*' (1976, p. 209; emphasis added). It was the orientation of actors towards the future that was most astutely recognized in this passage and subsequently given some due and prominence by Dilthey. He realized that the teleological, goal-directed nature of the constant pursuit by individuals of psychic satisfactions immediately gives their concerns a dynamic that is oriented against the limitations of the present and towards the prospects of the future. He saw the problem for actors this way: 'We are facing a decision. In this situation we ponder existing conditions and those which might arise in the future: with all our vitality and experience we project ourselves testingly [*versetzen uns probierend*] into those conditions' (quoted by Ermarth, 1978, p. 172). Actors are always located in and experience reality as a present, and they must use their remembered past experiences as the most readily available mediating guide to the expected nature of the future if they wish to exercise any control over how it will turn out. Thus, in each momentary synchronic view of the psychic nexus, the present includes 'memory pictures of the past and *pictures of the future in which possibilities are imagined and selected as purposes.* So the present is filled with past events and contains the future' (1976, p. 235; emphasis added; cf. Ermarth, 1978, pp. 324f; Bulhof, 1980, pp. 170ff). Thus, as they are experienced by actors, 'every form of historical life is finite, it contains a distribution of happy forces and of restraint, of enlargement and of narrowness of life, of satisfaction and of need' (quoted by Bulhof, 1980, p. 166).

Even more specifically, within this view Dilthey recognized the concept of the *plan* as characteristic of its future orientation and the importance of its links to the meaning of the past: 'Every plan for your life expresses a view of the meaning of life. The purposes we set for the future are determined by the meaning we give to the past. The actual formation of life is judged in terms of the meaning we give to what we remember' (1976, p. 236; cf. Rickman, 1988, pp. 28f). He made the important, if more or less self-evident distinction between actors' perspectives concerning the past and the future. 'When we look back at the past we are passive; it cannot be changed. . . . In our attitude to the future we are active and free. Here the category of reality which emerges from the present is joined by that of possibility. We feel that we have infinite possibilities' (1976, pp. 209f). But, 'the more links, such as moods, outer events, means and goals, there are between the filled present and a moment of the future the greater is the number of possible outcomes, the more indefinite and nebulous the picture of the future becomes' (1976, p. 209). In this respect, as Dilthey sensed, the luxury of apparently infinite future possibilities is given an uncertain and per-fidious twist for individuals to cope with. He did not go on to explore the real import of these facts of life or consider how individual actors may try to cope with them in designing their purposive actions. Nonethe-less, the insight was posited and potentially ready for development by others.

It is apparent that what has been progressively emerging in the foregoing argument is the idea that not only is the conduct of actors more than mere behaviour, their conduct interests science most when they act purposefully *within, through and on* their inherited environment to bring about consciously intended change. In this sense they are more than actors and should be referred to as *agents*, and the totality of their actions is more than conduct and should be referred to as *agency*. In sum: 'The purposiveness and the nexus which are located in the relation-ship of . . . instincts and feelings to intellectual processes, on the one hand, and to volitional conduct on the other, confer on the . . . emergent psychic alterations the character of an adaptation between the indi-vidual and his conditions of life' (1977, p. 95). Human science should, according to Dilthey, recognize that 'the individual [agent] is born into those systems and thus encounters them as an objective situation which existed before him, remains after him, and influences him through his arrangements. They thus present themselves to [an analyst's] scientific imagination as independently existing objective facts' that must be represented in any depiction of the situations of agents (1988, p. 106). These conditions, comprising the situations of active agents, direct the processes by which satisfactions are achieved. The form and processes of this direction will be dealt with in the next two sections below.

4.3 Human agents in their life-world situations

As Dilthey was to emphasize in great detail, individuals can experience and act, and thereby create their history and its manifestations, only within their given situational environments and in accordance with their varied biographically developed values and world views. This sort of contained existence constitutes 'the germinal cell of the historical world [and] is the experience in which the subject discovers himself in a dynamic relationship with his environment. The environment acts on the subject and is acted on by him. It is composed of the physical and cultural surroundings' (1976, p. 203). From the perspective of these actors as subjects, 'it is inherent in the unity of human consciousness that [the] experiences it contains are conditioned by the context in which they appear. From this ensues the *universal law of relativity which governs our experiences of external reality*' (1988, p. 309). World views formed by actors, then, are the joint product of their individual qualities and of the situations within which they must live their lives.

The phenomena that human individuals as active agents generate can therefore only be understood by rendering them discursively in a manner that maintains a meaningful contact with the external realities of their actual existence and their cumulative effects on the way agents see their life-world. At the same time, Dilthey ascribed a fundamental importance to ensuring that the free-will capacity of individual agents be explicitly recognized in human science: 'the theory of will constitutes the real working foundation of the human sciences...' (quoted by Ermarth, 1978, p. 120). Such freedom is exercised by most agents within a framework of situational responsibilities and sanctions, and of situational constraints and opportunities. Ermarth's summary of Dilthey's position is precise in its reference to the situated conditioning of agents' freedom as it is exercised in the practices of everyday life: 'Dilthey stipulated that will is "free" in a quite special sense....: not free *from*

conditions, but free to *respond to* a multiplicity of conditions as
mediated through consciousness and cultural forms. Freedom is thereby
defined in terms of a range of possible responses and choices within a
concrete situation' (Ermarth, 1978, p. 121, cf. pp. 225ff; original
emphasis).

External environmental conditions of all sorts, natural and human-
made, affect agents because they necessarily become involved with them
through the instincts, feelings and values that lead them to actions
directed towards achieving satisfied and satisfying states. At 'the center
of our psychic structure is a bundle of instincts or drives and feelings'
and it is these 'instincts and feelings [which] constitute ... the real
agency which drives onward' (1977, pp. 87, 95). But, 'it is only as ...
external conditions produce a sense of pressure or intensification in the
sphere of feeling that a striving to maintain or to modify a given
[personal} state arises' (1977, p. 86). Human agents as free-willed beings
were thus thought of by Dilthey as meaningfully and actively engaging
their inherited, but dynamically changing life-world situations. It is their
mode of participation in their life-world and constitutes the means of
establishing their existential identity. 'The course of life imposes on
each man a continual determination of his circumstances. The formation
of his nature [*Wesen*] always the further development for everyone ...
[and] he always finds that the extent of new prospects within his life and
the inner variation of his personal being [*Dasein*] is limited' (1977,
p. 134).

Dilthey was adamant that it makes no sense to try to understand
individual agents in isolation from their external world. Agents are
not purely subjective in the sense that they have a self-sufficient and
independent inwardness. Rather, 'self-consciousness and consciousness
of the world are two sides of the same consciousness' (quoted by
Ermarth, 1978, p. 126). And, as Dilthey observed, '*each self finds itself
conditioned by an external world and reacting to it*. ... Since this living
unity finds itself thus conditioned by the milieu in which it lives and to
which it in turn reacts, there emerges an articulated organization of its
inner states. This I call the structure of psychic life' (1977, pp. 81f;
emphasis added). Psychic states experienced by individuals are 'the
form of ... conscious life itself' as it is shaped by the relationship of
'the self and the objective world', and by the objective world itself
'which exists for each of us, which preceded me, which will survive me
and which, as limitation, is correlative and opposed to the self ...' (1977,
p. 82). So, Dilthey reasoned, 'all reflection upon the self is therefore at
the same time a reflection upon its relation to an external reality and

upon the origins and justification of determinations about that reality'
(quoted by Ermarth, 1978, p. 126).

Active agents exhibit two crucial characteristics in the operational
engagement with their life-world situations, including their relations
with others for whatever purpose. First, they exercise their free-will in
a contained and constrained way that stems from their pragmatically
oriented interpretations of the *meaning* their situations have in relation
to their pursuit of satisfactions. It becomes apparent to them that the
entities of their situations comprise *facilitations for*, as well as constraints
on their preferred conduct. So, it becomes integral to their concept of
free-willed conduct to accept volitionally the directional dictates of their
environment (cf. Rickman, 1988, p. 27). Agents rarely could, or would
want to, act in isolation from their external environment. Dilthey
showed some awareness of this point in passing (reiterating here a piece
previously quoted): 'the external conditions in which the individual
finds himself . . . [may be] obstructive or beneficial', but this is not an
idea that he followed through so as to expose its more important
implications (1977, p. 95). Secondly, they are selective in all that they
do in their confrontations with their situations. They observe other
agents, as well as confront problems and phenomena generally on the
grounds of relevance to the pursuit of their own goals and satisfactions.
In doing so, they also exercise selectivity in the application of their
psychic talents to problem-solving and in the details of their engage-
ments with the manifold and complex situations in and through which
they must operate in working up such solutions. This idea of selectivity
on the basis of practical relevance is one which can apply to the total
situational environment confronted by agents.

The situations confronting, locating, conditioning and directing
agents have a multiplicity of dimensions and as active agents 'we find
ourselves constantly conditioned by external causes both physically and
psychically' (1977, pp. 92f). Situational and conditioning dimensions of
concern here may be meaningfully categorized as natural–physical and
human-made physical–technical structures, along with the social and
institutional environment. This latter environment consists of *virtual*
entities in the sense that they exist only in their instantiation by the
actions of agents who are collectively their constituents. That is, they
are very real for agents, but have no necessary physical or perceptual
presence beyond these interdependent actions and an agent's location
within them. They may, of course, include a physical dimension, but
this is not sufficient to define their existence. Examples include families,
markets, firms and corporations.

Human agency *per se* has an obvious physicalist dimension, in that the agents as physical bodies act on the natural and human-made physical elements of their inherited situations. Human agents are fundamentally corporeal entities induced to act in a physical manner by a complex of physiological and genetic composition, psychic instincts and somatic drives, all of which shape reactions to particular environmental circumstances and conditions. Rickman is especially aware of this aspect of Dilthey's representation of human agents: 'Man ... is imbedded in nature. He is a physical creature with a biological makeup and physiological needs. He expresses himself by physical means and confronts a physical world.' Consequently, Rickman continues, 'history, sociology, and economics all deal with the interplay between ideas and physical facts – people shaping their environment according to their purposes, which, in turn, are affected by their environment and physical needs' (Rickman, 1988, p. 82; cf. Ermarth, 1978, p. 114). The conduct of agents is intimately dependent on some specification of their knowledge of the natural world as a primary influence on them (Dilthey, 1988, pp. 83ff). Considered from a naturalistic perspective, human agency in itself is initiated by and comprises physical and physiological changes in the human body and brain.[6] Also, that agency is manifested as physical interchanges with the material world comprising those in accordance with its purposes and, most probably, those that were not intended as well. In acting as agents engaging nature, 'when we *exercise volition*, when we influence nature, simply because we are not blind forces but wills which determine their ends through deliberation, we are dependent on the order of nature' (1988, p. 86).

The dependence of human agency on nature, including on the innate instincts of agents themselves, is mitigated by a process of adapting to and learning how to override its conditions, restrictions and limitations. Agents confront the natural world of their instincts and surroundings and have the psychic capacity to make the best they can of it. In this respect, agents become increasingly autonomous by means of their sovereignty over nature so that 'along with dependence which is implicit in adapting to natural conditions, we see a mastery of space so bound up with scientific thought and technology that mankind historically achieves mastery precisely by means of its subordination' (1988, p. 87).

As indicated earlier, the situations of agents must also include human-made dimensions. On the most fundamental level, the relevant human creations here are those of a physical nature, such as tools and infrastructure. These are utilitarian and technical constructions built by agents and subsequently taken up and selectively used for their own purposes. They act to direct and contain, and to assist or impede, the goal-directed conduct of agents. This facet of understanding agency is vital where it concerns the physical processes of production, but such a direction of inquiry was of little explicit importance to Dilthey.

He focused primarily on the general social facets of agents' situations as comprising the most obvious of the human-created dimensions of the life-world. We have seen how he depicted individual agents as self-contained, purposeful psychophysical units as a matter of principle. So it may be, he reasoned, that at first sight the 'interaction of individuals seems accidental and haphazard ... [and] the emotions, and the narrow egoism which strut so in the forefront of life's stage ... confirm the view of observers of human nature who see in social life only the play and counterplay of the interests of individuals influenced by chance ...' (1988, p. 107). But, Dilthey noted, no agent has ever appeared in a form that 'did not interact with society and as if he existed *before* society', so that 'the human being as a fact which precedes history and society is a fiction of genetic explanation. The man whom sound analytical science studies is the individual as a component of society' (1988, pp. 93, 94). The social relations and activities into which agents enter comprise the most fundamental and general systematic dimension of their existence.

To the extent that these structured social contacts between them are directed at seeking to expedite the satisfaction of their life-world needs and goals, and are thus likely to be important enough to interest human scientists, the key operational characteristic is that some understanding must exist between the agents. Efforts to understand others pervade the day-to-day life-world activities of agents (Plantinga, 1980, p. 6). Dilthey stressed this in asserting that 'our actions always presuppose the understanding of other people and a great deal of human happiness springs from empathy with the mental life of others' (1976, p. 247). In particular, 'understanding first arises in the interests of practical life. Here, people interact with one another. They must make themselves understandable to each other. *One must know what the other is up to*'. In this context, Dilthey was led to draw on introspection and interpersonal analogy and extrapolation as the basis for mutual understanding between active agents. Here his notion that 'our consciousness of the world, just as our self-consciousness, issues from the life of the self' (1977, p. 78) was pertinent. That is, consciousness is an inner or mental reflection of the experiences of participating in the life-world. Now all individuals will be required to understand something of the consciousness of others: 'We complete [our] inner perception by the apprehension of other persons. We apprehend their inwardness. That occurs by means of a spiritual process which is equivalent to a conclusion from analogy' (1977, p. 80). This process amounts to 'carrying over our own psychic life into another' (1977, p. 80). Thus, the process of reaching an understanding 'is a rediscovery of the I in the Thou' (1976, p. 208).

Interagent knowledge that is integral to agents' operations depends on some understanding by each agent of the unobservable cognitive structures and processes of the others. This requires that all agents can presume that the others are just like themselves in certain core respects (cf. Rickman, 1988, pp. 99f). They can thereby attribute to others similar interpretations of conditions confronted and similar meanings and responses to those in their own experiences. Dilthey's psychology assumed for this purpose a set of universal and reliably present human qualities and categories of mind-structure, along with a common appreciation of the manifold objects of the mind-constructed world in which all agents must live. All the time, though, he was conscious of the extreme variations in and the consequent uniqueness of actual agents and he attributed this to quantitative and other differences of degree in particular agents' profiles of these qualities. More specifically, in expressing the fact that agents are a mix of similarities and differences, Dilthey adopted a typification approach to depicting human agents and their relationships with each other, although he was ever conscious that these typifications are constantly changing as agents learn and their situations change. This meant that the existence of secure interagent understanding can never be completely assured. Dilthey noted this limitation: 'Thus, there is something irrational in all understanding, just as life itself is irrational. It can be represented through no logically-derived formulae. . . . These are the boundaries which are set to the logical treatment of understanding by its very nature' (1977, p. 137). Interagent understanding was lifted by typification based on commonly relevant facets of life-world expressions one step above purely introspective speculation. The prospects for interagent understanding are further improved by the fact that typified agents at least have to contend with and employ a common environment of action when confronted with a particular life-world problem. Each agent can be sure that other agents of interest to them are, nominally at least, responding to similar conditions and gearing their conduct accordingly. The situational structures within and through which actions are undertaken have a significance in this respect which is further explored below.

Interactive agents are situated in and their actions instantiate a *society* which, as a whole, is 'like the most powerful of all machines, each one of its wheels and rollers functions in a particular way and yet also has a function to perform in the whole as well . . .' (1988, p. 99). At this stage, we should not read back into this observation all that we now know about the problems of functionalist interpretations of the nature of societies. Rather we should see only the naive, but nonetheless important view that the operational entities that are parts of society, and society as a whole, are means by which agents relate to others, organize themselves and effectively participate in their life-world. Such entities were considered by Dilthey to reflect 'the richness of an individual's life ... broken up into perceptions and thoughts, feelings and acts of will ... [and] by this fact alone (in virtue of the natural organization of psychical life) this living content makes possible a variety of systems in the life of society' (1988, p. 106). What were called *systems* in Dilthey's social theory are complexes of life-world purposes and comprise 'permanent structures, objects of social analysis' (1988, p. 101). These entities are human creations and have a virtual existence, being instantiated only in the performances in which their participant members engage. Dilthey posited two categories of systemic entities as comprising the extended social situation confronted by agents in their life-world. He called the first and primary set *systems of culture*, and the second *systems of external organization of society*. As we are about to see, each set had its own conception and coverage in the structuring of society in general (cf. Ermarth, 1978, pp. 124f).

Systems of culture arise 'when a purpose based on a component element of human nature (hence permanent in character) relates psychical acts of particular individuals to one another and thus organizes them into a complex of purposes' (1988, p. 101). The participation through forms of interagent cooperation in these systems, such as language, law, morality, religion, art and science, is undertaken volitionally by agents in pursuit of the satisfaction of their desires. Nonetheless, these systems confront agents as objectively defined and with an air of permanence. They demand certain profiles of conduct if participation is to be effective and rewarding for individuals. In short, they shape, but cannot determine, free-willed conduct as it occurs on a day-to-day basis. Any change in the participation by individuals through changes in the system is relatively slow and comes from the accumulated experiences and collective actions of individuals over time, mostly as unintended consequences.

The second category of extended social entities comprised systems of external organization of society. They have their origin in 'permanent causes [which] unite wills into an association as a whole ...' and comprise 'the web of permanent alliances of wills corresponding to basic relations of mastery, dependence, property, and community ...' (1988, pp. 101, 102). The crucial concept here is that of the association (*der Verband*), a form that will include institutions. It is 'a permanently established union of wills among a number of people for a specific purpose . . ., [where] their union goes beyond a mere amorphous sense of belonging together and community and beyond the closer sort of interaction in a group which is left to individual choice' (1988, p. 118). In particular, the bonding in 'this kind of voluntary union has a structure; the wills involved are bound together in a definite form of cooperation' (1988, pp. 118f). Such cooperation stems from the common purposes of its constituent agents, and 'the character of the [resulting] purposive system determines the character of a given structure; the purpose complex functions as a law of formation in shaping the association' (1988, p. 119, cf. p. 122). Although he did not use the terminology, Dilthey wanted to convey the idea of virtual structures constituted by the goal-directed interactive relations between agents. As indicated above, most commonly, these appear as what we call institutions.

As perceived by participating agents, systems may be viewed *subjectively*; that is, as consciously interpreted means of realizing the full richness of their human existence. Then *'one's experience* is that one discovers one's will in a nexus of external connections, in relations of dominance and dependence with regard to persons and things, and in relations of community' (1988, p. 115). The subjectively meaningful situation confronted by active agents presents a complex picture that reaches back behind the external organization into its ontological foundations.

> The same undivided person is at once [a] member of a family, director of a project, member of the community, citizen, member of a church organization, and at the same time, perhaps, [an] associate in a mutual association or political society. A person's will can thus be intertwined in an exceedingly complex web, . . . [and this] results in a mixture of a feeling of power and pressure, of community feeling and of self-interest, of external obligation and of freedom – all of which makes up a substantial part of our feeling of self. (1988, p. 115)

External associations between agents may also be viewed *objectively* as something standing outside them and something that they must confront as an ostensibly permanent and inherited potential mode of containment. Somehow they must consciously and actively enter into such systems if their purposes in the life-world are to be achieved. In so doing they confirm the permanence of the system. There exists, then, 'an external permanence independent of individuals themselves and [comprising] the character of massive objectivity of those systems', and they 'loom before us as great, manifest, objective facts' (1988, pp. 106, 112). What can be observed is that agents are situated in a society that comprises 'a nexus of relationships of community and of obligation into which [the] wills of individuals are fitted or tied, so to speak' (1988, p. 115). *In situ*, human agency 'is always subject to the general control of the external organization of society, which both assures a margin of free play to independent and reasonable activity of individuals and sets limits to it' (1988, p. 108). Moreover, existentially, each individual agent is constituted as 'a point of intersection of a plurality of systems which continue to become ever more subtly specialized as a culture moves forward. Indeed, one and the same living act of an individual can demonstrate this many-sidedness' (1988, p. 106).[7]

Such a multiplicity of interagent connections, varying priorities and external obligations acts in all the above contexts to exacerbate the contingent remainder of situated agents' conduct. In addition, two further qualifying factors were noted by Dilthey as influencing the contingency of the relationship that is actually observed between agents' conduct and their situations. One such factor was his explicit realization that situated agents always retain an inalienable right of autonomy in their conduct. No situations of normal concern to science can deprive agents of their volition and creative imaginations entirely, so that there will always be variations of reaction to problems they deal with even though their situations may be similar. It is always the case that 'free activity and regulated activity, self-seeking and community, confront one another as opposites . . .' (1988, p. 108). Indeed, as we have seen, in the all pervasive circumstance of deliberations concerning future oriented actions, imagination and volition are the very foundation of agency. The form of agency will depend upon the ultimate uniqueness of character profiles and of the resulting uniqueness in forming selective interpretations concerning the meaning of the life-world of agents. Dilthey noted that as an active agent, 'every process of thought which occurs to me is guided by an intention and an orientation of attentiveness. Even in the associations that seem to flow in me without willing, the interest determines the direction in which the connections are completed' (1977, p. 84). But such directed conduct has an undercurrent of contingency, for 'one comes here into obscure frontier regions: the volitional element in the permanent orientations of the human spirit, spontaneity as the condition for the fact that I experience constraint or influence'. And, he went on, 'it is necessary to acknowledge that it is the presence of volitional activities which can usually be least placed in evidence among all the psychic processes' because 'the volitional impulses completely enter into, are wholly submerged in, the formational processes having a representational nature . . .' (1977, pp. 84, 85).

Dilthey's second qualifying extension of the problematic of agents confronting their situated existence was the question of what agents can and do know about the situations they inherit and must operate in and through. He was struck primarily by the enormous multiplicity and complexity of the combination of natural and societal conditions that confront agents, much of it simultaneously. He was sceptical about what they could actually grasp of such a complex: the 'complexities [of society] are so great and the conditions of nature under which they appear are so manifold, and the means of measuring and testing them are so narrowly constricted, that difficulties which appear almost insuperable hinder knowledge of this structure of society' (1988, p. 97).

Quite apparently, all these considerations impede any endeavour by observer-analysts to establish regular and reliable links between a knowledge of agents' situations and their conduct in response to problems confronted. There was a need, then, for analysts to see that for situated human agents, whatever may be the determinate appearance of their conduct, autonomous and volitional elements of the application of reason cannot be avoided. Reaching any satisfactory understanding of human agency in the human sciences is preconditional on an ontologically established balance of the counterposed influences of containment and contingency being found in the case of relevant phenomena. In effect, they compound the problems of maintaining consistency between the representation of how human phenomena are generated ontologically from the situationally conditioned purposes, motives and deliberations of agents and the realities of the processes involved. This is the basis of the problematic confronted by the human sciences generally and by economics in particularly and it is the theme to which I turn in the next section.

4.4 Agents' expressions and the foundations of the human sciences

In the previous two sections, my objective has been to elicit an outline of Dilthey's subjectivist understanding of situated human agents and agency. Initially he focused on the descriptive psychology of individual agents as the foundation for understanding human conduct and the phenomena it generates. His adoption of agents' expressions as mediations for observers in attempting to provide an objectively grounded account of understanding, mitigated rather than transcended the difficulties associated with introspection as a psychological foundation for scientific inquiry. At the same time, he gave an explicit role to the multi-faceted situational conditioning of agents discussed in the previous section as the medium within and through which such expressions are generated by their actions. As we are about to follow through, he was thereby led to move from a purely psychological approach to the objective of *Verstehen* in the human sciences to one modelled on hermeneutics. This involved him in an extension of hermeneutics from its orientation towards interpreting unique historical expressions to a form that facilitates the understanding of generalized classes of typical phenomena of interest and concern to these sciences.

Dilthey's inclinations were to continue *to begin* from the premiss of introspection in the sense that any inferential understanding the psyches and cognitive processes of others can only be grounded in the presumption that they are essentially like us. In a (subsequently published) lecture on the theme of hermeneutics, he made the explicit claim that in interpreting the observed physical manifestations of the conduct of others, 'we have to reconstruct the inner source of the signs which strike our senses. Everything: material, structure, even the most individual features of this reconstruction, *have to be supplied by transferring them from our own lives*' (1976, pp. 247f; emphasis added). That is, all individuals as observers of other actors whose conduct they wish to comprehend must make some effort to represent to themselves the psychic exigencies of those others. Observer-analysts in the human sciences must claim and try to formalize knowledge of these consciousness states of those whose deliberated and purposive activities are their objects. This is necessarily the essential direction of their task, for their objects are ontologically accounted for only by the mental processes that comprise the deliberations prior to the actions of individuals. From the observers' perspective generally, Dilthey was sanguine that all actors must have some capacities of this sort in order to engage in relationships with others. Analysts must be expected to do the job more effectively on the grounds of their professional education and experience as psychological observers.

Observation of other relevant active agents can only reveal the manifested forms of expression through action (conduct, physical and virtual products) that the results of their psychical structures and processes take. Such expressions represent the objectified and most immediately observable form of lived experience accessible to interdependent active agents in their efforts to understand others. In our interdependence with other active agents, 'we *constantly* rely on interpretations of particular gestures, expressions, purposive acts, or related groupings of these' (1977, pp. 125, 129, emphasis added; cf. Ermarth, 1978, pp. 271ff). These, Dilthey argued, comprise 'the medium in which the understanding of other persons and their expressions takes place. For everything in which mind has objectified itself contains something common to the I and the Thou' (quoted by Ermarth, 1978, p. 277). As he put it elsewhere:

> Every *single expression of life* . . . represents *something common*. Every word, every sentence, every gesture or polite formula, every work of art, and every historical deed is understandable only because those who express themselves in it and those who understand it are connected by having something in common. The individual always experiences, thinks and acts within a sphere of commonality, and only within such a sphere does he understand. Because of this commonality, everything understood bears intrinsic features of familiarity, as it were. (Quoted by Plantinga, 1980, p. 2; Dilthey's emphasis)

It was Dilthey's belief that all active agents who need to comprehend the conduct and intentions of others will resort to some sort of *typification process* as a means to formulate the relational structures and agency processes around them (Tuttle, 1969, pp. 79ff). This gives the typification idea an ontological content and suggests that the typification process is imbedded in the deliberations of agents that precede their actions. Type formation is an extension of the commonality that he believed underpins interagent understanding by enabling them to overcome the uniqueness of individual expressions. 'In reality, . . . the expressions of life are for us at the same time representations of something general: we make an inference when we classify them under a type of gesture or act . . .' (1977, p. 137). Dilthey noted that 'we understand individuals by virtue of their interrelatedness and that which is common in them' (1977, p. 131). He introduced the analogy of 'distance' to signify decreasing degrees of commonality and mutual familiarity: 'The greater the inner distance between a given expression and him who understands, the more often uncertainties arise' (1977, p. 128).

The implication here was that more or less objectively devised types facilitate intelligibility and predictability of conduct between agents. In constructing the typology of their life-world situation, and in using it to give direction to their conduct, agents will be guided by practical relevance with respect to their motives and goals. They must set aside those facets of the others' individuality and their own situational environment that are of lesser consequence to them in making a particular decision. The resulting type classification is used to mitigate the uncertainty about what to do under the circumstances and about what these others may do in particular circumstances. Dilthey's perception was that 'the expression of life which the [active] individual apprehends is ordinarily not taken by him to be something isolated, but is rather, as it were, saturated with a knowledge of that which is held in common and with a relationship, given in this expression, to something inner' (1977,

p. 127). So, he reasoned, 'the particular expressions of life which confront the subject who understands them can thus be comprehended as belonging to a sphere of communality, to a type' (1977, p. 127). As a consequence, 'there arises between us and the other person *a certain type which the person represents to us, which type colors and conditions our perceptions of his expected actions*' (quoted by Ermarth, 1978, p. 172; my emphasis added).

In all these ontological respects, the containing influence of typification by agents on their conduct reinforces the importance of situational conditions. Social and economic systems evolve as constructs that, to a large extent, comprise roles and rules within which agents volitionally apply their motives and pursue their goals (Tuttle, 1969, p. 89). The teleological-meaningful types of agent conduct are those most situationally conditioned, and it is these that are likely to be of primary concern to a human science like economics. This is for the reason that all significant economic conduct is the result of complex deliberations. In their decision processes, when coping with such complexity, agents need all the help and objective direction they can get. The effect is to reduce the degree of contingency of conduct confronted by observers, in part because typification enables agents more reliably to anticipate what relevant others will do.

The contingency of agents' conduct is further mitigated by the fact that particular types of situated agents confront a definable range of typical problems that may be resolved for the most part by typical responses drawing upon a typical quantitative profile of human qualities. These typologies become part of the human psyche and render much of day-to-day life much more manageable. As Dilthey saw agents' experience, there is a need for them to recognize that 'in every portion of human expression there arises a type which represents their most appropriate execution. This type designates their norm, since it lies between deviations on both sides' (quoted by Ermarth, 1978, p. 177, cf. pp. 262ff; cf. also Makkreel, 1969, pp. 439f and Rickman, 1988, p. 59).[8]

Consequent upon the vital existential status ascribable to expressions, 'the objectifications of life', Dilthey advocated that they be given a fundamental place in the metatheory of the human sciences. Thus 'a realization of the objectivity of life, i.e. of its externalizations in many kinds of structural systems, becomes an additional basis for the human studies' (1976, p. 191). Lived experience is manifested in these external expressions and observers can understand them only through a process of *interpretation* that seeks to establish the *meaning* of the expressions to the active, creative agent. Indeed, 'meaning is the comprehensive category through which life can be understood' (1976, p. 235). And, he continued, '*by understanding I mean the process in which we use expressions given to the senses to gain knowledge of mental life*' (1976, p. 260).

Dilthey was led by this awareness of the role of expressions to supplement his psychological insights and the *Verstehen* approach with an adaptation of a theory of interpretation, usually found in hermeneutical studies of historical texts, to human science inquiry. Thus, he noted, *I call this methodology of the understanding of recorded expressions hermeneutics*', where expressions now included all human products (1976, p. 261). The hermeneutical method of inquiry thus comprises

> a special case of methodological *Verstehen* in the human sciences, involving description, abstraction, analysis, typification, comparison, and generalization. It attempts to reproduce or re-evoke at the conceptual level the original content of what is 'there-for-us' in lived experience, but goes on to examine this phenomenological content in relation to sociocultural forms and certain typical patterns of thought. (1978, p. 327)

Thus it requires a 'methodical "interpretation of interpretation", that is, a kind of meta-interpretation or general hermeneutic of life-attitudes' (1978, p. 328).

Dilthey adopted what he thought of as cognitive processes directed at understanding (*Verstehen*) as the metatheoretical core of the human sciences (cf. Ermarth, 1978, pp. 241ff). Their objective was, in effect, to get at and discursively to represent in reasoned formal argument the generation of human phenomena as the expressions (or products) of human agents and agency (cf. Bulhof, 1980, p. 212 n. 13). The resulting argument is expected to provide a cogent insight into the origin of the phenomenon in focus without further appeal to other forms of cognition. By virtue of the ontological nature of their objects, *understanding as an objective* (cf. Rickman, 1988, pp. 44ff, 51) in the human sciences depended in turn upon analysts establishing the meaning of the expressions confronted to those who perpetrated them. As Rickman puts it, 'Dilthey's whole methodology hinges on the claim that grasping a communication is a distinctive, intellectual process. His purpose in narrowing and refining the everyday meaning of "understanding" was to pinpoint this distinctive cognitive process' (1988, p. 53).

In this process of achieving understanding, it was interpretation by observers that retained a central role because all the expressions of life embody the purposes and meaning intended by their creators. They effectively 'speak' to the analyst in the same way that texts do, albeit less explicitly (Bulhof, 1980, p. 99). As Dilthey put it, 'absorbed into the context of the epistemology, logic and methodology of the human

studies the theory of interpretation becomes a vital link between philosophy and the historical disciplines, an essential part of the foundations
of the studies of man' (1976, p. 260; cf. 1977, pp. 124, 132ff). Ermarth's
reading of Dilthey gives strong emphasis to this hermeneutical orientation of his methodology (and cf. Rickman, 1988, pp. 55ff). Most
especially, there is a sense in which life itself is hermeneutical because
it is underpinned by the unrelenting need for human beings to interpret
all facets of the reality they confront, including the expressions of others.
In recognition of this, Ermarth writes, 'Dilthey established that the
process of interpretation is not something secondary to a preexisting
reality but a primary attribute of being alive; interpretation is the original condition of life itself, not the subsequent refraction of an
antecedent reality. The world of our experience comes to us already
interpreted' (Ermarth, 1978, p. 347; cf. pp. 232ff).

Dilthey was concerned that human scientists should stress the unity
of all facets of the external world and agents' experience of it. His own
vision was that

> dealing with the whole man in history and psychology led me to take the
> whole man – in the multiplicity of his powers: this willing–feeling–perceiving
> being – as the basis for explaining knowledge and its concepts (such as outer
> world, time, substance, cause), even though, to be sure, knowledge appears
> to weave these concepts solely out of raw material it gets from perceiving,
> imagining, and thinking. (1988, p. 73; cf. Rickman, 1988, pp. 134f)

The problem of the 'hermeneutical circle' was implicit in the ideas of
this passage, as Dilthey clearly sensed. In Rickman's summary, 'the aim
of a methodology is to consider how a subject – in this case man and
his works – can come to be known. Yet Dilthey demands that this
methodology should itself be guided by an idea of what man is like'
(Rickman, 1988, p. 79; cf. pp. 98ff). Plantinga refers here to what he
calls 'the basic Diltheyan question: how is the whole to be understood
out of the individual?' (1980, p. 156). Dilthey realized that reaching an
understanding of the expressions and wholes of the human world by
reference to the individuals who comprise them cannot be unambiguously and immediately pursued at the same time as reaching and
understanding of the individuals in terms of their expressions and their
situations within those wholes (cf. Tuttle, 1969, p. 37). There can be no
uniquely defensible starting point within this ongoing mutual interaction
and interdependence. Rather, the analyst is required to break into it at
some point and reason from there (Rickman, 1988, pp. 43f, 64ff).

Later in his manuscripts, Dilthey recorded this 'hermeneutical circle'
issue as an 'Aporia', that is, a 'philosophic problem without a solution'

(1976, p. 262 and ed. n. 44). But he chose to devise a practical solution by breaking into the 'circle' and proclaiming the priority of actually existing human agents as they are observed in their life-world expressions. His belief was that:

> the most important elements of our image and knowledge of reality – such as the unity of life in the person, the outer world, individuals apart from us, their life in time, and their influence on each other – are all things we can explain from ... [the] totality of human nature, whose real life process manifests itself in its various aspects through willing, feeling, and imagining. (1988, p. 73)

Or, as Dilthey put it elsewhere, 'I start from the structure of mental life, from the system of urges. The point at which I plant my feet ... is the psychologically knowable nature of man, as it constitutes our human mental life, consciousness of self, etc. The mental structure which we find in ourselves I consider a fixed standpoint' (quoted by Rickman, 1988, p. 79). But as Rickman so clearly indicates, while it is quite inappropriate to assign any absolute status to this or any other starting point within the bounds of the 'circle', all productive intellectual inquiry must begin from a belief that observation and sense data indicate something about the actual nature of reality. Frankly put, 'all cognitive achievements must be treated prima facie as provisional and corrigible. At best they are facets of the truth. ... If this is intellectually unsatisfactory, well, this is just too bad because we have to live with it' (Rickman, 1988, pp. 66f). It was to an empirically based theory of situated human agents as they exist and operate in their life-worlds, however insecure it may be epistemologically, that Dilthey turned to in an endeavour to provide the hermeneutical human sciences with sound metatheoretical foundations.

4.5 Conclusions and inconclusions

In Dilthey's own metatheoretical endeavours, then, the priority of methodology over substance that he found in positivist efforts with human science was reversed. He intended to defend the idea that primacy had to be given to a meaningful representation of the identifying structural and operational essentials of an object reality, with methodology being worked up to ensure that this is so, whatever the form thus required. The effect was to stand the burgeoning metatheory of the human sciences, including psychology and economics, on its head, as it were.

In the human sciences, Dilthey realized, priority had to be given to the subjectivist ontology of phenomena in terms of their generation as the means of understanding them. As a consequence, he could not resort to imposing by fiat any methodologically determined mode of transcending the problematics of human agency. Rather he had to struggle with the notion that some regularizing conditions need to be identified within the ostensibly ineffable exigencies of real-world human deliberations and actions. Some form of ontologically grounded normalization had to be postulated if the human sciences were to be viable at all in the sense that their discursive arguments could maintain consistency with the subjective and individual nature of their phenomena.

One step that Dilthey took to get beyond the confines of a subjectivism grounded in introspection, as we have seen in the foregoing inquiry, was to recognize that active subjective agents are chronically situated and that their conduct cannot be understood without explicit cognizance of this fact. He gave some indications that he wanted to be clear about the nature of active agents' dependence on and interaction with the integrated complex of situational conditions that they confront and actively engage in the process of solving their day-to-day problems. These conditions play a dominant part in forming their psychic constitutions and their observed conduct, along with the consequent phenomenal results. It follows that it is the influence of situational conditioning that is of primary concern in any attempt to account for phenomena that are pervasive and regular enough to be objects of human science inquiry. Such phenomena are open to interpretation as reflecting typical agent conduct in addressing typical problems of the life-world within and through commonly inherited situational conditions. This renders the *in situ* typical conduct universally valid in a sense that can allow it to be discursively represented in ontologically grounded terms. It is important to note that Dilthey confined the capacity of *Verstehen* to the systemically situated, typical and purposeful conduct of agents. This meant leaving aside a range of more impulsive and non-deliberative conduct and expressions. But, it is really the former that are of concern to non-clinical human sciences such as economics, so this criticism, whatever its validity or otherwise, is not pertinent here (cf. Tuttle, 1969, pp. 91f).

Dilthey did not explore fully the import of physical and virtual, natural and social-institutional situations for regularizing the volitional and creative conduct of active subjective agents. Most especially he failed to see the need fully to inquire into and to understand the balance of influence on their conduct of the fact that situational conditions of all sorts can both *facilitate and constrain*. These conditions are the primary operational mediations that agents must confront in their deliberations and actions within the situational framework that they confront. It was by means of the agents' capacity for reflexive experience that the elements of their situations become an integral part of the flow of experience rather than standing external to it as given modifiers. Any dualism between agents' psyches and their situations is only apparent. The meaning of the situations to individuals can only be evident when their elements are fully integrated into the experience, but the flow of experience itself cannot be completely appreciated by the agents without due allowance for the impact of the situations confronted. In this subjective sense, the agents and their external world are existentially interdependent.

Dilthey came to realize that his structural-descriptive version of psychology, even as it was extended to provide an hermeneutical understanding of the essentially situated nature of human agents and their expressions of agency, could not provide the self-sustainable foundations that the human sciences needed. It is well established that the idea of hermeneutic inquiry in the human sciences has inherent difficulties. Rickman points to some of these pertinent to his treatment of Dilthey. The key to his critique is that it is sometimes impossible to attribute a human phenomenon fully to the conscious, subjectivist intentions of the agents concerned (1988, pp. 75ff). First of all, agents act in part in response to motives, intentions and influences of which they are not fully aware. These include especially some aconscious somatic functions (glandular functions, blood pressure, ageing effects) and some deep-seated subconscious motives that the agent may not bring to consciousness in a particular context. On the collective level, there are the well-known puzzles associated with the unintended consequences of individual agents' intended purposes and goals. Here, too, hermeneutical insights into agents' actions cannot account for the phenomenon without supplementary accounts of how the actual actions interacted together and with the situational environment to generate the unintended result. Neither of these sorts of factors negates the usefulness of the hermeneutic approach, but they serve as a reminder of its limitations. These limitations were not confronted squarely by Dilthey in the currently available writings.

In spite of all the ontological complexities that have been alluded to above, Dilthey realized that some methodological principles appropriate to the human sciences had to flow from his inquiries. At one point, he summed up his methodology as follows:

> The logical ideal of the real sciences of man is to arrive at the separation of
> that which is essential and meaningful in the individual phenomenon from

that which is purely incidental and meaningless – and to bring the former to clear consciousness. The need to place the individual phenomenon in a coherent and valid order of concretely intelligible causes and effects compels these sciences to ever more refined constitution of concepts which can encompass the individual reality through the selection and synthesis of characteristic traits. (Quoted by Ermarth, 1978, p. 309)

The observer-analyst's role in the human sciences is, then, to apply to the available and relevant empirical data 'the devices of reason: analysis and abstraction' (1988, p. 92).

In this respect, Dilthey maintained that it is possible to identify sufficient coherence and regularity in the production of human expressions to warrant their treatment as intelligible in a loosely nomo-logical sense. That is, they exhibit patterns of structures and formations, of meanings and types, which are grasped by experience. But such patterns do not reflect a strict necessity of causation and thus cannot be expected to have the reliability of natural science laws nor the capacity to predict. Instead, human science must settle for the derivation of functional empirical laws. The resulting analyses should be directed at the provision of reasoned and formalized pieces of discursively argued understanding of relevant phenomena as types. As such, these under-standings are subject to constant revision by means of the critical assessment of ever changing circumstances. Of this, Dilthey wrote that 'every empirical and comparative procedure can only extract a rule from the past, whose validity is historically limited; it can never bind or determine what is new or may appear in the future. This rule func-tions only backwards and does not contain a law of the future' (quoted by Ermarth, 1978, p. 308). For any pragmatically oriented theoretical human science, such as economics with its eye to policy management, this represents a severely limiting conclusion as it stands. What remained open to further development was the extent to which the sorts of typification procedures cited by Dilthey, in combination with the reg-ularizing effects of specific situational containments and conditioning, can render reliable the relevant categories of human agents' conduct. That is, sufficient reliability effectively to mitigate the potential for agent contingency to the degree necessary to allow analysts to form coherent and generalized discursive representations of human phenomena.

Menger and Dilthey were contemporaries. They were both concerned to give the human sciences ontologically defensible subjectivist and individualist foundations. As we have now seen, although they were much more deeply philosophical and abstract than Menger's, the contri-butions of Dilthey pursued similar metatheoretical themes and exposed

similar difficulties. In their works, the most fundamental redirection of
human scientific inquiry to be given emphasis was that methodological
and epistemological outcomes were correctly a matter of logical consequence rather than logical priority. For them, the apparent merits of
natural scientism were not given the automatic status they had come to
enjoy in positivist science generally. Menger more so than Dilthey
sought to retain some dimension of objective and universal theory
for economics in particular. Dilthey followed out the methodological
implications of human inquiry to their inconclusive end. Ultimately,
the methodological problematic posed by the priority of maintaining
ontological accuracy in human science was left incompletely resolved
by them both.

Dilthey's critics were intent upon bringing some epistemological
objectivity to the human sciences that would overcome what appeared
to them to be his open-ended ontology of subjectivism and psychologism. The way ahead for subjectivism as a cogent ontological
foundation for the human sciences was to be quite severely impeded
by the diversions of the Baden Neo-Kantians in their reactions to his
work. It was to take the genius of Max Weber and of Ludwig von Mises
ultimately to sort out the confusing legacy as best they were able. The
nature of these metatheoretical diversions and a critical assessment of
the responses to them by Weber and Mises are the subjects of my next
three chapters.

Notes

1. It warrants noting that dealing with the contributions of Wilhelm Dilthey to the
metatheoretical foundations of the human sciences, and to our understanding of
the role of situated subjective human agency in particular, poses several unusual but
crucial problems of intellectual historical inquiry. Ermarth is moved to refer to a
'Dilthey problem' in this respect (1978, pp. 4f). Most prominent among the complexity
of Dilthey interpretation is the fact that, in spite of the vastness of his extant written
output, he rarely completed any component of his intended life's work, with many
of his key ideas fragmented and scattered across his published and unpublished
writings. The result has been that Dilthey interpretation has required a more than
usual input from the scholar to ensure coherence of argument (cf. Tuttle, 1969, pp. 1,
15, 24f, 77f, 80, 82, 111; Betanzos, 1988, p. 11). A second characteristic of his work,
that of his style of writing, compounded these problems. Very early on in Dilthey
interpretation, Rickman drew attention to this difficulty. He noted how Dilthey had
a 'preference for abstract rather than concrete expression... [and a] tendency to
express his sense of the complexity and interrelatedness of things in the very structure
of his sentences' (1961, p. 20; cf. Betanzos, 1988, p. 11; Ermarth, 1978, p. 4). And, to
compound the import of this difficulty, the fact that it was all written in the professorial
German so characteristic of nineteenth-century scholars makes interpretive study a

demanding and problematical process for second-language readers (cf. Rickman, 1988, p. 13). I have, therefore, as far as possible, deferred to the translations of others in my all too brief outline of Dilthey's ideas. The third problem to be confronted is the vast bulk and wide-ranging substantive scope of Dilthey's intellectual legacy. His inquiries were not bounded by any of the recognized disciplines that we are accustomed to today and what he wrote took human scientific inquiry as a whole (cf. Rickman, 1988, pp. 33ff). Most of his resulting output is locked up in his unpublished papers, a *Nachlass* that runs to some 100,000 pages of papers written in an impressionistic sort of handwriting (Ermarth, 1978, p. 6). Obviously, this presents us with an insurmountable problem if we take seriously the assertion by Rickman that Dilthey 'has to be read in bulk' (1961, p. 20). The true bulk of his work that is now apparent makes this an impossibly open-ended challenge, and one that must be left aside here. For my limited purposes it must be sufficient to dip into selected examples of Dilthey's main available writings and to defer to selections from the vast secondary literature for support when appropriate. Central will be the first parts of the never to be completed *Einleitung in die Geiteswissenschaften* published in 1883 (translated as *Introduction to the Human Sciences*, 1988, carrying the indicative subtitle 'An attempt to lay a foundation for the study of society and history'). This main published work was accompanied by a range of shorter pieces published in limited circulation monographs and in the journal literature. In particular, I have supplemented my reading with some additional insights worked up in the 1894 piece 'Ideen über eine beschreibende und zergliedernde Psychologie' (translated as 'Ideas concerning a descriptive and analytical psychology' in Dilthey, 1977), from the 1910 article 'Das Verstehen anderer Personen und ihrer Lebensäusserungen' (translated as 'The understanding of other persons and their expressions of life' in Dilthey 1977), and from the selected manuscript and other pieces assembled by Rickman in Dilthey, 1976. It has also been helpful to quote some less accessible passages from Dilthey that are used in the secondary literature. And, finally, there is the problem that while some interpretations of Dilthey's work claim the existence of continuity, consistency and overall unity in his core contentions, there are evident shifts of emphasis, too. Moreover, he made changes to his position and emphasis without noting explicitly that he had done so (Tuttle, 1969, p. 3). That such shifts are only to be expected over such a long and active intellectual life does not reduce the need to take account of them in representing Dilthey's ideas (see, for example, Tuttle, 1969, *passim*; Ermarth, 1978, pp. 9f; Plantinga, 1980, pp. 13ff, 44ff, 51, 58ff; Betanzos, 1988, p. 12; Rickman, 1988, pp. xi, 4f, 68, 160).

2. In this chapter, all references by date not explicitly attributed to a particular author are to works by Dilthey listed in the bibliography. In quotations from Dilthey's writings, all emphases are in the original unless otherwise stated.

3. This observation does not conflict with Plantinga's (1980, pp. 36, 63, 157f) view that Dilthey was not concerned with ontology as the philosophy of being *per se*. My intention is only to convey his concern with those dimensions of existential reality that account for the generation and nature of observed human phenomena.

4. The overriding problem of interpretive translation here remains that both parts of this concept, stemming from *der Geist* and *die Wissenschaft*, have more diversified and yet more unified meanings than any English equivalents (Ermarth, 1978, p. 359 n. 1). As is well known, *die Wissenschaft* refers to an organized body of formalized knowledge about any coherently identifiable facet of nature or human existence, without any implied epistemological claims. Dilthey explicitly rejected any inclinations to narrow the scope of what constitutes legitimate knowledge for this purpose on these latter grounds. In this respect, he noted that 'the so-called positivists . . . derive the content of the concept "science" from a definition of knowledge developed for the most part in the pursuit of natural science, and they decide on the basis of that kind of content what sorts of intellectual activities merit the name and rank of "science"'. Dilthey judged this to be an aberration based on 'an arbitrary notion of knowledge', which resulted in the positivists 'shortsightedly and arrogantly' refusing to acknow-

ledge any discipline that did not conform (1988, p. 78). He chose to set such restricted conceptions aside and allow *die Wissenschaft* to retain its more open meaning. For our purposes, we may accept this meaning and allow that it may be translated as science or study. However, in line with Ermarth's reasoning, I prefer the term science as it appears to be more in accordance with Dilthey's hopes for the future of these disciplines as formal, empirically grounded and relevant understandings of the human life-world. Ermarth writes that 'the rather flaccid "human studies" fails to convey Dilthey's concern for methodological rigour, general validity, and critical self-consciousness . . .' (1978, p. 359 n. 1; cf. Bulhof, 1980, p. 199 n. 45). The concept of *der Geist* requires careful conceptual interpretation by German readers, as well as involving compounded problems of conceptualization and translation for English readers. Literally, the term can mean ghost, spirit, intellect or mind, but its meaning is very much dependent upon the context: compare its use in *der Zeitgeist*, the 'spirit of an age', with that in *die geistige Fähigkeit eines Menschen*, the 'intellectual capacity of a person' (cf. Rickman, 1976, p. 28).

5. Even more emphatically he ruled out, at least as a viable option for his own time, the ever more influential notion that physically and chemically grounded genetico-physiological structures and functions of the brain itself could be elicited as the foundation for understanding human ideas and actions (1977, pp. 43f, 48f; 1988, p. 96).

6. This is a fact of life quite independently of any claims to *understand* human agency by genetico-physiological means. We have seen in note 5 that Dilthey rejected any such claim.

7. The example used by Dilthey to illustrate the point here was the writing of a book by a scholar. The book may be a manifestation of the scholar's professional commitment, it becomes part of its science, it will involve the scholar and the publisher in a contract sanctioned by the legal system, and it will become part of the substance of the publishing and bookselling industry (1988, p. 106).

8. To give an example pertinent to economics, the typologies of agents, relations, communications and other issues involved in negotiating a supply contract are very different from the analogous matters involved in the deliberations by corporate agents leading to an investment decision in an industry characterized by oligopolistic competition.

5. Metatheory of the sciences of culture and of Man

5.1 Historical–cultural science and the science of Man

Attention to Dilthey's metatheory of the human sciences was diverted for a time by the epistemology and methodology of the Southwest German (Baden) School of Neo-Kantians. Its core members, Wilhelm Windelband and his more influential student Heinrich Rickert, stood out as rejecting subjectivist metatheory in the human sciences. In their search for appropriate foundations for history and the sciences of human phenomena generally, it was the Neo-Kantians' intention to distance themselves from any ontological, especially psychologically oriented, principles. They redefined the objects of knowledge for the human sciences and wanted to claim for these sciences a non-naturalistic but objective epistemological status. In doing so, though, they focused on the unique and individual phenomena of the historical and cultural world as their objects of study. They made little attempt to provide generalized accounts of categories of such phenomena that were akin to the concerns of natural science.

The historicist inclinations of the Neo-Kantians emphasized the historical character and understanding of the human life-world and all its phenomena, and their neo-idealism was aimed at reasserting the role of human consciousness in the historical process. But they aimed at establishing the distinctive metatheoretical nature of human sciences on objective grounds that did not depend on the deeply ontological arguments, with their psychologistic references, employed by Dilthey (Willey, 1978, pp. 9, 23, 137f). Dilthey's idea that the identifying criteria for separating the natural and the human sciences could be found in the different ontologies of their respective phenomenal objects, with the ontology of the latter linked back to the immanently structured psychology of agents, was decisively rejected by the Neo-Kantians. This was a reflection of their return to Kant in response to the post-Hegelian uncertainty in German Philosophy in the second half of the nineteenth century (Willey, 1978; Schnädelbach, 1984). Kant's philosophy attributed an unreachable existential independence of reality-in-itself that could only be represented in the human psyche by means of an imposed categorial structure. The latter had its origins in experience, but was not constituted by experience in the manner of Dilthey's psychology. Indeed, the NeoKantians would have nothing to do with any ontological inquiry, for they were intent upon providing historical science with an objective foundation that could be defended through the exigencies of established cultural influences (Oakes, 1986, pp. vii, xiif).

Windelband's vision that historical sciences could be independently identified by what he called their *idiographic* status was concerned with knowledge the purpose of which is to grasp the distinctive properties of the unique events in themselves. He saw this as a contrast with the *nomothetic* inquiries pursued by natural sciences in the search for transphenomenal universal laws. These sciences have no intrinsic concern for the individual events of concrete reality. Rather, they abstract from the unique existential properties of actually observed real phenomena in order to develop the laws on which they are supposed to depend (cf. Oakes, 1986, p. x). Windelband was thus perceptive enough clearly to see the problem that 'there is no set of nomological statements, regardless of how exhaustive and precise, from which any description of an individual event can be deduced'. So, as 'the occurrence of individual events cannot be explained by general laws' usually associated with the procedures of natural sciences, the puzzle remains as to how knowledge of such events can be made available. In response to this demand, Windelband had little to offer, indeed 'nothing more than a few obscure metaphorical suggestions' (Oakes, 1986, p. xiii).

While Rickert chose to accept the absolute dualism of unique historical reality and its conceptual representation posited by Windelband, he tried to formalize the understanding of that reality by objectifying the abstraction process through which concepts are formed. In so doing, he claimed to be espousing the representation of the phenomena of reality in a way that captures all their essential and meaningful dimensions as these are dictated by the theoretical concerns of analysts. These concerns, it was argued, are a product of the extant *objectively valid* value system of the analysts' own cultural environment. In the process, Rickert shifted the focus to what he termed cultural sciences (*Kulturwissenschaften*) as an alternative to the concept of human (mental, spiritual) sciences (*Geisteswissenschaften*) used by Dilthey and others. Rickert did so to reinforce his rejection of ontological differences as providing the demarcation criteria between his focus and the natural sciences, and as a reflection of the cultural source of the objective values on which their version of the historical sciences depended. Ultimately, though, his defence of this mode of dealing with metatheory cannot be considered successful in any rigorous sense. But, it was influential nonetheless, as we shall see later on, through the critical endeavours of his colleague and friend Max Weber (Oakes, 1986, pp. vii and n. 2, xxiiiff, xxx; cf. below, Chapter 6).

Rickert expressed what drove his inquiries as 'the conviction that a lack of philosophical understanding of the nature of the historical sciences is one of the most serious defects of the philosophy of our time' (1986, p. 16).[1] He railed against 'the absurd attempts to treat history as a natural science' and against the idea that 'historical objectivity consists in a mere reproduction of the facts without any ordering principle of *selection*' (1962, p. 85). Especially was he also concerned that 'although we have "theories of the human sciences", we have no logic of the disciplines that do not fall within the natural sciences' (1986, p. 132n. 18). In particular, then, Rickert sought an independent logic that could replace the positivist and naturalistic, as well as the historicist metatheories in the realm of human phenomena. There was, he accepted, a sense in which all empirical phenomena are the potential objects of science, so that 'there is *nothing* that could be exempted as a matter of principle from an investigation of the kind specifically conducted by the natural sciences'. From this perspective, 'the proposition that there can be only *one* empirical science is altogether valid . . .'. The result, he reasoned, was that 'the concept of empirical science then seems to coincide with the concept of *natural science* in the broadest, formal sense of the term, and it appears that *all* science that deals with real existence must aim at discovering the general concepts or the natural laws under which its objects can be subsumed' (1962, pp. 13, 53). But, it was Rickert's crucial point that scientific inquiry could legitimately be directed by interests, values and epistemological standards other than those involved in natural science. It was this alternative direction that demanded distinctive metatheoretical foundations for the non-natural sciences.

Although Rickert's work was largely chronologically and thematically juxtaposed to Dilthey's, there was 'the sharpest imaginable contrast' between them (Schnädelbach, 1984, p. 129). The contrast was twofold: in the first place, Rickert pursued a science of human phenomena that was intent upon discursively representing in conceptual form the individual and unique characteristics of historical–cultural events in a manner that avoided any claims about their generalized origin or content; secondly, his metatheoretical objective was primarily epistemological and methodological, with concerns for an object's ontological origins, especially where these involved any hint of psychology, set aside as beyond the scope of and unnecessary for his strictly logical inquiries (cf. Oakes, 1986, p. xii n. 10). He shifted attention away from the *Geistes-wissenschaften* that in Dilthey's work focused on the ontological distinctiveness of the objects of the human world and those of the natural–physical worlds. For Rickert, the very idea of the *Geist* as an object of inquiry had become too deeply steeped in unacceptable metaphysical and psychological connotations. He remained conscious of the fact that the non-natural sciences 'do deal *predominantly* with psychical existence, and it is therefore not strictly a departure from the truth to refer to them as *Geisteswissenschaften*, i.e. as sciences dealing with manifestations of the human "mind" or "spirit"' (1962, pp. 11f). Nevertheless, he defined the non-natural sciences as *historischen Kultur-wissenschaften* (historical–cultural sciences: 1962, p. 16 and ed. n.) in which historically oriented inquiries were concerned with individual phenomena of mainly human origin. His point was that the ontologically distinct human objects that were to be dealt with could not, *per se*, account for the *logical* requirements of such sciences (1962, p. 71). The intellectual separation from the natural–physical sciences of such inquiries could be correctly established only by their different epistemo-logical and methodological perspectives (1962, p. 12).

5.2 Neo-Kantian historical–cultural science

We have seen that Windelband's seminal idea was for the historical–cultural sciences to have an exclusively *idiographic* orientation in seeking to comprehend on their own terms the *unique and individual* empirical facts, conditions and events of the real-world. Explanations of the generalized and permanent dimensions of reality were to be left to the *nomothetic* natural sciences in which universal laws applied. Rickert's modified view was that all of empirically experienced reality comprises unique and individual objects. Accounting discursively for their perceived appearance can be developed by one of two methodologies: the *individualizing* or the *generalizing*, with a continuum of integrated methodological possibilities in between. For Rickert, the result was to be the formation of '*two purely logical, and hence purely formal, concepts of nature and history*' with the repeatedly emphasized characteristic that these are 'not two different *domains* of reality, but the same *reality* seen from two *different points of view*' (1962, p. 56). Even more decisively put: '*Empirical reality becomes nature when we view it with respect to its universal characteristics; it becomes history when we view it as a particular individual*' (1962, p. 57, cf. pp. 99ff).

Windelband and Rickert opposed any naturalistic notion that the metatheoretical foundations established by the natural–physical sciences could be exclusively relevant for historical and cultural inquiries. The reason for this was that where individual objects are in focus, these cannot be grasped by means of the general laws that comprise the substance of natural–physical science. Nomologically argued theories are simply not of sufficient reach to enable any individual object to be fully accounted for in its observed detail. Windelband left the metatheoretical problematic of his idiographic inquiry without a satisfactory conclusion. Rickert took up this challenge and developed a defence of the individualizing methodology as a legitimate scientific form (cf. Oakes, 1988, p. 48).

It was especially the general and fundamental requirement of establishing knowledge in all empirical sciences that they form *concepts* as the mode of discursively capturing the perception of real-world objects. However, as Rickert expressed it, 'the goals of *generalizing* and *individualizing* ... are formally *different* from each other, and for this reason there must also be formally *distinct types of concept-formation* which serve for the attainment of these goals' (1962, p. 57). In this respect the concept formation pursued by the natural sciences was severely limited in that it sought only those abstract concepts that enabled it to express the universal and general characteristics of particular categories of phenomena. In historical and cultural inquiries, the aim of knowledge was discursively to capture the unique and individual characteristics of empirically observed phenomena and Rickert sought 'to discover the inner logical structure of all historical concept formation' (1986, p. 4, cf. p. 29). His approach was 'to undertake an investigation of the *limits of natural science* in order to achieve clarity concerning the nature and the philosophical significance of the historical sciences' (1986, p. 17).

The question thus posed was how legitimate, conceptually expressed knowledge of individual phenomena could be established: 'Is it at all *possible* to form *concepts* of individuals? This, essentially, is the *logical problem of the method of history*' (1962, p. 71). The question required cultural scientists and historians to confront the fact that the substantive specifications of such individuals are, and are perceived to be by agents, effectively infinite in their complexity and thus irrational in that they are, *per se*, beyond the reach of human reason. That is, scientists must confront the implied intellectual void between the empirical reality of individual phenomena, as they are actually perceived, and any conceptual grasp of them. Rickert accepted this void as unbridgeable and he searched for a metatheory into which it could be explicitly integrated.

Guy Oakes's concise interpretive summary shows that the results of

Rickert's search may be represented as five links in a chain of reasoning (Oakes, 1986, pp. xviff). First, Rickert pursued a particular *phenomenology of experienced reality* devoid of any ontological links or implications; secondly, he inferred from this phenomenology a rejection of *epistemological realism*; thirdly, in ruling out realism, Rickert adopted instead an alternative epistemology that included a *theory of cognitive interests* and a *theory of concepts*; fourthly, he investigated the established metatheory of natural science as a mode of formal inquiry with the intention of exposing its *limits of concept formation*; and fifthly, he sought *metatheoretically* to differentiate natural sciences from the *Kulturwissenschaften* consistently with all of the above predilections, but especially with respect to their distinctive modes of concept formation. My argument below appropriates these links as a frame of reference and draws some substantive guidance from Oakes's critical reading of Rickert.

5.3 Empirical reality and scientific inquiry

Rickert pursued a particular phenomenology of experienced reality devoid of any ontological links or implications (1962, pp. 30ff). Such a phenomenology meant that reality comprised only the agent's consciousness of it. Empirical objects as we experience them through perception, rather than as they are 'in-themselves', are also exposed as comprising an effectively infinite spatial and temporal complexity: 'Empirical reality proves to be an *immeasurable manifold . . .*' (1962, p. 32). The experienced reality of the natural and human worlds is extensively infinite in that it is limitless and endless and cannot be exhaustively encompassed by any perception. Rickert called this 'the theorem of the *continuity of everything real*' (1962, p. 33). Furthermore, each individual phenomenon as it is experienced is an intensively infinite complex of a limitless number of elements and descriptive properties. This he called 'the theorem of the *heterogeneity of everything real*' (1962, p. 34, original emphasis). So it is that phenomenal experience as a whole and in its elements is irrational in that because it appears to be open-ended, it is beyond the powers of reason fully to grasp as an object of knowledge. Most generally put, '*the rational is not restricted to the real, and what is only real is not yet rational*' (1986, pp. 6f), which is to say that the rationally manageable facets of reality-in-itself can only be a product of the intervention of the mind of the observing agent in the Kantian manner.

For Rickert, a consequence of this phenomenology, with its absence of any claims to ontological insight, was a rejection of epistemological realism in which conceptual analyses are treated as integral and essential expressions of the reality that they represent. Realism entails that representative conceptual argument has an immanent ontological status. In Rickert's own words of rejection, he tried 'to demonstrate the emptiness of the doctrine according to which the common elements of things are the same as the essential features of concepts' (1986, p. 3). In this respect he referred to the *'impotence of concepts'* for the purpose of discursively copying reality (1962, p. 34). The irrational reality to which Rickert referred was as we experience and perceive it, wholly or in part. Its infinite complexity meant that there could be no claim that experience captures things as they are 'in-themselves'. In Rickert's words, it is the 'combination of heterogeneity and continuity that impresses on reality its peculiar stamp of "irrationality"; i.e. because it is, in its every part, an *heterogeneous continuum*, it cannot be conceptually grasped as it is' (1962, p. 34). That is, 'the "object" of knowledge ... with which conceptual knowledge must conform ... can be equivalent neither to an absolute real being nor to empirical reality – what we know is not the actual [*wirkliche*] or really [*real*] existing "objects" of concepts in natural science or history' (1986, p. 216).

Indeed, it is the aim of natural science to achieve just the opposite to expressing our actual experience of the empirically real. Rickert informed us that 'a theory in natural science is more advanced the more it has surmounted this infinity and thereby reduced the irrational to the rational', and 'a natural scientific theory is more complete the *less* its concepts contain of the immediately given and infinite reality of sense perception'. Moreover, 'a *mere* duplication ... [of reality] would be worthless; and most important, it would have no *theoretical* significance' (1986, pp. 43, 44). However, he was just as definite that even though the abstractions of science rely on the mediating values of and judgements by investigators and do not intend to copy reality, there must remain a sense in which reality as it is originally perceived validates the non-real conceptual forms used to express it discursively. Thus, he wrote, 'a cognitive content can be ascribed to the generalizing concept formation of natural science only if the general it represents holds *validly for* individual reality'. So, concluded Rickert, 'the concepts of the natural sciences are true, not because they reproduce reality as it actually exists but because they represent what holds *validly* for reality' (1986, p. 44, cf. pp. 45f).

By ruling out realism, Rickert was led to adopt an alternative epistemology comprising a theory of cognitive interests that directed the substance of scientific inquiry and a theory of concepts that provided the mode of discursive representation of that substance. In his view, 'if we assume that empirical reality is the only [object] material of science, and if empirical reality forms an infinite manifold whose purely factual rendition can never be provided by science, it is self-evident that science is possible only by means of the [conceptual] reshaping undertaken by the [observing] subject' (1986, pp. 217f). In pursuit of this concept formation process, Rickert posited a selective principle of cognitive interests that centres on those facets of an experienced phenomenon deemed important to analysts or agents in accordance with the values they hold. It is these values that give purpose and direction to inquiries within the infinite of reality and thus to the construction of knowledge itself. The result is a strictly non-real mode of scientific representation in which concepts provide the medium of the construction of knowledge. These concepts simplify, reformulate and transform experienced reality on the basis of the concerns they are intended to address. They consist, therefore, of logical constructions designed to meet a particular cognitive purpose (cf. Oakes, 1986, p. xix). That is, conceptual argument can express only a *logical* relationship between concepts and the observed object. The arguments are ontologically empty because concepts are merely intellectual instruments of discursive expression. Reality-in-itself cannot be contained within or reproduced discursively by means of conceptual constructions. The effect of this belief was to ensure that only imposed values could give legitimacy to the necessarily non-real grasp that observers could have on the phenomena of nature and on mental and physical activities of other agents. It is to be noted that because conceptual constructs have no immediate ontological contact with the reality that comprises their object, it is value consistency that becomes the test of the objectivity, validity and truth of any representative argument.

In his approach to setting up the identifying character of the historical sciences, Rickert investigated the established metatheory of natural science as a mode of formal inquiry with the intention of exposing its limits of concept formation (1962, pp. 40ff, 1986, *passim*). The crucial characteristic of natural science is its pursuit of universal theory of generalized categories of objects. It does so through the formulation of abstract conceptual complexes that comprise nomological relationships, the laws of nature. Such abstractions and laws enable scientists to transcend the infinite continuity and heterogeneity of empirical reality. Thus the irrationality of perceived reality is overcome by abstracting the common and universal features of a type of phenomenon. In doing so, they set aside the unique and non-repeating aspects of individual observations of the phenomenon (1962, pp. 41ff).

The consequence of this process for Rickert was that generalizing science ends up with non-real discursive representations of phenomena that take the form of concepts and their relationships. Such representations do not seek to encompass the individual perceptual qualities that characterize phenomena as empirical objects of experience, and in this respect their epistemological reach is consciously limited. The 'meaning and purpose' of natural science, then, Rickert argued, is 'to establish an opposition between the content of *concepts* and the *reality* of sense perception that is as rigorous as possible' (1986, p. 37). This applies to all objects that constitute reality, including human individuals and their products, both mental and physical. Rickert put it emphatically: '*What fixes the limits of natural scientific concept formation, and which the natural sciences can never surmount, is nothing but unique empirical reality itself*, just as we directly experience it in sense perception, in its *concrete actuality* and *individuality*' (1986, p. 40; cf. 1962, p. 46). Especially was he concerned to show how generalizing natural science, even when it is extended to encompass sciences of the human world, effectively removes any individuality of its object world from the conceptual forms that are its discursive substance (1962, p. 42, 1986, pp. 37ff). What, then can be said of the search for conceptual knowledge of empirical objects in their individuality, especially as it applies to the historical–cultural sciences?

5.4 A metatheory of the historical–cultural sciences

It was in addressing this vital question concerning the discursive representation of individual phenomena that Rickert set out meta-theoretically to differentiate concept formation in the natural sciences from that in the *Kulturwissenschaften*. His rejection of epistemological realism meant that this differentiation could not ultimately be grounded in any distinctions involving the respective ontologies of their phenomena. Rickert accepted that such distinctions do exist, but he claimed they were just not of primary concern to concept formation in science. Scientific discourse could not, and was not intended to capture reality at this existential ontological level, rather confining itself to working with perceptions of experience by means of judgements under the guiding directions of values and cognitive interests. Empirical phenomena of natural and human origin, of physical and psychic form, were both of equal experiential status for observers in this sense (1962, p. 47). What was different for natural and for historical–cultural scientists was the value and interest orientations of their pursuit of valid knowledge. While natural scientists were satisfied to express the perception of objects as nomologically constructed conceptual complexes that are self-consciously generalized and remote from reality, scientists of history and culture were intent upon expressing the empirically individual characteristics of their perceived objects. These latter objects were to be discursively represented so as to preserve their unique identifying qualities: 'Wherever this *interest* in reality is present, we can do nothing with natural scientific concept formation' (1986, p. 46; cf. 1962, p. 55). That is, for Rickert it was the interest orientation alone that elicited and validated the pursuit of classes of knowledge.

The fundamental claim of Rickert's endeavour to isolate the problem of concept formation in the historical–cultural sciences was that 'we understand by the word "concept" *every* idea comprising the scientifically *essential* constituents of a real entity. This extended usage is seen to be warranted as soon as it is realized that conceiving [i.e. concept formation] and generalizing need *not* coincide' (1962, p. 80). In his metatheoretical alternative for the development of these sciences of perceived reality, 'if there is to be a representation of reality with reference to its uniqueness and individuality, a science is required that diverges logically from natural science in essential points concerning the form of its concept formation'. Rickert's consequent task was 'to identify the logical structure of this science, to distinguish its mode of concept formation from that of every natural science . . .' (1986, p. 47). More explicitly, his intention was to focus on the '*logical* opposition between nature and history' (1986, p. 34).

Historical–cultural science has as its objects observed empirical phenomena. It must, therefore, confront the fact of their intensive infinity of existence as heterogeneous individuals. As we have seen, Rickert emphasized that no science can be expected conceptually to reproduce the full dimensions of the perceived reality that it addresses. Now he was advocating a science for which viability and validity depend on its actually capturing the very individuality of at least the intensive reality of its unique objects. Such an endeavour seemed to defy the void between the real and the conceptual that he had accepted as incorrigible. It followed that the only way this science could be realized was through some form of conceptual transformation from reality as it is perceived into a discursively manageable form that preserved its individuality to some extent deemed adequate and meaningful. This could not be facilitated, though, by any resort to a generalized nomological frame of reference constructed from non-real concepts as in the natural sciences. Laws cannot discursively express individual objects to any sufficient extent. Rickert asserted that 'historical science and nomological science are mutually exclusive concepts ...', and 'the *concept* of the "historical law" is self-contradictory'. To proclaim laws for the historical sciences was thus labelled a '*logical absurdity*' that would cause such sciences to fail in their objective of accounting for the individuals of reality (1986, p. 56).

The key to the historical–cultural '*science of reality*' is the discursive preservation in conceptual form of individual identifying characteristics that are actually present in the makeup of the perceived part of reality that is of interest to the analyst. In this respect, although the concepts used 'cannot reproduce the content of reality itself, ... [they] still stand in a relationship to unique and individual reality that is in principle different from and actually *more proximate* than what holds true for the concepts of generalizing natural science' (1986, p. 52). However, it was immediately apparent to Rickert that this sort of claim still had to deal explicitly with the question: 'How can "irrational" reality be ... "rationalized" in such a way that ... its "individuality" does not disappear?' (1986, p. 53).

It was, then, quite apparent to Rickert that this metatheoretical criterion for founding the historical–cultural sciences defied the irrational infinity of their objects of knowledge. At the same time, it was essential that history did not degenerate into a relativistic description of perceived events with no scientific validity. So, the real challenge of '*the problem of concept formation in history ... is whether a scientific analysis and reduction of perceptual reality is possible that does not at the same time – as in the concepts of natural science – forfeit individuality ...*' (1986, p. 78). As we are soon to see, such individuality can be preserved only if 'concepts comprise what is abstracted from the [object] material of knowledge as "essential". Their significance for knowledge lies exclusively in the consideration that their content is united to form a necessary – in other words, a valid – unity' (1986, p. 46).

His response to these challenging criteria was to proclaim a principle of value relevances that posits cultural value sets which reflect the interest orientations of scientists (1962, pp. 19, 87ff). Conceptual formations relating to the individual objects of reality took a form that reflected these value relevances, the orientations of meaning and judgements of significance, of the investigators and the disciplines in which they worked. They were envisaged by Rickert as manifested in a principle of selection that enables analysts to discriminate within the infinity of their real objects and isolate the essential facets of them in accordance with their theoretical orientation and interests (1962, p. 36). It may be said, then, that the notion of value relevance is how Rickert addressed the problem of concept formation with respect to historical individuals (cf. Oakes, 1986, pp. xxiiiff; Oakes, 1988, p. 78). But such a claim begs the question: what is the source of such validating values?

Rickert construed the value set as a 'series of *presuppositions* that can be designated as the "*a priori*" of scientific concept formation'. Such presuppositions comprise 'the *law of nature* as ... an unconditionally general judgement' in the case of natural sciences, and 'the concept of the *cultural value* to which every historical object must be theoretically related in order to become a possible object of historical representation ...' (1986, p. 65). There must exist, then, an 'unconditionally and valid value more or less realized by the generally esteemed objects and institutions of cultural life in their capacity as expressions of individual complexes of meaning'. The objective validity of this value, Rickert claimed, results from the notion that 'every man engaged in any scientific enterprise implicitly assumes the more-than-individual significance of cultural life, of which he himself is a product' (1962, pp. 141, 144).

The accepted system of value relevances enables particular historical and cultural analysts to select for discursive expression just those elements of the perceived empirical complex that preserve the coherence and indivisibility of its essential and individual nature. There emerged the notion that there are two humanly conceivable types of individual phenomena: 'The one type of individuality is identical with the *concrete singularity of everything real* and eludes *every* science. The other is a definite *conception* of reality and can be incorporated in concepts' (1962, p. 83). Rickert chose to apply to the latter particular mode of existence the hyphenated term '*in-dividual*' in order to distinguish it from the more general infinite individuality that characterizes all raw phenomena. It captured the delimited interest of the historian and cultural scientist in an object phenomenon that had, nonetheless, to remain unique in this more confined sense.[2]

It was apparent to Rickert that this dependence of historical and cultural inquiry upon the principles of value relevance and selection on the part of investigators had the potential to degenerate into a mess of relativism (1962, pp. 137, 140). All observers could bring their own values, interest orientations and judgements to an inquiry and select their own essentials of the individual object for discursive representation. He was determined to contain this potential relativism and ensure the achievement of objective knowledge in the field of historical–cultural inquiry in the sense that all scientific observers could realize the same knowledge of an empirical object (cf. Burger, 1976, p. 17). To this end, he introduced four constraints on the value set to be applied by the investigator (Oakes, 1986, pp. xxvff, cf. Oakes, 1988, pp. 78ff).

First, the values must be those of the agents whose actions generated the object phenomenon in focus. Secondly, the values should not be private or personal, but rather should be those imbedded in the culture of the agents' environment. Thirdly, these cultural values are required to have an objective status that transcends the dictates of any empirical and normative immediacy. It was crucial for the defence of Rickert's claim that historical–cultural sciences were just as objective in their epistemology as natural sciences to be able to say that these are values with unconditionally general status. This was reinforced by the fourth constraint ensuring that the personal value positions of the investigators, their valuations, were not permitted to impede the objective, theoretical application of the pertinent, culturally defined value relevances. Rickert's belief was that 'even though history deals with values, it is *not a science that posits values*. Instead of concerning itself with what *ought* to be, it establishes only what *is*' (1962, p. 89). For, he claimed, 'the fact that *cultural values are universal* . . . is what keeps concept-formation in the historical sciences from being altogether *arbitrary* and thus constitutes the primary basis of its "objectivity". What is historically essential must be *important* not only for this or that particular historian, but for *all*' (1962, p. 97).[3]

5.5 Ontology in Rickert's metatheory

However persuasive Oakes's immanent critical exposition and its conclusions, they do not exhaust the difficulties and misdirections of Rickert's intellectual legacy. There is a further critical aspect to consider, one concerned with Rickert's failure adequately to confront the ontological dimensions of his attempts to reconstruct the metatheory of the sciences of human phenomena. That is, his failure to identify and deal with these phenomena as having qualities that originate in their generation by human agency and that must then set them apart from natural phenomena for whatever purpose is at hand. Moreover, his defence of the notion of value relevance as the foundation for concept formation in the historical–cultural sciences can be argued as necessarily ontologically dependent in that the pertinent values set cannot avoid confronting the choices of situationally conditioned human agents. Rickert was, in fact, led to grant a status to *meaning* in human affairs that entailed values having an ultimately ontological foundation. All this leaves any metatheory involving values with an unavoidable ontological dependence and renders all of Rickert's claims to be able to retreat to an exclusively logical inquiry invalid. His consequent demarcation criterion based on that logic is also shown to be of dubious status as the exclusive means of differentiating the sciences of nature from those of the human realm. The intention to subsume all such concerns within his value-based, individualizing methodology enabled him to avoid confronting the potential merits of a generalizing but non-naturalistic human science.

Recall that it was Rickert's idea to constrain the nature and conditions of involvement of values in the process of concept formation in the historical–cultural sciences. In doing so, however, he could not avoid relating values directly to agents whose actions are the ontological foundations for any historical–cultural objects. Even he himself observed: 'Human beings will always stand in the center of the reality that is the object of a historical representation. We have a historical interest in a reality only if it is truly connected with mental entities who themselves take a position on general human values' (1986, p. 131). And elsewhere he noted in a similar vein that 'the unity and objectivity of the cultural sciences are contingent on the unity and objectivity of *our concept of culture*, and these in turn depend on the unity and objectivity of *the values we acknowledge as valid*' (1962, p. 140; emphasis added). These are explicitly agent-centred remarks that link the relevance of values to the choices of agents.

In his belief that the values of historical inquiry must be those of the agents whose actions generated the object phenomenon in focus, Rickert referred to the position of these agents as 'historical centres'. It is they who posit values as an integral and fundamental part of the psychic and cognitive constitution by means of which they deliberate and decide to act. Values are in this respect practically relevant at the root of historical objects. This was consistent with Rickert's claim that the substance of historical objects comprises the expressions of mental life, including the physical and psychic situational influences that affect it directly and indirectly through the values agents form. Consequently, it is only possible for such values to be comprehended as ontologically dependent in that they are intimately attached to, and have no existence beyond, the subjective agents who generate the historical or cultural phenomena that are under study by the analysts. In Rickert's own words to this effect, 'the values governing conceptualization are always to be derived from the historical *material itself*. That is, they must always be values in regard to which the beings or centers themselves – the objects of the representation – act in a valuative fashion' (1986, p. 127, cf. 1962, p. 88)

Rickert also expressed his belief that historical values were not private or personal, but those imbedded in the culture of the agents' environment. As such, they are the products of the cumulative influence of acculturation (including socialization) on agents who have grown up and come to operate in particular situational life-world conditions. Understanding of the life activities of individual agents requires an understanding of the values to which they grant validity. But the values themselves are prior to, and not dependent upon this adoption: values comprise 'an autonomous sphere [*Reich*] that lies *beyond subject and object*' (quoted by Oakes, 1988, p. 101; Rickert's emphasis). Objectively general and valid cultural values were thus to be taken for granted as definitive for the very existence of cultural phenomena. Such existence did not depend in any way upon the private, and so contestably valid, valuational inclinations of any agents.

For agents to be warranted as historically specific *in*-dividuals, and thus to qualify as historical centres in Rickert's senses of these ideas, they must be shown to act on the basis of the general cultural value set that was acknowledged or normatively expected at the time in their environment. This acknowledgment was thought of by Rickert in social terms: agents are socially situated and so adopt what are social values from this perspective (1986, p. 131). It is this ongoing, ontologically fundamental status of values for agents that brought him to recognize that their influence is one that mediates in the *meaning* that agents attach to their social and cultural situations. The fact of this meaning then distinguishes the objects of historical–cultural sciences from the meaningless objects of the natural sciences that are totally detached from values. In Rickert's thought, this distinction remained epistemologically based in that the natural objects are so interpreted because their concepts are abstract and generalized. He referred to the distinction as one of 'substance', but he was resolute that it was not to be read as ontologically dependent. It could only be interpreted as the consequence of the different value and interest orientations of the observers of the phenomena concerned. That is, the objects were defined in terms of the methodology by which they were to be analysed and discursively accounted for (1962, pp. 20f; cf. Oakes, 1988, p. 84). Because of the ontological intimacy necessarily involved in all subjectively meaningful accounts of human phenomena, such a claim is impossible to sustain beyond the semantics.

Rickert's strategy of metatheoretical inquiry ostensibly gave primacy to logic rather than to ontology. This was a judgement that reflected his disinclination to pursue the appropriate foundations for any generalizing science of human phenomena. His focus was on inquiries that have historically generated phenomena as objects and the logic he developed then entailed that all such phenomena were to be scientifically dealt with as unique and individual. For Rickert, the expression *Kulturwissenschaften* was the appropriate name for the non-natural sciences: 'By "culture" everyone understands those realities that have an intelligible meaning for us because of their value relevance' (1986, p. 147). And, 'to the extent that this [cultural] material consists of meaningful realities, its unity or totality . . . occurs only by means of the *meaning* configurations of culture that it embodies' (1986, p. 148). Finally, on the basis of such reasoning, Rickert concluded that the required interpenetration of cultural values and conceptual formations that comprise the representation of cultural objects as individuals meant that 'the generalizing method of natural science is unable to do justice to the substantive content of the material' (1986, p. 147).

Nevertheless, there was no lack of awareness on Rickert's part that there were extant endeavours to deal with human phenomena in terms of *generalizing logic*. And he even gave serious and extended critical consideration to the ontologically distinct nature of these phenomena with which such a logic would have to cope. However, as we are to see, his efforts in these directions ultimately amounted to an attempt to distance himself from any orientation towards this alternative approach (1986, pp. 116ff, 138ff). He argued resolutely to the effect that all human scientific inquiry that purported to begin from the distinctive ontological nature of human phenomena could not avoid dependence upon his axiological premises.

Rickert was prepared to grant that history and culture are 'in fact primarily concerned with *mental* or *psychic* processes' and was conscious of the associated ontological issues raised by focusing on the *content* of the historical–cultural sciences: 'To give precedence to form, as we were obliged to do, is not to *ignore* content completely' (1986, p. 117). In more explicit detail, he wrote:

> All students of the disciplines that do not fall within the natural sciences –
> the theologian, the jurist, the philologist, the historian, and *the economist* –
> feel that, in comparison with natural scientists, they belong together. If we
> inquire into the reason for this, we will always be disposed to regard the
> concept of the 'spiritual' – in other words, the concept of the psychic – as
> the bond that ties the nonnatural scientific disciplines together into a unified
> whole. In fact, their objects are and must be predominantly mental. Thus it
> is easy to understand why anyone who proposes to survey the entire domain
> of scientific activity and its differences would divide the sciences into natural
> sciences and human sciences, or sciences of mental phenomena. (1986, p. 128;
> emphasis added)

In order to compound the contrary case for rejection of the primacy of ontological concerns in human science, Rickert often reiterated his view that it is the value-relevant, individualizing metatheory of historical–cultural inquiry that overrides the existential form taken by its objects. It is 'from the *formal* concept of historical method . . . [that we] arrive at the *substantive* character of the historical *material*' (1986, p. 121). His argument was that any attempt to grasp an historical phenomenon as manifesting mental activity must involve the intervention of values, which confirmed the aptness of the value-relevant approach to representing the phenomenon as an individual.

However, Rickert also claimed to be directly concerned with the 'interpenetration of object and method' in recognizing that 'it is cultural realities, and above all their mental centers, that *require* a value relevant, individualizing representation by history' (1986, p. 145). This requirement, he claimed, gave historical inquiry the metatheoretical grounding that depended upon values *and* gave due recognition to the human ontological nature of its object phenomena. Thus he wrote that 'the content of [historical] meaning can be interpreted only with reference to values' (1986, p. 147). Rickert's now ontologically oriented reasoning was that 'the historian will best do justice to the distinctive character of his material in a thoroughly "objective" fashion *only* if he is led in the selection of what is essential by *the same* values that provide the basis for the meaning of the cultural life of the . . . human beings that appear in his material' (1986, p. 145). Thus, 'the distinctive central *material* of historical science . . . is represented in such a way that the values that endow it with meaning at the same time provide the governing principles of concept formation with the help of which historical science appropriates its material' (1986, p. 145). The more explicit import of this idea was that 'the value character of the meaning configurations that appear in the material of history . . . *determine the method of historical concept formation*' (1986, p. 147; emphasis added). On the basis of these assertions, we can see that Rickert was ultimately led to the position where the metatheory appropriate to the sciences of human phenomena could not be designed on logical grounds alone. Reference to consistency with the ontology of the objects to be studied could not be avoided. What this meant for Rickert was that while any human science that began with and pursued exclusively existential particularities could not be justified, preserving the importance of ontological insights remained necessary for his own metatheoretical alternative.

5.6 Rickert's rejection of human science

Rickert's conception of the demarcation between the sciences does not enable us to address the metatheoretical potentials and requirements of the non-naturalistic, *generalizing human science* that was taken seriously by a number of philosophers of his time, most prominently Dilthey. All human phenomena are existentially historical, but our scientific interest in them is not confined to the individuality that is of concern to historians *per se*. As Rickert recognized, 'of course, culture as well, like every reality, can be brought under the concepts of natural science. In other words, it can be represented in a generalizing fashion'. However, he was prepared to put aside such an alternative as 'alone never sufficient for culture' (1986, p. 64). However, more than this was involved in endeavours such as Dilthey's. What Rickert really had to confront and show to have no negative import for his own individual-izing metatheory of the human realm was the idea that there existed a legitimate mode of inquiry into that realm that began from ontology and was generalizing in its results without resorting to the methodology of naturalism and positivism. As we shall see, he remained steadfast in his view that such inquiry could not but *depend upon and be subsumed by the logic of his own axiological reasoning*. That is, human science that applies naturalistic methodology to create exact theory was to be the only viable, independent generalizing alternative to the *Kulturwis-senschaften*.

Recognition that 'most historical sciences are predominantly con-cerned with mental processes' led Rickert to express the misgiving that 'in representing a real mental process, ... the historian lacks access to the object of immediate experience' (1986, p. 118). He quoted Dilthey, referring to his use of external expressions as the mediation for psychic inquiry: 'We call that process *understanding* in which we acquire knowl-edge of something that is inner on the basis of externally given perceptual signs.' But Rickert's response could only be to ask of Dilthey: 'What is an "inner" process?', for '[e]verything depends on this ques-tion' (Rickert, 1986, p. 159 n. 29). In his view, access to such private, inner *realities* of the psyche was epistemologically problematical: 'The signs that are "externally" given must make it possible to acquire knowledge of more than a real "inner" process. Otherwise they will remain unintelligible' (1986, p. 159 n. 29). Crucial to Rickert's case was the idea that 'historical understanding cannot only signify the under-standing of the real mental or psychic existence of the past.... The task of history rather lies in the understanding of culture, which is *more* than a real psychic phenomenon' (1986, p. 65). That is, 'the historian does not represent the real event for the sake of its reality, but only to the extent that it is linked with something that points beyond its *mere* real existence', where this 'something' comprised the cultural values that direct selective representation of the individual phenomenon (1986, p. 139).

Understanding the generation of human phenomena as expressions of psychic and cognitive processes in general theoretical terms was always a legitimate objective of science. Rickert was well aware of this and he made some effort especially to reach a compromise with Dilthey's direction of inquiry. Rickert clearly recognized this direction: 'It is, of course, possible to begin with differences in the *material* that the sciences investigate in order to show how, for example, the acquisition of knowledge of *mental* life in history poses other difficulties – and thus requires other methods of investigation – than the acquisition of knowledge of corporeal nature'. In such circumstances, he continued, 'we might quite rightly place concepts like that of historical "understanding" – in contrast to the concept of "explanation" in natural science – in the foreground' (1986, p. 29). In particular, he defended in detail the view that 'the logic of history need not *conflict* with investigations concerning the nature of history that have a different orientation. At least it has its own theoretical value *alongside* them' (1986, p. 29). As I have already indicated above, however, Rickert believed that this juxtaposed existence of an ostensibly independent human science in Dilthey's sense could not be isolated from his own axiologically grounded metatheory.

The reasons for this claim take us back to Rickert's fundamental thesis that the void between our perception of empirical reality and its unreal conceptual reflections is intellectually unbridgeable. This applies with a vengeance, he noted, when the empirical reality to be captured conceptually is a phenomenon whose origin is 'the real mental life of historical personalities or mass movements' (1986, p. 157). It was his understanding that the human sciences dealing directly with ontologically defined objects claim to understand and thereby to be able discursively to represent these objects as they are in their essential reality. Rickert's view was that conceptual expressions could not achieve this level of representation for any object. Conceptual formations were for him non-real in that they were dependent upon the mediation of values and meanings. In his parlance, 'what does not have *value* and *meaning* in some sense or other remains "unintelligible"' (1986, p. 159), so that 'the understanding of real historical material can never be concerned with the *merely* real – and thus value-free and nonmeaningful – mental life.... [T]he real is an object of understanding in the sense that and to the extent that it is the "bearer" of nonreal meaning' (1986,

p. 162). Thus 'the unity in the *material* of history, which consists of meaningful realities, is based not on the reality but on the meaning embodied in it' (1986, p. 160). Ultimately, then, Rickert's claim contra Dilthey was that 'in its pure reality ... mental life remains just as "incomprehensible" for us as a purely real material object, such as a stone lying in the street' (1986, p. 162). It is not possible in Rickert's case merely to respond that only human phenomena of mental origin can sensibly have meaning, anyway, for he argued that meaning is always a function of values applied. As he saw things: 'Meaningful mental life is a special type of the value-relevant event as such.' The consequence was that 'the concept of understanding as knowledge of a meaning is necessarily related to *our* theory of the historical representation of cultural processes and their centers' (1986, p. 161).

This need for values in concept formation could be further attributed to the fact that 'the real mental life the historian hopes to grasp in its actual individuality is never his own, but is rather always the mental life of *another* person. And . . ., nothing psychic that really transpires in other individuals can ever be *directly* accessible to the historian. In other words, it cannot be immediately "experienced" as real existence' (1986, p. 164; original emphasis). It is as a result of a set of commonly available cultural value relevances that 'as regards *the meaning of the mental life of other persons, we may perhaps acquire direct access to the individuality of its nonreal meaning, but never to the individuality of its real existence*' (1986, p. 164, cf. p. 167). Rickert's conclusion here was that:

> historical re-creation is always concerned with the reconstruction of the individual mental life of the past that is meaningful because the goods of culture were expressed in it. Thus without our concept of the *value-relevant and individualizing science of culture* whose central material is constituted by the meaningful mental life of cultural human beings, both the concept of human science and that of re-creative understanding remain without any logically useful meaning. (1986, p. 175)

So what Rickert effectively chose to de-emphasize, and ultimately to render pointless, in all of this was the pursuit of an independent non-naturalistic, generalizing metatheory of the human sciences. The science of human phenomena that transcended naturalism could only be individualizing according to his reasoning (1986, p. 175). In response, it may well be justifiable to grant that the science of *history per se* quite aptly requires the individualizing metatheory that he sought. Nonetheless, the fact that all phenomena of human origin have an historical existence does not mean that they are always most appropriately dealt with as objects of history in this particular sense. This was Dilthey's not wholly successful line of inquiry. Merely nominating human objects more broadly as cultural and value oriented had an ontological legitimacy, but it could not justify Rickert's extension of the historical logic as the exclusive mode of scientific treatment of these objects.

5.7 Rickert's legacy

We have now seen how Rickert sought to defend the independent scientific status of the historical and cultural sciences from the inroads of naturalist scientism. At the same time, he endeavoured to develop a metatheoretical foundation for these sciences in their individualizing form. He began from the premiss that no science can grasp in conceptual form the causal forces that generate the infinite reality-in-itself of its objects. This was the problem of the 'extensive manifold' of empirical reality. It did not matter, Rickert continued, how empirically delimited the object might be, the problem of an infinite causation remained as the 'intensive manifold'. In short, reality-in-itself was beyond the reach of human reason to encompass and in this sense Rickert labelled it as 'irrational'.

This impossibility of grasping scientifically the heterogeneous causality of an infinite empirical reality of objects that are of interest to science had to be confronted nonetheless. The knowledge construction procedure to be adopted, according to Rickert, could only be that some metatheoretical criteria had to be specified by means of which the 'manifolds' could be simplified. That is, some of the heterogeneity had to be removed under controlled methodological conditions. For this purpose, Rickert developed his theory of concept formation. He designed this to facilitate the discursive presentation of selected, empirically 'essential' components of reality as constituting knowledge of a phenomenon. The question begged by this intention was the nature of the 'selection' procedure that could claim access to these 'essentials'.

As a Neo-Kantian, for Rickert it was out of the question that the principles of selection could in any way be inherent in the ontology of reality itself. The 'essentials' that he referred to were not those that would be sought by an Aristotelian realist. They could only be designated by the fiat of the knowing subjects, the observer-analysts. Their effort was directed at simplifying the reality of an object in a way that retained its 'essentials' according to some criteria constructed prior to an inquiry. These criteria were manifested in the conceptual forms abstracted by analysts to capture discursively those facets of the reality required for its consequent meaningful representation as knowledge.

The remainder of the reality was thereby left aside as not essential for a sufficient understanding of the phenomenon's causal origins. One crucial result of this procedure was effectively to close the void between reality and conceptual forms. The void disappeared rather than being bridged in that reality came to be defined only in terms of the concepts selected to represent it.

It is apparent that for Rickert, it was an integral part of this concept formation procedure that it enabled the analyst to dichotomize the fields of science between the natural and the historical–cultural. This separation was grounded in the distinction between generalized concepts of universal nomological meaning that comprise the arguments of the natural sciences, and the individualizing concepts that capture only the causal 'essentials' of particular empirical phenomena in the historical–cultural sciences. As far as he was concerned, there was little to trouble the metatheorist in the notion of natural science. It was the defence of the independence of the historical–cultural sciences that had not received sufficient and satisfactory attention. Such a defence could only be legitimate if some mode of abstract concept formation could be argued in which the individual and unique character of an empirical phenomenon under study was shown to be preserved. That is, can there be a science in which reality is simplified in a manner that retains its individuality in spite of the need for abstraction? To achieve this, Rickert combined his non-realist epistemology with the process of individualizing concept formation so as to advocate a discursive representation he called the 'historical individual'. This abstraction comprised empirically oriented causal explanations that made no claim to realism in the very particular sense that there was no access 'back' to reality-in-itself from the conceptual construction. The epistemological and methodological defence of the construction had to consist in its meeting the imposed criteria of the inquiry set prior to its formation.

The selection criteria on which Rickert asserted the abstracted concept formation should depend comprised the values and interests that could be attributed to the observer-analysts operating in a particular realm of empirical inquiry. These axiological choice criteria effectively isolated the 'essentials' of individual phenomena in a manner that enabled the resulting representation to exhibit their uniqueness as the analysts perceive it to be on a case by case basis. The immediate implication here was that the selection is subjective and the resulting analyses relativistic. But, Rickert went on to add, where it can be claimed that an established and agreed set of value relevances exists in a culture or community, the axiology takes on a semblance of delimited 'objectivity'. His view was that this was all that could be expected epistemologically in the historical–cultural sciences.

It was to be Max Weber especially who selectively adopted some of the main tenets of Rickert's position and made them an integral part of his *search* for a metatheory of the human sciences. These included the notion of the infinity and irrationality of reality-in-itself, the problem of the potential void between the world of concepts and the world of realities, the principle of concept formation as the correct mode of scientific inquiry, the generalizing and individualizing dichotomization of science, the resulting idea that historical–cultural sciences are sciences of perceived concrete reality, the notion of the 'historical individual' as the object of empirical science, and the principle that historical–cultural meaning is defined by value relevance. It was a *search* nevertheless because he found Rickert's legacy to be deficient in certain crucial respects. We turn to what Weber made of these and other metatheoretical guidelines in his pursuit of objective knowledge in the human sciences in the next chapter.

Notes

1. Rickert's most important epistemological work was *Die Grenzen der naturwissenschaftlichen Begriffsbildung*, written and published in two instalments between 1896 and 1901, with the first complete edition in 1902. Ultimately the work ran to five editions, the last in 1929 (translated as *The Limits of Concept Formation in Natural Science*, 1986). This work elaborated on themes that Rickert had also outlined less formally in his *Kulturwissenschaft und Naturwissenschaft*, first published in 1899 and finally in its seventh edition in 1926 (translated as *Science and History*, 1962). In the remainder of this chapter, references shown in parentheses are to the works of Rickert, and emphases in quotations from these works are in the original, unless otherwise indicated.

2. For example, Goethe as a male member of the human race was an individual. But Goethe as an historical personality, defined by those characteristics and qualities pertinent to his status as a literary genius, was an '*in*-dividual' in the delimited sense. For the interest of analysts in him stems from a set of cultural value relevances commonly accepted as setting him apart from other individual members of the population of contemporary literati of which he was a member (1986, p. 89; cf. Oakes, 1988, pp. 74ff).

3. In a detailed exposition and subsequent critique that cannot be pursued here, Oakes establishes convincingly that on its own terms, Rickert's claim to have delivered an objective axiological grounding for the historical–cultural sciences as he defined them is not defensible (Oakes, 1988, pp. 91ff and 111ff). In short, the choice of a pertinent value set defining a cultural context remains subjectively determined by the predilections of the analysts. Cultural values are, then, ultimately those of the analysts' own *Weltanschauungen*. They must decide which values to apply in their inquiries. The subjective nature of values and the relativism of their application were never negated by Rickert's arguments.

6. Human agents and rationality in Max Weber's metatheory for the human sciences

6.1 Preamble

In his contributions to the methodology of the human sciences,[1] Max Weber has, on the basis of his own testament, been classified as a neo-Kantian follower of Heinrich Rickert (Oakes, 1975, 1988; Burger, 1976). As we saw in the previous chapter, one of the fundamental premisses of this neo-Kantian philosophy was its non-ontological epistemology. Weber's understanding and explanation of socio-economic and historical phenomena were ostensibly argued in terms of conceptual constructions that complied with this premiss. That is, the concepts were constructed without any claimed ontological links to the real nature of the object under investigation (cf. Oakes, 1986, pp. xvf and 1987, pp. 439f).

In this chapter, I suggest that contrary to his neo-Kantian intentions in this particular direction, there is much textual evidence that Weber was not consistent in following them through. He found it impossible to insulate his methodological investigations from concerns about the distinctive ontological nature of object phenomena originating in individual, socially oriented subjective human action. As a consequence, it will become apparent below that what he wrote was, in fact, rich in subjectivist and individualist insight. And, adherence to ontological integrity in representing this insight was ultimately prominent in the methodological foundations that he devised for his social and economic empirical inquiries.

For Weber, concern with understanding and accounting for social and economic phenomena as the products of situated human agents was always paramount. His analyses, in both their form and substance, were oriented to reflect this fact explicitly, whatever the methodology required and whatever the epistemological status of the resulting analyses. Consistently with this orientation in the case of economics as a human science, Weber made plain his belief that 'the subject matter of economics is human action. Human action is a product of both natural and historical conditions' (1975a, p. 96). In their economic actions, individual agents act with self-consciousness, for they are 'endowed with the capacity and the will to take a deliberate attitude towards the world and to lend it *significance*' in a subjective sense (1949b, p. 81). In relation to his objective of understanding human phenomena as the products of individual action, Weber wrote that 'human behavior, "external" or "internal", exhibits both relational contexts (*Zusammenhänge*) and regularities in its course, as do all occurrences. Unique to human behavior, however, . . . are relationships and regularities whose course and result can be *intelligibly* interpreted' (1981, p. 151). These essentially human foundations for socio-economic science led Weber to pursue its objective of *Verstehen*, that is, of making intelligible and thereby understanding the causes of human events and phenomena. In his own words, a *verstehende Soziologie* 'is a science which attempts the interpretive understanding of social action in order thereby to arrive at a causal explanation of its course and effects' (1964, p. 88).

The themes taken up in this chapter begin in the next section with some introductory background to Weber's work, especially its situation with respect to other intellectual developments around him. Section 6.3 examines Weber's claim that as exact theoretical economics had adopted natural-scientistic methodological preconditions, it was induced on this basis to misrepresent human agents as *homo oeconomicus*. The main objective in section 6.4 will be to establish the deeper understanding of individual human agency that can be found in his writings. He was concerned that social economics should emphasize that its object phenomena originate in intentional, deliberated and meaningful human action. As agents in social and economic processes, human beings are also contained within and constrained by the structured situational complex comprising their many and varied social connections with others. It is the containing and shaping influence of such social situations that comprise the next stage of my analysis of Weber's ontological insights in section 6.5. The products of this situationally conditioned individual and collective agency are the objects of inquiry in the social economics. How Weber attempted to apply his understanding of situated human agency to the causally adequate explanation of these objects by means of the concepts of agent rationality and the ideal type is the subject of section 6.6. In the end, though, as the concluding section 6.7 reveals, the dependence on agent rationality as the fundamental methodological mediation raised a number of problems that Weber failed fully to address. In particular, he understated the subjectivist contingency of human agency and he fell short in understanding the nature and influence of the situations within which agents must operate. So, as I will conclude in this final section, Weber's seminal search for an objective methodological legitimacy consistent with maintaining an ontologically valid representation of social and economic phenomena remained incomplete. The endeavour was, nevertheless, enclosed within a rich set of subjectivist ontological and methodological insights.

6.2 Introduction to Max Weber

Among Weber's extensive written output are to be found the results of several interrelated research orientations. Perhaps the most obvious of these was his dominant interest as an historian and human scientist in providing a comparative historical sociology of past and present problems affecting economy and society (Kalberg, 1994). The empirical range of his inquiries in the human realm was wide, including economic, social, political and religious matters. Within this range, much of his emphasis was on those life-world agencies, structures and phenomena that had an economic origin and/or orientation. The phenomena of concern to Weber were those that originated in the intentional and meaningful actions of individual human beings. He well understood that these individual actions are driven by pluralistic motivations and are most frequently carried out in social concert with others and within a complex of situational conditions of all sorts. The elements of this total social and structural situation that agents assess as relevant under particular circumstances shape and direct their otherwise individually subjective action responses to problems confronted.

It was the unsettled state of metatheoretical matters that had surrounded him since his student days that gave Weber the impetus to take up inquiries that were intended to give a cogent and coherent foundation and legitimacy to his empirical research. In this endeavour, he set out to provide a critical assessment of the contemporary state of controversy and crisis that dominated the literature concerned with the methodology of history and the human sciences (see especially Weber, 1949c, 1975a, pp. 93ff and 1977). The resulting research in the crucial decade or so from 1903 onwards turned out to be an immediate reflection of the ongoing *Methodenstreit* around him (cf. Oakes, 1975, pp. 17ff). For the most part, the debates by this time were about the proper construction and role of theory in economics, and we have seen in a previous chapter how Carl Menger and Gustav Schmoller in particular were involved.[2] Weber's own background in economics was as a selective student and advocate of the 'Historical School'. In particular, archive material indicates that Weber gained his insight into and attitudes towards the study of the economic dimensions of the human lifeworld and society predominantly from his contacts with Karl Knies (1821–98) (Hennis, 1987).[3] It was into the unresolved metatheoretical controversy that Weber injected the neo-Kantian orientation and principles he had acquired from his studies of Rickert. He made it quite explicit that it was one of his intentions to 'test the value of his [Rickert's] ideas for the methodology of economics' (1975a, p. 213n. 9). As we are to see, this juxtaposition of historicist and neoKantian influences became a characteristic of Weber's fragmented metatheoretical inquiries during the first two decades of this century.

It may be suggested with some justification that Weber wrote his methodological pieces in spite of himself, to some extent, because he had an aversion to such investigations unless they were undertaken immediately to assist in addressing substantive issues (Oakes, 1975, pp. 12ff and 1977b, pp. 10ff). For Weber, metatheory was never to be a separable intellectual development. Methodology had to prove itself in practice: 'Only by laying bare and solving *substantive problems* can sciences be established and their methods developed. On the other hand, purely epistemological and methodological reflections have never played the crucial role in such developments' (1949c, p. 116). It was always an explication of existing practices in the human sciences: 'methodology can only bring us reflective understanding of the means which have *demonstrated* their value in practice by raising them to the level of explicit consciousness . . .' (Weber, 1949c, p. 115; cf. Hekman, 1983, p. 18; Giddens, 1987, p. 184). That his own contributions were exposited in a fragmented form and sometimes left in an incomplete state probably was, in part, a reflection of this lack of a separable commitment. There is evidence, though, that he did not consider these characteristics to be a deficiency in his work. Rather they were the result of a concern to avoid any impression that the metatheory of the human sciences could be ultimately defined in a manner that would render it universal and transhistorical. He believed that the ever-changing and dynamic nature of the phenomena with which these sciences must deal made this impossible (Oakes, 1975, pp. 8ff; 1977b, pp. 4 and 39n. 3).

What ultimately dominated Weber's critique of extant methodology in the human sciences was his concern to preserve the best aspects of the Historical School of economics while keeping in contact with acceptable facets of Neo-Kantianism. Historicists were realists and empiricists who sought 'the *descriptive* reproduction of reality in its full actuality' (1975a, p. 55). They either rejected theory altogether or, more importantly for Weber's critique, argued that it could only be exposed inductively by means of extensive 'factual' investigations. It was the Historicists' objective, for the most part, to espouse this combined descriptive and ultimate theoretical ideal for human science. In Weber's case, he declared that his focus most generally, and consistently with the broad intent of the empirical aspect of the Historicists' methodology, was on the 'type of social science' that comprises 'an *empirical science* of concrete *reality* (*Wirklichkeitswissenschaft*)' (1949b, p. 72). The consequent aim of individualizing scientific inquiry was 'the understanding of the characteristic uniqueness of the reality in which we move. We wish to understand on the one hand the relationships and the cultural significance of individual events in their contemporary manifestations and on the other the causes of their being historically *so* and not *otherwise*' (1949b, p. 72). To achieve this aim, some means would have to be found to realize a discursive understanding that transcends the infinitude of characteristics and causes that comprise the individual events and objects of empirical reality. In neo-Kantian style, Weber adopted as the basis for confining infinite reality within discursively manageable limits the principle that analysts must confine themselves to some finite portion of reality as their object. To achieve this, some selection criteria are required to separate those dimensions of what is observed that are somehow essential to the concerns of the analyst. Basically, the selected portion is that considered by analysts and their science to be of sufficient interest to warrant the effort of formalized inquiry. The crucial questions remained as to 'what are the criteria by which this segment is selected?' (1949b, p. 72) and how can we form concepts that '*approximate* a representation of the concrete actuality of reality by selecting and unifying those properties which we regard as "*characteristics*"'? (1975a, p. 57).

According to Weber, the critical error made by most Historicists was to assume that the only criterion for selection was that of inductively identified regularities of causal relationships that could be designated as laws. He cited Roscher, for instance, as one who had 'no doubt, in principle, that the relations between economic phenomena can be and should be conceived exclusively as a system of *laws*. "Causality" and "nomological regularity" are identical from his point of view. The first exists only in the form of the second' (1975a, p. 60). Weber identified a similar limitation in the work of his teacher Knies (1975a, pp. 96, 206f). The perception adopted by Roscher applied both to individual phenomena and to the temporal development of phenomena (cf. 1975a, pp. 73ff). The claim was, then, that 'the "laws" we are able to perceive in the infinitely manifold stream of events ... contain the scientifically "essential" aspect of reality' (1949b, p. 72). It followed that 'as soon as we have shown some causal relationship to be a "law"... a great number of similar cases order themselves under the formula thus attained' (1949b, pp. 72f). The result was that 'the ideal which all the sciences, including the cultural sciences, serve and towards which they should strive ... is a system of propositions from which reality can be "deduced"' (1949b, p. 73).

Most fundamentally, the crucial metatheoretical issue here was, with respect to the construction of knowledge in the historical–cultural sciences, how are we to 'conceive [of] the logical relation between law and reality in the course of history?' (1975a, p. 60). The historicist methodological premiss, as Weber read it, was that the required concept formation 'is to be acquired and slowly perfected through the observation of empirical regularities, the construction of hypotheses, and their verification, until finally a "completed" and *hence* deductive science emerges' (Weber, 1949b, p. 106; cf. Schön, 1987, p. 62). However, whatever may be the 'extraordinary *heuristic* value' of correlations and generalizations revealed by cumulative empirical observations, he believed that their discovery 'cannot be conceived [of] as the ultimate *goal* of any science: neither a "nomological" nor an "historical" science ...' (1975a, p. 63). The correlations and generalizations themselves cannot have any causal status, for they constitute at most the data that warrants scientific investigation (1975a, pp. 63f).

In claiming that universal theoretical results could be expected as the outcome of their inductive fact gathering, the Historicists made theory an objective, an end in itself, rather than the means to the end of empirical understanding that Weber believed it to be. The metatheory of the natural sciences that Weber rejected in its baldest forms as inappropriate for the human sciences depended upon the formulation of narrowly defined and universally valid concepts and laws of human conduct. It demanded attempts to elicit explanations of and predictions about human reality by logical deduction. Theory was used as a means in this case, but he believed the objective it pursued to be an impossible one. Weber's neo-Kantian epistemology told him that the no reality could be reached by processes of concept formation and logical deduction alone. Moreover, there remained the problem of how the Historicists expected to derive the abstract concepts of exact theory from the empirical concepts required to express their descriptive studies.

Some Historicists nevertheless remained inclined to believe in the veracity and merits of generalized theoretical constructs and in the 'classical–scholastic [realist] epistemology' upon which such theory had been grounded (1949b, p. 106). Weber's reading was that Historicists, as in the case of Roscher cited above, were of the opinion that 'it is the end and the goal of every science to order its data into a system of concepts...' (1949b, p. 106) characterized by relationships with the status of general laws. Thus, Roscher saw 'the basic scientific task of economics as the formulation of economic *laws*' (1975a, p. 81). Knies, too, claimed that 'whoever sees economics as a science cannot doubt that it is concerned with the laws of phenomena' (quoted by Weber, 1975a, p. 206). And, according to Weber, it was believed by the Historicists that this basic objective could be extended so that 'the concrete actuality of economic life is *in principle* analytically comprehensible in the form of laws. Of course, "innumerable" natural laws – but nevertheless *laws* – are necessary for an exhaustive analysis of economic life' (1975a, p. 85).

In Weber's view, the Historicists' realist approach to the nature and construction of theory also led them to misrepresent theory. For them, the 'function of concepts was assumed to be the *reproduction* of "objective" reality in the analyst's imagination' (Weber, 1949b, p. 106). He saw Roscher, for example, as believing that 'all concepts are ideational images of reality' (1975a, p. 70). As a Neo-Kantian, Weber could not accept this notion: 'When it is said that history seeks to understand the concrete *reality* of an "event" in its individuality causally, what is obviously not meant by this... is that it is to "reproduce" and explain causally the concrete *reality* of an event in the totality of its individual qualities' (1949c, p. 169; cf. 1975a, p. 255n. 54). His view was that the Historicists had stood the methodology on its head as a consequence of their realist epistemology. When it is understood, he argued, that 'concepts are primarily analytical instruments for the intellectual mastery of empirical data and can be only that...', then 'the relationship between concept and historical research is reversed...' (1949b, p. 106). So it was, he continued, that 'the goal of the Historical School... appears as logically impossible, [for] the concepts are not ends but are means to the end of understanding phenomena which are significant from concrete individual viewpoints' (1949b, p. 106).

The simple fact of the matter was that it was logically untenable for the Historicists to have it both ways in their intention to produce empirically realistic *and* nomological theoretical accounts of human phenomena by means of ever more observations and the discovery of empirical correlations of conceptual elements. The generalized, universal concepts required for exact theory were, by definition, empty of just the empirical content demanded in meeting the former characteristic. In Weber's words, 'the formation of "laws" – relational concepts of general validity – is identical with the progressive depletion of conceptual content through abstraction. The postulate of the "deduction" of the content of reality from general concepts . . . is logically absurd . . .' (1975a, p. 218n. 23, cf. pp. 64, 69f). It could be concluded, then, that 'it does not make sense to suppose that the ultimate *purpose* of concept formation in the historical sciences could be the deductive arrangement of concepts and laws – discovered by employing [empirical] correlations – under other concepts and laws of increasingly general validity and abstract content' (1975a, pp. 65f). For Weber, both Roscher's and Knies's endeavours to formulate an historical economics were classic cases in point that could not but be ultimately contradictory (1975a, pp. 79ff, 89f, 96ff).

In the end, then, Weber saw the need for an alternative metatheory for the empirical human sciences that avoided the fallacies and misrepresentations that he identified in the received work around him. In particular, the seemingly paradoxical demand was that concept formation and theory construction had to eschew claims to realism and yet must they be cognitive processes that facilitate an understanding of the perceived real phenomena of the human life-world. How Weber tried to meet this challenge will be taken up in the following sections.

6.3 The problem of human agency in economic theory

In the exact economic theory of Weber's era, methodological orthodoxy gave priority to formalist principles adopted from the natural sciences. This demanded that the human agent be represented strictly as *homo oeconomicus* in order to meet the regularity and reliability of response required to ensure logical tractability. Very early in his academic career, in a manuscript piece written in 1898, Weber saw the limited nature and status of such a *methodologically driven* choice of *homo oeconomicus* as the exclusive means of representing the human agent. His expression of these limitations contained a number of critical insights into the ontological problematic that economics must contend with if it is explicitly to recognize the human origins of its object phenomena.

> To ascertain the most elementary life conditions of economically mature human subjects it [abstract theory] proposes a *constructed* 'economic subject', in respect of which, by *contrast* with empirical man, it
> (a) *ignores* and treats as *non-existent* all those motives influencing empirical man which are *not* specifically *economic*, i.e. not specifically concerned with the fulfilment of material needs;
> (b) *assumes* as existent qualities that empirical man does not possess, or possesses only incompletely, i.e.
>   (i) complete *insight* into a given *situation* – economic omniscience;

(ii) unfailing choice of the *most appropriate means* for a given end –
absolute economic rationality;
(iii) complete dedication of one's powers to the purpose of acquiring
economic goods – 'untiring acquisitional drive'.
It thus postulates an *unrealistic* person, analogous to a mathematical
model. (Quoted by Hennis, 1987, p. 35; Weber's emphasis)

In this passage, Weber made reference to the restricted interpretation
of motivation, the presumed omniscience and the absolute rationality of
choice claimed for such a human agent. It was the concern about the
unreality of *homo oeconomicus* on these counts that would ultimately
resurface throughout his fragmented methodological writings.

The import of such an approach here is that the pseudo-ontology of
human agency in accounts of economic phenomena are *imposed* by the
dictates of the methodology. Arguments that comprised the legacy of
the nineteenth-century Classicals' theories were thus able to become,
Weber observed, 'apparently a matter of "deductions" from fundamental psychological motives' (1949b, p. 89).[4] He rejected the scientistic
notion that all social inquiry should pursue this exclusively hypothetico-
deductive methodology based on *assumptions* about human agents and
centred on the discovery of laws. A main point of this critique was that
such theory continued to give priority to the demands of methodology
at the expense of ontological integrity. The idea that human agency
could adequately be represented by an imposed *homo oeconomicus* was
an extreme example of such a perverse methodological strategy.

Weber had some stern and pointed criticism for the dominance of
naturalistic exact and abstract theory that had become so much a part
of economics. There was extant even in the Germanic literature a
well-established predilection for arguing causal conduct in relation to
economic phenomena in strictly nomological and generalized terms.
During the classical period, and subsequently in the efforts of Carl
Menger to revise the theory of value and distribution, the theory
espoused was of this type. In arriving at its logical form, analysts of this
persuasion 'take it to be a fact that we always have a direct awareness
of the structure of human actions in their reality. Hence – so they think
– science can make human behavior directly intelligible with axiomatic
evidentness and accordingly reveal its laws' (1949b, p. 87). The axiomatic element involved depended on the belief that 'the psychological
isolation of a specific "impulse", the acquisitive impulse, or of the
isolated study of a specific maxim of human conduct, the so-called
economic principle' could provide a sufficient foundation for deductive
accounts of economic phenomena. Such theory led to 'the fantastic
claim' that 'abstract theories of price, interest, rent, etc. ... can, by

ostensibly following the analogy of the physical science propositions, be validly applied to the derivation of quantitatively stated conclusions from given real premises, since given the ends, economic behavior with respect to means is unambiguously "determined"' (1949b, p. 88).

Nonetheless, Weber's critique of generalized theory centred on its *misrepresentation and misuse* rather than on any outright rejection of the need for it in human science (cf. Schumpeter, 1954b, p. 819). For instance, he held economic theorists such as Menger and Böhm-Bawerk in high regard, and whatever the limitations of their work in relation to his own views on theory, he was intent on identifying their merits (Weber, 1975b, p. 33 and n. 15). Formalized abstract theory had been misrepresented by aligning it with Aristotelian realism. Weber identified such realism within theoretical economics, and the implications of the approach were that 'the "true" content and essence of historical reality is portrayed in . . . theoretical constructs' or through the 'hypostatization of . . . "ideas" as real "forces" and as the "true" reality which operates behind the passage of events and which works itself out in history' (1949b, p. 94).

Those among the theoretical economists referred to by Weber as the 'extreme free-traders' even conceived of pure economic theory in a manner that combined misrepresentation with misuse as 'an adequate picture of "natural" reality, i.e. reality not distorted by human stupidity, and they proceeded to set it up as a moral imperative – as a valid normative ideal . . .' (1949d, p. 44). Misuse in particular, then, arose in drawing any unqualified conclusions concerning the real economy, actual or potential, from the immediate application of economic theory in its abstract and exact form.

A further problem was in the use of theoretical constructs 'as a procrustean bed into which history is to be forced', where history includes all past economic events and phenomena (1949b, p. 94). Any attempt to undertake 'an *exhaustive* causal investigation of any concrete phenomenon in its full reality is not only practically impossible, but simply an absurdity' (1949b, p. 78: translation modified, cf. 1973a, p. 178). Weber was thus led strongly to express what he regarded as 'the meaninglessness of the idea which prevails occasionally even among historians, namely, that the goal of the cultural sciences . . . is to construct a closed system of concepts, in which reality is synthesized in some sort of *permanently* and *universally* valid classification and from which it can again be deduced' (1949b, p. 84).

Above all, though, what this theoretical approach failed to grasp was that because of their human origins, the phenomena of the human sciences could and should be understood differently. Among the reasons given by Weber as to why such a nomothetic view of human science consistent with naturalistic principles was impossible was an ontological one. He stated quite explicitly that unlike the natural realm in which it was the '*quantitative* and exact aspects' of empirical objects that were to be grasped in explanations, it is the more open-ended '*qualitative* aspect of phenomena [that] concerns us in the social sciences' (1949b, p. 74). However, his understanding was that the nomological view of science was intent upon 'the most radical reduction possible: the qualitative differences of concrete reality are reduced to precisely measurable quantities' (1975a, p. 56). The crucial and identifying characteristic of inquiries in the human sciences was that 'we are concerned with psychological and intellectual (*geistig*) phenomena the empathetic understanding of which is naturally a problem of a specifically different type from those which the schemes of the exact natural sciences in general can or seek to solve' (1949b, p. 74). However, it is important in the present context to recognize that this ontological distinction was not taken by Weber to be the ultimately vital point of departure in the search for an independent metatheory for the human sciences. He remained true to his neo-Kantian premises in this respect and sought explicitly to avoid the temptation to isolate the human sciences exclusively on grounds that their objects are psychological in its broadest sense and thus existentially distinctive. This originating facet of the objects of human sciences remained an important fact of life, but not one that should have a determining impact on the metatheoretical problematic of constituting the form of these sciences.

6.4 The individual human agent and rationality

In his approach to understanding the intelligible manifestations of human action that are the objects of the social and economic sciences, Weber was nonetheless quite explicit about the *subjectivist* and *individualist* ontology that he adopted. He recognized that 'action in the sense of a subjectively understandable orientation of behaviour exists only as the behaviour of one or more *individual* human beings', for in all social inquiry, 'the object of cognition is the subjective meaning-complex of action' (1964, p. 101). And, while for certain analytical purposes, it may be 'convenient or even indispensable to treat social collectivities, such as states, associations, business corporations, foundations, as if they were individual persons', such an approach could never provide adequate causal understanding of the phenomena with which they are involved. The subjective interpretation of such classes of actions required that they be 'treated as *solely* the resultants and modes of organization of the particular acts of individual persons, since these alone can be treated as agents in a course of subjectively understandable action' (1964, p. 101).

Weber gave every indication that he was well aware of the existential complexity of human agents as individuals. Nonetheless, he had a very strong belief that human agents should be understood as being at least notionally and intentionally rational in a practical and instrumental sense. That is, they are universally capable of action that is the result of personal 'best practice' reasoning applied to perceived circumstances under the direction of self-interest. In problematic situations, they seek to do their best in selecting and applying the most appropriate means to the realization of their preferred ends and goals. Practical rationality demands the 'methodical attainment of a definitely given and practical end by means of an increasingly precise calculation of adequate means' (Weber quoted by Sadri, 1982, p. 622).

Rational action is, as Weber realized, a highly subjective procedure, dependent upon expectations, plans, situational adaptations, deliberations, opinions, orientations, and a host of other human contingencies. There can be no assurance, therefore, that any action will be objectively rational in the absolute sense that it achieves any end optimally or maximally in accordance with the complete, technically defined means and circumstances (cf. Brubaker, 1984, pp. 49ff).

The pursuit of calculated self-interest within particular problematic circumstances, depends upon the assumption that agents can know and have the necessary capacities to adapt their conduct to the requirements of the problems that they choose to confront. That is, active agents must be presumed to have the required intellectual capacities, the necessary information and the accurate foresight to turn the self-interest into a realized outcome by way of reasoned deliberation. As Weber saw the decision process involved, 'the acting person . . ., insofar as he acts rationally', weighs up:

the 'conditions' of the future development which interests him, which conditions are 'external' to him and are objectively given as far as his knowledge of reality goes. He mentally rearranges into a causal complex the various 'possible modes' of his own conduct and the consequences which these could be *expected* to have in connection with the 'external' conditions. He does this in order to decide, in accordance with the (mentally) disclosed 'possible' results, in favour of one or another mode of action as the one appropriate to his 'goal'. (1949c, p. 165)

This passage from 1905, quite early in Weber's methodological inquiries, contained a crucial appreciation of the necessary deliberation and decision processes of agents. In it, he showed an awareness that human action has a future orientation, that agents need to rely on expectations, that they are required to formulate alternative anticipated scenarios about the results of their actions and that they must irrevocably choose only one such scenario to pursue. Unfortunately, these revelations and their profound importance for the idea of agent rationality were never developed more fully in his subsequent work.

From time to time, Weber did make some reference to the particular problem of understanding the contingency of action attributable to human free-will. His primary concern, though, was to dispel the idea that free-will leads to agents behaving 'irrationally', thus rendering their observed conduct in particular situations incoherent. He believed that from the subjective perspective, we as agents 'associate the highest measure of an empirical "feeling of freedom" with those actions which we are conscious of performing rationally – i.e., *in the absence of physical and psychic "coercion", emotional "affects" and "accidental" disturbances of the clarity of judgement*, in which we pursue a clearly perceived end by "means" which are most adequate in accordance with the extent of our knowledge, i.e. in accordance with empirical rules' (1949c, pp. 124f; cf. 1975a, pp. 96, 191f). But at the same time, agents manifest in their actions and artefacts a multiple of innate and cumulatively conditioned psychic and cognitive processes and motivational influences. They carry highly variable inherited and learned characteristics, comprising, for example, 'certain sociologically relevant qualities and drives, . . . the capacity for rational orientation of action in general, . . . or certain other specifiable intellectual qualities in particular' (1981, p. 153).

Whatever their characteristics and cognitive capacities, the contingency of agents' conduct is compounded by the fact that they freely adopt one or more motives as the directing force behind their actions. A motive was defined by Weber as 'a complex of subjective meaning which seems to the actor himself or to the observer an adequate ground for the conduct in question' (1964, pp. 98f). In understanding human phenomena, then, he argued that we must confront 'an extremely heterogeneous and highly concrete structure of psychic motives and influences' (1949b, p. 89). More directly put, as regards agents' conduct, 'behavior that is identical in its external course and result can be based on the most varied constellations of motives, and the most plausible motive may not be the one that really came into play' (1981, p. 151). Indeed, 'the "conscious motives" may well, even to the actor himself, conceal the various "motives" and "repressions" that constitute the real driving force of his action' (1964, p. 97). Moreover, 'actors in any given situation are often subject to opposing and conflicting impulses . . .', a condition that renders the operational balance between them adopted by the agents to be crucial in understanding their actions (1964, p. 97). And, as regards agents' interpretation of meaning, 'identical relationships of meaning are not linked to identical operative "psychic" constellations, although it is certain that differences in one can be influenced by differences in the other' (1981, p. 153; cf. 1964, p. 97).

In an endeavour to sharpen the conceptual representation of subjectively motivated, goal-directed agent action, Weber introduced four specific types of rationality. Each was classified 'according to its mode of orientation' towards its essential objectives (1964, p. 115). All were of equal potential status and may be present to some degree in any observed action. First, the form of action designated *zweckrational* was that which is directed at 'a system of discrete individual ends' through 'expectations as to the behaviour of objects in the external situation and of other human individuals, making use of these expectations as "conditions" or "means" for the successful attainment of the actor's own rationally chosen ends' (1964, p. 115). That is, it is action that is rational by virtue of its successful achievement of one or more preconceived ends by what agents presume to be the correct choice of the means to do so. Secondly, conduct that is rationally oriented 'to an absolute value of some ethical, aesthetic, religious, or other form of behaviour, entirely for its own sake and independently of any prospects of external success' was called *wertrational*. A third potential orientation of action was that with an *affectual* orientation, especially linked to the emotions, and directed by 'the specific affects and states of feeling of the actor'. The fourth orientation was that of *tradition* 'through the habituation of long practice' (1964, p. 115).

Now, of these categories of agent action, the last two, affectual and traditional, stand 'very close to the borderline of what can justifiably be called meaningfully oriented action, and indeed [are] often on the other side [of it]' (1964, p. 116). The type of concerns, and the emotional or habitual nature of the conduct involved, will most often mean that agents use a minimum of rational deliberation, calculation, planning and self-consciousness in designing their actions (1964, p. 117). This renders their potential role in understanding scientifically relevant agency minimal when considered in isolation. In *wertrational* action, the agents do deliberate and plan, and the action is self-consciously meaningful, and carried out in order to satisfy, some absolute value(s) they hold in each case (1964, p. 116). In such action, 'the more uncon-

ditionally the actor devotes himself to this value for its own sake, ...
the less he is influenced by considerations of the consequences of his
action' (1964, p. 117). Whatever additional insights these categories of
conduct might bring, in understanding the phenomena of concern to
the social sciences, especially those of concern to social economics, by
far the most significant type of action is that called *zweckrational*. It
was the category that provided Weber with the archetype of goal-
directed human agency with which economics is concerned, at least as
a matter of first principle: 'Action is rationally oriented to a system of
discrete individual ends when the end, the means, and the secondary
results are all rationally taken into account and weighed' (1964, p. 117).
And, he continued with a definition of *economically rational action* as
that which is 'rationally oriented, by deliberate planning, to economic
ends' comprising 'the satisfaction of a desire for "utilities"' (1964,
p. 158). The implication may then be that the other categories of action
cited above, those bringing affectual, traditional and value criteria to
bear on otherwise *zweckrational* action, have the potential to complicate
and divert the agents' operationally rational intentions and capacities.

Weber believed that in the cases of volitional, self-conscious and
purposeful action in response to particular problem circumstances that
are of concern to social economics, 'the goal, the "motive", the
"maxims" of the actor' are manifested in the means applied. This
was because 'all strictly teleologically (purposefully) occurring actions
involve applications of empirical rules, which tell what the appropriate
"means" to ends are ...' (1949c, p. 125; cf. 1981, p. 151). He reasoned
in this respect that 'even the empirically "free" actor – i.e., who acts
on the basis of his *deliberations* – is teleologically bound by the means
for the attainment of his ends, means which, varying with the circumstances of the objective situation, are nonequivalent and knowable'
(1975a, p. 193). Weber's thesis was that 'the immediately "most understandable kind" of meaning structure of an action' is action that is
'subjectively, rigorously, and rationally oriented toward means that are
(subjectively) held to be unequivocally adequate for the attainment of
(subjective) unequivocally and clearly comprehended ends' (1981,
p. 154). And, when we understand human action as 'determined by
clearly conscious and intended "ends" and a clear knowledge of the
"means" required for these "ends"', it is then 'incontestable that
the degree of "self-evidence" attained ... is unique' (1975a, p. 186).
This analytical self-evidence is attributable to the circumstance that 'the
relation between "means" and "ends" is intrinsically accessible to a
rational *causal account which produces generalizations*, generalizations
that have the property of "nomological regularity"' (1975a, p. 186). In

this respect, Weber adhered explicitly to his notion that the teleological nature of such ends and means accounts of human conduct comprise regularized causal explanations (1975a, pp. 187, 191 and 274n. 93).

As economic examples, Weber cited 'the manufacturer in the competitive struggle' and 'the broker on the stock exchange'. In the operations of either agent, existential notions of the freedom of will are of little concern or interest, for 'he has the choice between economic destruction and the pursuit of very specific maxims of economic conduct' (1975a, p. 193). For an agent confronted with a market situation of competitive price determination, 'the "pure" expression of this situation leaves the individual trapped within the market a choice between only the following two alternatives: "teleological" accommodation to the "market" or economic ruin' (1975a, p. 202). It follows that in any such situation, if the agents chose not to act rationally in accordance with the known 'maxims', one possible explanation might be that they lacked the freedom of will that allows *Zweckrationalität* in their process of choice. Weber concluded consequently that 'every purely rational interpretation of a concrete historical process . . . *presupposes* the existence of "freedom of the will" . . .', including 'the "laws" of economic theory' (1975a, p. 194).

The suggestion of a teleological reliability of agents' conduct in these claims was, then, tempered by a recognition that their actions are inevitably complicated to varying degrees by affectual, traditional and value oriented diversions and other limitations that render them 'irrational', or at least less than perfectly rational (1949c, p. 125; 1964, pp. 92, 96). As further sources of such irrationality, Weber made reference to 'where either the "objectively" correct conditions of the instrumentally rational action had been unheeded or, what is different, the subjective instrumentally rational considerations of the actor had been largely ruled out (a stock market panic, for example) . . .' (1981, p. 154). Such irrationality was ontologically argued in terms of the actual form that human actions can be observed to take. Empirical conduct by agents has, effectively, a penumbra of complexity around the logic of its rational core because 'irrational "prejudices", errors in thinking and factual errors', as well as '"temperament", "moods" and "affects"', influence what they decide to do (1949c, p. 125; cf. 1964, p. 112). Thus, whatever may be the presumed rationality applied by agents in their decision processes, the realized outcomes will most often deviate from those intended or expected ex ante. It may then be possible for an observer, or the agents themselves, retrospectively to identify what alternative decision would have been more completely 'successful' (1949c, p. 165).

With phenomena attributable to conduct by agents that is considered to be irrational, Weber considered it 'necessary, above all, to determine how the . . . limiting case of pure instrumental and correct rationality *would have* proceeded'. For 'only when this is determined . . . can the course of action be causally attributed to both objectively as well as subjectively "irrational" components . . .' that deviate from the ideal (1981, p. 154). The effect was that when observed actions to be understood do not conform to the tenets of rationality, when they are 'irrational' in this sense, he took them to be divergent from the core rational course in ways that can be made explicit. This was a claim that had a significant methodological import for him and it will receive more attention below.

6.5 Human agents *in situ*

For Weber, the *individual and always subjective* nature of action could be more fully understood if the agents concerned were represented as specifically situated in, and operating through, a prestructured environment that surrounds them and influences and shapes their conduct (cf. Kalberg, 1994, pp. 30ff). He thought of human agency as having a definite situational orientation and as thereby conditioned and directed: 'action, for the interpretive sciences, is to a very considerable degree meaningfully related to the "outer world" . . .', be that world of social or physical constitution (1981, p. 153). *In situ*, then, agents' otherwise internally motivated and directed actions are conditioned by the subjective meanings they attribute to the relevant elements of their situations. The potential meanings include perception as constraints on and as providing facilities and opportunities for their actions. The volitional or coerced conditioning they experience contains and regularizes the patterns of their actions.

Regularities of agents' actions were accepted by Weber as, in part at least, the consequence of the fact that they choose or are required to act in and through given structured and functionally congenial situations in contending with problems or in engaging in activities of their lifeworld (cf. Hekman, 1983). He wrote that volitional regularities of conduct may be said to be 'determined by the exploitation of the opportunities of his situation [that are] in the self interest of the actor', if and in so far as the 'probability of its empirical performance is determined by the purely functionally rational [*zweckrational*] orientation of the actors to similar ulterior expectations' (1964, p. 121: translation modified, cf. 1973a, p. 571). In such situations, he went on, the regularity of action depends entirely on the requirement that it is 'in the nature of the case best adapted to the normal interests of the actors as they themselves are aware of them' (1964, p. 122). For instance, 'action which is ... primarily economic, is orientated to knowledge of the relative scarcity of certain available means to want satisfaction, in relation to the actor's state of needs and to the present and probable action of others, in so far as the latter affects the same resources' (1964, p. 126n. 50).

The most prominent situational influences on agents in Weber's analyses were social ones involving the shaping of their actions in relation to their interdependence with others. Of basic importance was the concept of the 'social relationship' as one that comprised 'the behaviour of a plurality of actors in so far as, in its meaningful content, the action of each takes account of that of the others and is oriented in these terms' (1964, p. 118). The notion of social action (*Gemeinschaftshandeln*) that manifests these relationships was thus defined as 'human action [that] is subjectively related in its *meaning* ... [to] the actual or anticipated potential behavior of other individuals' (1981, pp. 159f). It 'may be oriented to the past, present, or expected future behaviour of others' (1964, p. 112). Much relevant individual action comprises conduct that '(1) in terms of the subjectively intended meaning of the actor, is related to the *behavior of others*, (2) is *codetermined* in its course through this relatedness, and thus (3) can be intelligibly *explained* in terms of this (subjectively) intended meaning' (1981, p. 152). Included were 'concepts of collective entities which ... have a meaning in the minds of individual persons, partly as of something actually existing, partly as something with normative authority'. Socialized agents accept the entities that constitute their situations and 'in part orient their action to them, and in this role such ideas have a powerful, often decisive, causal influence on the course of action of real individuals' (1964, p. 102, cf. p. 93; and cf. 1949b, pp. 88f; 1975a, p. 96). In this vein, Weber at one point drew attention to 'the fact that orientation to the situation in terms of the pure self-interest of the individual and of the others to whom he is related can bring about results that are very similar to those which an authoritarian agency, very often in vain, has attempted to obtain by coercion ...' (1964, pp. 122f).

Although social action 'is not the only kind of action significant for sociological causal explanation, ... it is the primary object of an "interpretive" sociology' (1981, p. 159; cf. 1964, p. 88). Weber emphasised especially that 'an important (though not indispensable) normal component of social action is its meaningful orientation to the *expectations* of certain behavior on the part of others and, in accordance with that, orientation to the (*subjectively*) assessed probabilities (*Chancen*) for the success of one's own action' (1981, p. 159; cf. 1964, p. 118). These expectations as between agents depend on their conduct being mutually oriented to some relevant extent, with the subjectively meaningful content of the relationship and action nevertheless remaining particular to each agent (1964, pp. 118f). Where a social relationship carries a constancy of meaningful content, it is 'capable of formulation in terms of maxims which the parties concerned expect to be adhered to by their partners, on the average and approximately' (1964, p. 120).

As a means of mitigating the degree of chance involved in the reliance on others, agents enter into tacit or explicit, formal or informal, understandings or agreements with them. In these circumstances, the agent 'believes that he has reason to expect compliance with the "agreement", according to the meaning which he himself attributes to it' (1981, p. 160). Such structured relationships were, for Weber, constructed around rules of various forms and purposes. Rules will be imbedded in the given situations in and through which agents normally carry on their life-world activities. Most rules involve the agents in mutual connections and communications with one or more others: they are then 'social rules' in his terminology (1977, pp. 98ff, 108ff).

Weber dealt at some length with what he called *legitimate orders* as the loci of formalized social relationships organized according to rules, maxims and conditions (1964, pp. 124ff). Within the situations confronted by agents, they recognize these orders as valid in the sense that they are prepared, to varying degrees, volitionally to conform to them (1977, pp. 129ff). He referred to such a social relationship as *associative* where 'the orientation of social action within it rests on a rationally motivated adjustment of interests or a similar motivated agreement, whether the basis of rational judgement be absolute values or reasons of expediency' (1964, p. 136). Self-interest remains the basis for such associations, but with 'agreement as to a long-run course of action oriented purely to the promotion of specific ulterior interests, economic or other, of its members' (1964, p. 136). However, in spite of the structured conditions within and through which agents act, there can be no guarantee that their responses will be fully and always in accordance with the rational demands of those conditions. Weber's idea was that some probability of expected response would need to be calculated *ad hoc* by those who require such information in deliberating on their own actions. Any formalized social relationship will be built around its meaning to the participants involved and 'consists exclusively in the fact that there has existed, exists, or will exist a probability of action in some definite way appropriate to this meaning'. Acceptance by analysts of the *ad hoc* nature of such mutual beliefs was important to Weber in order to 'avoid the "reification" of these concepts' (1964, p. 118).

Weber made explicit reference to the *functional association (Zweckverein)* as a key form of rule-based agent interdependence.[5] Such an organization involves 'associational action wherein *all* participants have rationally *agreed* on an order defining the purpose and the methods of their joint action' (1981, p. 163, cf. p. 174). The association of which they are part will have '(1) agreement on *general* rules and (2) a *staff* of its own' (1981, p. 164). Associations of this type have an ongoing existence in the sense that their continuity is not tied to particular individuals as participants: 'an association can be regarded as a continuing structure despite the turnover of members' (1981, p. 174). Weber wrote of social relationships that are closed, at least to the extent of allowing continuing membership only to the extent that member agents act in accordance with rules, as constituting what was aptly called a *corporate group*. Such groups have an order that 'is enforced by the action of specific individuals whose regular function this is, of a chief or "head" and usually also an administrative staff' (1964, pp. 145f). That is, these organizations carry out *corporate actions* either through the conduct of their executive heads and/or administrative staffs, or through the conduct of their members as directed by the administrators. There should be 'a probability that certain persons will act in such a way as to tend to carry out the order governing the group; that is, that persons are present who can be counted on to act in this way whenever the occasion arises' (1964, p. 146, cf. pp. 148f).

Weber's analyses outlined in this and the previous section suggest that he was intent upon identifying whatever regularity may be attributed to the deliberated actions of human agents. He was clearly aware that as subjective individuals, human agents are existentially capable of a multitude of calculated responses to problem situations. Of most concern to social scientists, however, are those categories of decision-making that occur in well-defined social situations. The situations act by means of facilitation and containment to shape the resulting actions in ways that render them more rational and regular than might otherwise be expected. How Weber envisaged representing these regularized categories of human agency in discursive argument is critically examined in the next section.

6.6 Ontology, rationality and ideal types

In the light of the complex exigencies of situated human agency elicited above, a pressing methodological dilemma emerged for Weber to contend with. It was his intention to orient his mainline of research towards understanding and explaining causally the generation of empirically observed human phenomena. At the same time he recognized that 'an *infinity* of causal factors have conditioned the occurrence of the individual "event" and that absolutely all of those individual causal factors were indispensable for the occurrence of the effect in its concrete form' (1949c, p. 169). Faced with this fact, social scientists are, nevertheless, to seek a tractable and coherent causal account of their objects of inquiry. In order to do so, both the manifested object and its claimed causal origins must be simplified. As he conceded, the required 'process of *abstraction* . . . proceeds through the analysis and mental isolation of the components of the directly given data – which are to be taken as a complex of possible causal relations – and should culminate in a synthesis of the "real" causal complex' (1949c, p. 173). It involves the 'production of . . . "imaginative constructs" by the disregarding of one or more of those elements of "reality" which are actually present, and by the mental construction of a course of events which is altered through modification in one or more "conditions"'. The result 'transforms the given "reality" into a "mental construct" . . .' (1949c, p. 173).

Clearly, such a methodology demands that some defensible means of selecting the defining essentials of the object and its causal elements from the complex of immediate reality must be found. Weber posited the principle that the analysis which 'the finite human mind can conduct rests on the tacit assumption that only a finite portion of this reality constitutes that object of scientific investigation . . .' (1949b, p. 72; cf. pp. 76, 78). That is, 'because of the logical impossibility of an *exhaustive* reproduction of even a limited aspect of reality', claims to know concrete reality can only mean 'knowledge of those aspects of reality which we regard as *essential* because of their individual *peculiarities*' (1975a, p. 57). In the case of the social sciences, he opened the way by expressing the belief that 'it is possible in the field of social action to observe certain empirical uniformities. Certain types, that is, of action which correspond to a typically appropriate subjective meaning attributable to the same actors, are found to be wide-spread, being frequently repeated by the same individual or simultaneously performed by many different ones' (1964, p. 120). The source of such regularity was to be found in a repeated or uniform responses by otherwise subjective and contingent agents to particular categories of goals, conditions and situations, responses that have thus become established and accepted practices under particular circumstances. Arguably, these regularized categories of human phenomena are the ones of most concern to social scientific inquiry. It was by means of the combination of agent rationality and the ideal type that Weber endeavoured discursively to represent situated human agency as the means of accounting for these phenomena (cf. Burger, 1976, pp. 115ff; Hekman, 1983, pp. 18ff; and Kalberg, 1994, pp. 84ff).

As he put it, the ideal type is the metatheoretical device which although 'it *is* no "hypothesis"' ... it offers guidance to the construction of hypotheses' and although 'it is not a *description* of reality ... it aims to give unambiguous means of expression to such a description' (1949b, p. 90). It served to ensure that 'in *all* cases, rational or irrational, socio-logical analysis both abstracts from reality and at the same time helps us to understand it ...' (1964, p. 110). It does so primarily because the origin of the ideal type itself is the ontology of empirical reality as it is perceived by a particular analyst. Properly derived ideal types are never the result of an analyst's isolated imagination. They are always ontologically specific and must be inductively distilled from observations by means of what Weber called 'idealizing abstraction' or 'exaggerating abstraction', the details of which are peculiar to the category of phenomenon and the interest orientations of the analyst. In this respect;

an ideal type is formed by one-sided *accentuation* of one or more points of view and by the synthesis of a great many diffuse, discrete, more or less present and occasionally absent *concrete individual* phenomena, which are arranged according to those one-sidedly emphasized viewpoints into a unified *analytical* construct. In its conceptual purity, this mental construct cannot be found empirically anywhere in reality. (1949b, p. 90)

Now although he was clear that neither agent rationality nor ideal types were intended to have any observable empirical manifestation, there was some ambivalence about their epistemological status. Weber's neo-Kantian predilections inclined him towards the perception that such concepts were non-real and need have no ontological connections in order to be valid and useful in explanatory analyses. What is to be emphasized here by way of clarification, though, is that there is a distinction to be drawn between such a claim about epistemological isolation from reality and the alternative claim that the concepts have no independent existential status. The latter allows ideal types explicitly to retain their ontological origins and links, a claim that I consider essential for any interpretation of Weber that is to make sense of his methodology. For as we have seen already, his understanding of the essentials of human agency was expressed in ontologically grounded terms. Moreover, as I am about to elicit, in some passages he explicitly envisaged deriving ideal types directly from observed samples of particular categories of phenomena. On these bases, he is better interpreted as having focused on the unreality of ideal types as an empirical rather than an ontological matter. That is, although the ideal type was intended as 'a conceptual construct (*Gedankenbild*) which is neither historical reality nor even the "true" reality' (1949b, p. 93), the causal explanations of empirical phenomena in which it is used 'represent a series of *conceptually* constructed events, which, in "ideal purity", are seldom, or even not at all, to be found in the historical reality of any particular time' (1975b, p. 34). As mental constructs, then, although they are cognitively ordered reflections of selected elements of actually perceived reality, rationality and the ideal type remained empirically non-real and could never be expected to be observed as pure forms within that reality (1964, p. 110).

Nonetheless, Weber expressed the idea that 'in the sociological analysis of understandable relationships, rationally interpretable behavior very often constitutes the most appropriate "ideal type": sociology begins, as does history, by interpreting "pragmatically", that is, on the basis of rationally understandable contexts of action' (1981, p. 152). And, for example, he recalled that 'social economics, ... in its rational construction of "economic man", proceeds in this way' (1981, p. 152). He also observed that 'economic theory is an axiomatic discipline ... [which] makes certain assumptions which scarcely ever correspond completely with reality but which approximate it in various degrees and asks: how would men act under these assumed conditions, if their actions were entirely rational? It assumes the dominance of pure economic interests and precludes the operation of political or other non-economic considerations' (1949d, pp. 43f; cf. 1964, pp. 96, 110f and 1975b, p. 32). So it was that now in the example of abstract economic theory, with its '"ideal" constructions of rigorous and errorless rational conduct' (1949d, p. 42), that the realist Weber found a conceptual construction that 'offers us an ideal picture of events on the commodity-market under conditions of a society organized on the principles of an exchange economy, free competition and rigorously rational conduct.... Substantively, this construct in itself is like a *utopia* which has been arrived at by the analytical accentuation of certain elements of reality' (1949b, pp. 89f). His return to *homo oeconomicus* in this context was more conciliatory now that its form had some specific status in relation to the reality of a total economic agent. Rather than being imposed by assumption, as an ideal type it was introduced in a controlled manner as part of an ontologically grounded methodology.

6.7 Conclusion: outstanding problems with agent rationality

The challenge for social science in applying an ideal–typical methodology was, according to Weber, to build the discursive causal account of an empirical phenomenon as it is actually perceived by the analyst. Such an account was to be constructed around a core model of rational ideal type categories, with the intention of making explicit the irrational dimensions of the phenomenon (1964, p. 92). As he put it, 'within the domain of *real* events, rational "evaluation" functions *exclusively* as an hypothesis or as an idealtypical construct. We compare the actual action with the action which is, from a "teleological" point of view and on the basis of general causal generalizations, rational' (1975a, p. 188). Most generally, he noted, having worked up an idealized scenario for any empirical human event in terms of the purely rational actions of agents, 'it is possible to compare this with the actual course of action and to arrive at a causal explanation of the observed deviations, which will be attributed to such factors as misinformation, strategical errors, logical fallacies, personal temperament [of the agents] . . .' (1964, p. 111; cf. 1949b, pp. 90ff; 1949d, p. 43; and 1964, p. 111). The ideal type, therefore, has 'the significance of a purely ideal *limiting* concept with which the real situation or action is *compared* and surveyed for the explication of certain of its significant components' (1949b, p. 93). It was Weber's argument that 'for the purposes of causal *attribution* [*Zurechnung*] of empirical events, we need the rational, empirical–technical and logical constructions, which help us to answer the question as to what a behavior pattern or thought pattern . . . would be like if it possessed completely rational, empirical and logical "correctness" and "consistency"' (1949d, p. 42: translation modified, cf. 1973a, pp. 534f).

Plausible though this methodology sounds, Weber's actual application of the notions of rationality and the ideal type in pursuit of discursively argued *Verstehen* involved him in two fundamental difficulties. One was that he failed to explore fully the notion of agent rationality itself, even though we have seen that he appreciated, albeit more or less in passing, some of the crucial exigencies involved. In particular, he referred to the fact that in the absence of agents' omniscience, it was necessary to make the dubious claim that they successfully apply reason in circumstances of uncertainty by means of expectations. So, even though he accepted the empirically unrealistic status of rationality, the problems with its conceptualization were much more deep seated in ontology than he chose to explicate. The other difficulty emerged in the comparisons with reality required in order to expose and 'add back' the irrational dimensions to the ideal rational constructs. If taken too literally, the comparisons required that he contradict his own position that no immediate intellectual grasp of reality is possible.

With respect to the ontology of agent rationality itself, there exist two crucial shortfalls in Weber's seminal efforts. First, his subjectivism and individualism did not extend to a sufficient recognition of the sources and degree of the contingency that potentially characterizes human action and renders it less than fully rational. It is in the fundamental and yet complex life-world deliberations and decision-making by active agents that give direction to their future-oriented actions that this contingency is most prominent. Subjectively rational processes directed at choosing means and realizing preferred ends and goals find agents located between an irrevocable past that can be known and a perfidious future that cannot. From the past they bring certain cognitive abilities, together with accumulated knowledge and experience. Agents' capacities, motivations and goals are all intimately related to their accumulated biographical experiences up to the present day. Such experiences are the products of what they have chosen to take from the multidimensional situations through which they have moved over time. At root in these processes, the particular inherited and learned capacities and beliefs of the agents involved are integrated with their specific motivations and intentions with respect to the problem about which they are currently deliberating. The information required in such deliberations is only to be had at a cost and agents must make decisions about acquisition for better or for worse. The need for additional information recognized *ex post* cannot be corrected for. At the very least, any understanding of the current processes should pay due regard to the need for agents to form expectations and to construct *ex ante* potential future scenarios between which some unique choice must be made. These are substitutes for the non-existent knowledge of the future as inputs to the decision process.

Secondly, there are issues concerning the constitution of inherited contemporary situations in which agents find themselves, and how they draw on and are conditioned by them, that require more detailed treatment than Weber allowed himself to pursue. The natural environment, physical–technical structures, social organizations and institutions all have a potential place among the many and varied dimensions of agents' situations. Weber was well aware of the place of such situational characteristics in social life and wrote much about various forms of human association. Nonetheless, the point remains that his treatment gave more emphasis to the collective dimensions of such associations rather than to their role in regularizing the conduct of individual subjective agents. Of particular concern in economic decision-making are the physical–technical structures of production, the organizations of production and distribution, such as firms and corporations, and the economically oriented institutions of the state. By means of judgements of relevance and priority, agents whose general objective is successfully to realize their plans and goals are inclined to conform to situational demands. Such demands comprise requirements that contain and constrain what agents volitionally choose to do in pursuit of their individual objectives. But, at the same time, situations include channels that mitigate difficulties and facilitate rational goal-directed and means-sensitive actions. Particular and empirically recurring categories of life-world problems may then be argued as confronted by agents in circumstances and situations that have a common core of relevant structural and operational characteristics at any point in time. The otherwise contingent actions of individual agents are thereby shaped and directed in particular ways that potentially have definite and specific shared ideal--typical qualities. By means of these regularities, analysts may give their representations some measure of discursive coherence.

With respect to the other difficulty identified above as involving comparisons between the rational ideal and irrational reality, Weber came close to contradicting his own position that all claims to knowledge of reality must be mediated by conceptual constructs. Immediate knowledge of reality as it exists was beyond the capacities of human observers. Indeed, he noted that 'if *this* type of knowledge were accessible to the finite mind of man, abstract theory would have no cognitive value whatsoever' (1949b, p. 88). He referred to the 'meaningless infinity of the world process ... on which *human beings* confer meaning and significance' (1949b, p. 81) and emphasized the analytical impossibility of any complete reproduction of even a limited aspect of observed reality. So, because of the inherent infinity of object characteristics, the knowledge of the so-called 'reality' against which the comparison must be made is necessarily itself already a selective conceptual construction. The result must be that Weber's recommended comparison was between one conceptual construction and another. Such an exercise cannot, therefore, provide any immediate empirical contact, or establish any confirmation or refutation, for the knowledge revealed by the ideal type in the manner that he suggested. The only apparent alternative was to accept that it is the personal, albeit socialized cognition and values of the analyst upon which constructing the compared 'reality' depends, perhaps defended on conventionalist grounds. Under these circumstances, *Verstehen* involves results that are necessarily tainted with relativism and must fail any test of 'objectivity'.[6]

Weber's investigations into the ontology of situated human agency and its methodological implications should be accepted for what they are: seminal endeavours to found social–economic inquiry on bases that avoided the dilemmas of naturalist formalism and historicist relativism. He was determined to design and sustain theoretical premises as the foundation for empirical understanding and explanation, but in a form that was consistent with the subjectivist and individualist ontology of object human phenomena. Not surprisingly, although his pioneering work can be shown to be replete with well-directed insights, the coverage and depth of intellectual penetration that he achieved was limited in certain crucial respects. The next step in the present context is to assess critically what Mises was able to make of the limited subjectivist legacies of both Dilthey and Weber.

Notes

1. Weber's contributions appeared in a number of papers collected in German as papers I to VI, VIII, X and XI in Weber (1973a), and available as English translations in his 1949a, 1964, 1975a, 1975b, 1977, 1981 papers. He brought many of the ideas forward into the methodological Part I of *Economy and Society* (1964, 1968) that was written towards the end of his life and published posthumously. In this chapter, all reference citations are to the writings of Weber, and all emphases are in the original, unless otherwise indicated.

2. In passing, it is worth noting that Weber was thoroughly familiar with Menger's metatheoretical views. This is apparent especially from the fact that his own extensively annotated copy of the *Untersuchungen* still exists in the Alfred Weber Institut in Heidelberg (Schön, 1987, p. 69n. 5).

3. Weber attended Knies's lectures at Heidelberg in 1882 and made an intensive study of his *Die politische Oekonomie vom geschichtlichen Standpuncte* in its second edition of 1883. This was 'the economics textbook that indicated to Weber, while still a student, the path his research would later take' and its contents demonstrate 'the *overwhelming* importance of Knies in Weber's socioeconomic education' (Hennis, 1987, pp. 33 and 41, original emphasis; cf. pp. 49, 56n. 79). Most importantly, it is Hennis's view that 'Weber's theoretical orientation to *action* can be traced directly back to Knies' (1987, p. 42; original emphasis).

4. The links into modern orthodox microeconomics of this observation can be found in the critical works of Spiro Latsis on what he calls 'situational determinism' and in which he reflects on Karl Popper's 'Rationality Principle' (Latsis, 1972, 1983).

5. In Weber (1981, (pp. 163ff), this is translated inappropriately as *voluntary association*. This non-literal form may be intended to convey the supplementary significance of many such associations that their members participate in their own volition.

6. Guy Oakes (1982, 1987, pp. 444f and 1988, pp. 150ff) accepts this critical point.

Thomas Burger had earlier made reference to it (1976, p. 208n. 8), but went on to dismiss it because the required '[empirical] facts ... can be known without being conceptualized (in Weber's sense)'. It is unclear how this latter procedure could work, and it is doubtful that Weber would have made such a claim given his consciousness of the primary need for conceptual forms in representing reality.

7. Mises and the subjectivism of economic action

7.1 Introduction

Much of Ludwig von Mises's subjectivist foundations for economics consists of a mixture of ontological claims and epistemological positions concerning the nature of human action. A study of the secondary literature that deals with these facets of his work reveals a bewildering array of suggestions relating to their philosophical alignment.[1] In his own writings, a number of these alignments appear to be more important than others in shaping his subjectivist economics.

As an Austrian educated scholar, Mises stood simultaneously within two distinct Germanic intellectual heritages. These have recently been identified and cogently argued out by Barry Smith (1986a, 1986b, 1990a, 1990c; cf. Kauder, 1957). Summarily put by Smith, 'Austria and Germany are different' (1990c, p. 212). The particular difference at issue concerns their fundamental philosophical traditions and a number of important philosophical principles that they espoused. In terms of the ontological connections encompassed by the conceptual constructs of the mind, the German strand was inclined to follow the legacy of Kant's epistemology of the *a priori*, with its synthetic but unreal representation of knowledge based on experience. Some followed the Southwest German (Baden) neo-Kantian revision of Kant's epistemology as a rationalistic theory of concepts isolated from experience, but validated by axiological premisses (see Parsons, 1990). In the sharpest contrast to these Kantian pursuits is the evidence that Austrians were influenced by the Aristotelian and Scholastic heritage of realism, with its emphasis on knowledge as an expression of the ontological form of observed objects. It is quite evident, as I will show, that each of these traditions, along with the writings of Carl Menger and Max Weber, impinged upon Mises to some extent at the outset of his search for the proper foundations for the human sciences in the 1920s (1960)[2] and then remained prominent throughout his work.

From an ontological perspective, Mises's emphasis was upon situated and conditioned human agents as the active generators of the phenomena that constitute the objects of study. Epistemological argument shifted his focus to observer-analysts' concerns with what can legitimately claim to be known about the world of human action and phenomena. He recognized that the two philosophical dimensions are intimately related in that the epistemological status of claims to knowledge of an object world are dependent upon and shaped by the ontological nature of the objects. It is for this reason that claims to realist knowledge in the human sciences were apparently more difficult to defend than in the sciences of nature. The variable and contingent origins of human phenomena in individual actions give such phenomena an appearance of impermanence and disorder that defies scientific generalization. The temptation, all too obvious in so much of orthodox economics, is to impose the required permanence and order by assumption. Mises, as with all subjectivists, refused to take this naive escape route.

Establishing the nature of the interface between these two philosophical dimensions and the balance of antecedent influences that shaped the approach to them in the foundations for Mises's subjectivist economics is no straightforward matter. Nonetheless, as I intend to show in this chapter, the pursuit is warranted. In particular, I will use his writings on these themes to elicit, and thereby to expose the limitations of, the insights into the essential problematic of subjectivism that this founder of Austrian economics left as his legacy.

My inquiries in this chapter are organized as follows. In section 7.2, I examine a number of the key alternative philosophical orientations that have been attributed to Mises in the secondary literature. Most important were the Aristotelian milieu of his education and his critical study of the Neo-Kantians and Max Weber. Then, in section 7.3 I elicit textual evidence for the philosophical ambivalence that Mises displayed in formulating his praxeology. It will be argued that there are clear indications of the neo-Kantian epistemological roots and orientations evident in his writings, situated alongside passages in which he emphasized the ontology and epistemology of Aristotelian realism. Section 7.4 pursues Mises's treatment of the nature of human action as it originates in the deliberated choices of situated human agents. Two levels of analysis appear in his writings on this core theme: one is the pure thesis of praxeology as an ontology of rational human action, and the other is the study and explanation of observed economic phenomena. Here I argue that this distinction of levels enabled Mises ultimately to establish the meaning of the tenets of praxeology as necessarily manifested within the reality of observed economic phenomena. It becomes apparent in section 7.5, however, that the praxeological requirement of giving agent rationality an ontologically *a priori* status is not readily defended once the contingent realities of human agency situated in time are examined. It will be quite evident that Mises was aware of these temporally conditioned realities, but he chose not to link them to the rationality thesis upon which his subjectivist economics depended. I go on to show in section 7.6 that although Mises developed his ideas of praxeology as an *a priori*, and purely general science of human action, its rationale and utility could only be in its application to the understanding and explanation of empirico-historical phenomena. Finally, in section 7.7, I draw together the evidence and reach the conclusion that it was the immediately ontological interpretation of the axioms of human action, and the contingencies of such action thus exposed, that rendered indefensible the epistemological foundations for subjectivism that Mises was inclined to pursue. Contrary to what he expressly sought to do at a number of points in his writings, he was unable to provide rational action with a sustainable defence as an ontologically relevant axiom. As a consequence, he failed to give his praxeology a cogent realist grounding and left its appropriate links to observed human action unresolved.

7.2 Philosophical orientations

7.2.1 Aristotelian influences

Mises looked back to Carl Menger as the father of the Austrian tradition from which he took his intellectual cues (1978, pp. 33, 121f, 127). In some prominent quarters, Austrian intellectual life was under the influence of the realism and essentialism of Aristotelian and Scholastic thought (Kauder, 1957; Johnston, 1972, pp. 68, 290ff; Smith, 1990a, 1990c). Menger's acceptance of ontologically rooted 'exact theories' in the realm of human conduct was arguably a consequence of this influence. The point upon which Menger depended was that 'Aristotle had insisted that there are qualities, for example, of action or knowledge or of more complex social phenomena, which are knowable a priori' (Smith, 1986a, p. vii). And, more graphically put, 'the ontological grammar of economic reality that is sketched by Menger can be seen . . . as providing a pre-empirical qualitative framework in whose terms specific empirical hypotheses can be formulated . . .' (Smith, 1990a, p. 279).

It is evident that in choosing to ground his economics in what he believed to be *a priori* axioms of human action, Mises was inclined to argue them in formally logical terms as prior to, and apparently isolated from, particular observations of their empirical manifestation. This is consistent with the dominant perception of the very idea of *a priori* knowledge as logically arranged mental categories that exist prior to and independently of observer experience. However, the status of *a priori* knowledge is not necessarily so restricted. Rather, it may be argued that the coherence and content of such knowledge is attributable to one of two alternative sources (Smith, 1990a, pp. 275f). The first involves the domination of cognition and concept formation that flows from experience by the imposed structural and categorial qualities of the observing mind, whatever the source of these qualities may be argued to be. In this 'impositionist' case, the claimed knowledge of observed reality is the mediated product of the mind's pre-existing capacities to deliver a particular logical co-ordination and order to an inflow of raw sensory experience. The alternative 'reflectionist' version of the *a priori* holds that knowledge expresses the primary existential order discovered in the essentials of reality and immediately grasped by the mind. The claim is then that cognition and concept formation are processes that report rather than construct the ordered and intelligible state of reality. Clearly, this latter form of *a priori* knowledge must be thought of as making ontological statements about the existential nature of reality as it is in itself, something that the 'impositionist' stance could never claim to do. *A priori* knowledge claims that depend exclusively upon the imposition of pre-existing mental constructs are appropriately thought of as Kantian, while the 'reflectionist', ontologically connected *a priori* claims are a heritage of Aristotle's essentialism and realism. As we are to see, in understanding Mises's use of the *a priori*, it will be important to keep this distinction in mind.

One scholar who recognized that the Aristotelian realist epistemology had been carried forward into Mises's work was Emil Kauder. He wrote of Mises as referring to praxeology comprising 'reflection about the essence of action' that maintained 'the ontological character of economic laws' (1957, p. 417). According to Kauder, Mises could be aligned with both Wieser and Böhm-Bawerk as carrying forward the Aristotelian roots of subjectivism in the very particular sense that 'all three authors are social *ontologists*. They believe that a general plan of reality exists. All social phenomena are conceived in relation to this master plan' (1957, p. 417; original emphasis). Kauder's insight here hints at the theme that I will pursue in more depth below: that the ontological status and content of praxeology, even in its purest form as expressing the essence of rational human action, was emphasized by Mises as a consequence of this Aristotelian heritage.

By contrast, other students of Mises have rejected the idea that this orientation is to be found so prominently displayed in his work.

Lachmann, for example, in assessing Mises's relationship to Menger, cited the latter's adherence to Aristotelian realism and essentialism in which 'exact laws' captured ontologically 'essential as well as necessary relationships between phenomena'. But, apropos Mises, Lachmann concluded that 'in this respect Mises was unable to follow his master. He was no essentialist'. And, although 'to him reason was inherent in human action, to be sure . . . few of what are usually regarded as typical manifestations of the Aristotelian tradition in European thought he found to his taste' (1982a, p. 35).

Barry Smith's reading stands in contrast to Lachmann's. In Smith's work on the philosophical origins of Austrian economics, Mises's thesis of praxeology in its pure, abstract form is assigned epistemologically to the Kantian camp (1986b, pp. 8, 18; 1990a, p. 279). In relation to this form, the suggestion is that Mises was inclined to adhere to an analytical rather than synthetic perception of praxeological constructs. In so conflating the *a priori* with an analytical logic, what appears to be certain is that his position could not be compatible with 'reflectionism' because analytical concepts and arguments have no ontological content. On this Smith observes that 'we know . . . that there is an Aristotelian alternative to the Kantian form of apriorism. This alternative seems not to have been explicitly recognized as such by Mises . . .' (1990a, p. 279).[3] However, it is the word 'explicitly' that is significant here, because for Smith, there is a very definite Aristotelian connection to be found implicit in the extended scope of Mises's economic analyses. He is, indeed, led to conclude of Mises's work as a whole that it represents 'one of *the most sustained realizations of the Austrian Aristotelian idea in the literature of economic theory*' (1990a, p. 282, emphasis added). For in spite of such 'impositionist' metatheoretical directions being clearly evident in Mises's writings, Smith suggests that most of his praxeological understanding of economic phenomena actually fits into the Aristotelian mould as synthetic and realist. This turn around comes in what Smith calls 'Mises's *practice*' as distinct from his 'methodological self-interpretations' (1990a, p. 282; original emphasis). The broad sweep of Mises's economic inquiries made it necessary for him to give the core axiom of human rationality a substantive form and context. Smith's finding is that there exists in Mises's work an ontologically grounded, pre-empirical structural framework comprising 'a family of *a priori* categories and categorial structures' (1990a, p. 283). These are so diverse and extensive that they could not have been derived from any singular axiom of rational human action by purely analytical arguments. He concludes, therefore, that they must rather have had their origin in the order inherent in economic events and are, therefore, aptly treated as ontologically rich, synthetic representations of a slice of reality. This essentialist approach to the causal interpretation and understanding of economic phenomena brought Mises into line with his Aristotelian heritage.

However, it remains unclear from Smith's analyses what meaningful status can ultimately be attributed to the axiom of rational action and some closely related categories. Rational action appears to become just another member of the 'family of a priori categories'. In Smith's otherwise helpful diagrammatic representation of the 'family' relationships involved in Mises's praxeological foundations for economic inquiry, the really critical issues are avoided (1990a, pp. 283ff). There are boxes containing the labels 'agent', 'choice', 'knowledge' and 'expectations', but there is no accompanying consideration of the ontological meaning, if any, given to them in Mises's writings. They are, without doubt, ontologically rich categories with an essential status in understanding economic action as rational or otherwise. But, as I will argue below, making them parts of a universal *a priori* structure for realist economic inquiry defies the contingent nature of the human agency to which they refer.

7.2.2 Kantian and neo-Kantian influences

It is readily made apparent, however, that juxtaposed to this Aristotelianism, Mises sought his epistemological foundations by reaching into and selectively adopting certain key principles of Kantian and neo-Kantian thought. A number of prominent Austrian scholars have observed this in passing, but few have pursued the textual evidence in detail.[4] Lachmann, for example, commented that Mises sought 'a reputable philosophical position that would supply him with enough intellectual armor to withstand the onslaughts of positivism and to espouse the cause of rationalism in human affairs . . .'. And, although Lachmann shied away from giving us details, he read Mises as 'driven to seek refuge in NeoKantianism', but added the rider: 'How far this endeavour was successful is a matter of debate. Some have held that no epistemology that fails to grant major status to experience is entitled to claim affinity with Kant' (1982a, p. 36). These observations fail fully to explicate Mises's position, for as I will show, his rationalism cannot be consistently identified with the ontologically unreal conceptual forms envisaged by the Baden Neo-Kantians. Upholding my argument then negates Lachmann's concern that in Mises's rationalism, there is a neglect of the Kantian thesis that knowledge originates in experience. It will become evident in this respect that Mises's epistemology of the *a priori* was closely akin to Kant's in the very particular sense that both demanded experiential input in order to make meaningful claims to know anything about reality.

S. Parsons is one of the most recent interpreters to devote some sustained inquiry to Mises's Kantian and neo-Kantian connections.[5] After quoting the above comments by Lachmann, he, too, is diverted towards the notion that 'although Mises's neglect of experience may indicate a break with Kant, it also reveals a continuity with neo-Kantianism' (1990, p. 297). Parsons grants some affinity between Mises and Kant, but adds that 'despite these similarities, Mises's intellectual heritage leaves him susceptible to a critique from the position of Kant' (1990, p. 310). The main objection in Parsons's Kantian critique of Mises that is of concern in the present context is the treatment of time and its link to his allegedly extreme rationalist view of knowledge. On the treatment of time, Parsons's criticisms are ontologically oriented and he finds Mises to have lacked completeness in dealing with the implications for agents' conduct of this vital facet of economic decision-making. I will suggest below, however, that the criticism levelled by Parsons is more aptly attributed to Mises's revealed lack of philosophical sophistication in pursuing appropriate epistemological principles than to any failure to appreciate the extent of the ontological problem. It is quite apparent in Mises's arguments that he understood the problematic of time in relation to the subjectivism of human action. Indeed, he did so in very much the same terms as George Shackle, but for some reason lacked the inclination to pursue the issues further.

It should be mentioned in passing, though, that Parsons picks up one quite relevant point in Kant's own concerns about reason in relation to the treatment of the import of time. He quotes Kant's second thoughts on the issue to the effect that reason *per se* is autonomous and out of time (1990, p. 314). It is my understanding that this was precisely the position taken by Mises. He warned of confusing timeless logical constructions that comprise reasoning *per se*, such as that employed in mathematics, with the logical essentials of human action (1966, pp. 99f). Reason is projected into time by the fact that the ontology of action has a necessary time dimension. And, recognizing the intended status of praxeology as prior to, but for practical purposes, never independent of the manifested phenomena of economics proper, is also relevant here. For once this is allowed for, the epistemological puzzles of how time enters our knowledge of human action seems less significant. Moreover, if Kant was in doubt about the matter, Mises could hardly have been expected to sort it out.

Parsons is on less certain ground in attempting to tie the time problem to Mises's epistemology, claiming that 'for Mises, knowledge was understood rationalistically, as involving analytical judgements' (1990, p. 312, cf. p. 315). As I will elicit below, while there is evidence of Mises's Neo-Kantianism and accompanying conceptual rationalism, there is also much in his writings to counter such an attribution. Passages that align him with the vital role of experience in the constitution of knowledge, as found in Kant's synthetic *a priori* and in the epistemological import of Aristotle's realism, are readily identified. Parsons concludes on rather too heavily philosophical grounds that 'Mises's science [of economics], like logic and mathematics, was... concerned with universally valid knowledge...', and that 'in common with Baden [Neo-Kantians], he defined knowledge rationalistically: it involved the analysis of concepts, independently of possible experience' (1990, p. 318). My interpretation will indicate that in making this claim, Parsons has taken a very narrow perspective and thus left much aside that is of relevance in understanding Mises's contribution to the foundations of Austrian subjectivist economics.

In particular, Mises appeared to lean towards neo-Kantian recognition of the infinite irrationality of reality as it is perceived by the human mind. He wrote in this vein that 'human reasoning does not have the power to exhaust completely the content of the universe. In the sciences of human action it goes as far as conceptual thinking can go' (1960, p. 48). He reiterated elsewhere that 'the exuberance and variability of human life and action cannot be fully seized by concepts and definitions. Some unanswered or even unanswerable questions always remain, some problems whose solution passes the ability even of the greatest minds' (1958, p. 320). He emphasized that because 'the main fact about human action is that in regard to it there is no... regularity in the conjunction of phenomena' it could not be 'a short-coming of the sciences of human action that they have not succeeded in discovering determinate stimulus–response patterns. What does not exist cannot be discovered' (1958, p. 9). Consistently also with this neo-Kantian orientation, Mises held that 'concepts are never and nowhere to be found in reality; they belong rather to the province of thought' (1960, p. 78). And, even more unequivocally expressed, 'it is true... that between reality and the knowledge that science can convey to us there is an unbridgeable gulf. Science cannot grasp life directly. What it captures in its system of concepts is always of a different character from the living whole' (1960, p. 46). Elsewhere he expressed the same strongly neo-Kantian sentiments: 'The imaginary constructions that are the main – or, as some people would rather say, the only – mental tool of praxeology describe conditions that can never be present in the reality of action. Yet they are indispensable for conceiving what is going on in this reality' (1962, p. 41).

7.2.3 Mises and Max Weber

It warrants emphasis here, too, that Mises found largely congenial the Kantian and neo-Kantian roots of the foundations of human science developed by Max Weber. The merits of the neo-Kantian approach seem to have been confirmed to Mises through his study of Weber. There are good reasons, then, to agree with Ludwig Lachmann's assertion that while 'Max Weber can hardly be called an Austrian economist, . . . he made a contribution of fundamental significance to what in the hands of Mises became Austrian methodology' (1976, p. 56). Mises had met Weber when the German spent a semester at the University of Vienna in 1918–19 and as Lachmann observed, he 'was struck by Weber's genius and admired his work' (1982a, p. 35; and see Mises, 1960, p. 74; 1978, pp. 9, 69f, 104, 122f; 1990, pp. 39, 44). Although Weber's impact on intellectual life in Vienna was never great, his *verstehende Soziologie* did become a frequent topic of discussion in Mises's own *Privatseminar* from its inception in the early 1920s (Haberler, 1981, p. 123).

When he reviewed Mises's magnum opus, *Human Action*, on an earlier occasion, Lachmann was one of the first to notice that 'it is the work of Max Weber that is being carried on here' (1977, p. 95). On yet another occasion Lachmann observed that Weber's writings 'provided the main focus of orientation for the methodological essays Mises began to publish in the German journals in the second half of the 1920s'.[6] And, Lachmann went on significantly to add that 'even where he disagrees with Weber, . . . it is clear that, throughout, his thought reflects the impact of Weber's work' (1982a, p. 35). The crucial questions that these claims beg are the meanings to be given to 'carried on' and to 'reflects the impact of Weber's work'. These matters require more careful exegetical attention in the respective writings of these two authors than they have hitherto received. Richard Ebeling (1988) makes a cogent case for the Weber to Mises link, but he concentrates his extended discussion upon how far the connection allowed the latter to give due emphasis to the role of time, uncertainty and expectations in human action. Jeremy Shearmur finds a complementarity between the work of Weber and Mises that comprises a duality in the conception of subjectivism (1992, pp. 104, 113). This involves setting the praxeological subjectivism of Mises, with its axiomatics of human action, against the historical or institutional subjectivism of Weber, with its depiction of human agency as ideal types tied to the historical situation. Parsons, by contrast, chooses to ignore the mediation of Weber in the neo-Kantian connection.

Mises read Weber as essentially continuing the dichotomy drawn by the Neo-Kantians between different perspectives on a consistently infinite and cognitively inaccessible empirical reality. Such reality included all phenomena of either natural or human origin. Natural sciences then comprised all those inquiries grounded upon generalizing, nomological methodologies, including the 'exact' theoretical economics that had been pursued by Carl Menger. Mises's opinion to the contrary was that 'the social sciences owe their progress to the use of their [own] particular methods' and that these 'methods' are devised 'along the lines which *the special character of their object require*. They do not have to adopt the methods of the natural sciences' (1990, p. 15, emphasis added). It was this 'special character' of the phenomena originating in human action; their ontological uniqueness, that Mises would focus upon in devising and defending his unique vision of human science.

The implication here was that the notion of a generalizing and abstracting metatheory had no immediate relevance for the human sciences with an empirico-historical orientation. In this respect, though, Weber modified his neo-Kantian principles of concept formation in an endeavour to conceive of and situate theory in a form that allowed it to have a crucial role in developing these sciences. Mises was well aware of this vital shift by Weber towards conceiving a logically prior status for theory and quoted his work in detail to this effect (1960, pp. 75ff). There was a sense in which this shift brought the German closer to Mises's own treatment of the nature and role of theory in the causal explanation of empirical phenomena. For as Mises put it, 'we explain a phenomenon when we trace it back to general principles. Any other mode of explanation is denied to us' (1960, p. 130).

It will be an integral part of my argument that in distinguishing his own metatheory, Mises failed to give due emphasis to the extensive common ground with Weber that can be shown to exist in the results of their investigations. He really failed, therefore, fully to express the crucial significance of Weber's contribution for the operational viability of his own praxeology in its application to understanding economic phenomena. It may well be, as Mises claimed, that 'if Weber had known the term "praxeology", he probably would have preferred it' when referring to the fundamental status of rational action involving the pursuit of subjectively designated ends by chosen objective means (1966, p. 126n.5). However, Weber's intended understanding of the term's import could never have been consistent with Mises's apriorism. I will suggest that if Mises's axioms of human action are to be given their

proper place in the foundations of human science, they demand more
critical scrutiny in order to establish their proper status. If this status
can be settled upon by well-reasoned argument, it can then be shown
to follow that the apparent failure of praxeology to be immediately
operational in meaningful analyses can be set aside. Two writers in
particular have noticed this alleged failure (Buchanan, 1982, pp. 14f;
Smith, 1990a, pp. 279ff). Another has made the related point, equally
unnecessarily as it will turn out, that there is a need to distinguish
Mises's limited subjectivism from a more directly applicable Weberian
alternative (Shearmur, 1992).[7]

Having identified the complementarity between the two authors, it is
nonetheless still important to realize that the resulting metatheory
remains in an incomplete state relative to what is required if subjectivism is to be taken seriously as an alternative and more ontologically
legitimate paradigm in economics. There will be no suggestion that
somehow adding a stronger Weberian consciousness to Mises's theses
will somehow resolve all the problematical elements that beset the
latter's metatheory for economics. One particular matter will be at issue
in the critical assessment of their joint intellectual legacy: the extent to
which the combined subjectivist insights of Weber and Mises actually
encompass the existential intricacies of the generation of economic
phenomena by the processes of human agency. Only once this is established will it be possible to examine the manner in which their
metatheoretical insights can be built upon and then applied in the
construction of cogent discursive theory in economics.

Mises pursued his own critical connection with Weber in one of his
earliest metatheoretical essays, 'Sociology and history', published in
1929 (1960, pp. 68ff). He recalled some years later that in this essay he
had intended, by means of the axioms of praxeology, to redirect the
science of human action away from the immediately empirico-historical
focus that Weber had given it in his visions of sociology and economics
(1978, p. 123). Of the intention of the essay, Mises wrote that 'my
essay was directed especially against Max Weber's epistemology, against
which I raised two objections: (1) its failure to comprehend the epistemological characteristics of economics; and (2) its distinction between
rational action and actions of other kinds' (1978, p. 123; cf. 1990,
pp. 43ff). His claim at the time was that the Neo-Kantians and Weber
had not recognized the potentially legitimate nomothetic status of sociology and economics as deductive sciences of human action. They saw
any approach to the study of human phenomena that depended upon
'laws' as necessarily naturalistic, while Mises was convinced that the
human sciences warranted an independent metatheoretical defence that

made due allowance for the status of nomological argument. Mises tempered his critique with a recognition that these antecedents had distinctively defined the independent human sciences as immediately, necessarily and exclusively empirico-historical. By this they meant that human phenomena can only be taken up as empirically observed and then understood and explained only as individual and unique occurrences. As far as Mises was concerned, Weber had reasoned correctly that the metatheoretical problems of history and the empirical human sciences could not be resolved by the mere application of principles established by the natural sciences. But, he continued, where Weber 'went beyond this and attempted to determine the character of sociological investigation, he failed and had to fail because by sociology he understood something entirely different from the nomothetic science of human action . . .' (1960, p. 78).

Mises was troubled by the appearance of the ideal type as the conceptual form that was to constitute the immediate substance of discursive theoretical argument for Weber. In Mises's opinion, 'the basis of Weber's misconceptions can be exposed only by consideration of the question whether the concepts of economic theory do in fact have the logical character of the "ideal type"'. His response was unequivocal: 'This question is plainly to be answered in the negative' (1960, p. 78). But in interpreting this response, it should be emphasized that for Mises 'economic theory' could only mean praxeology and thus it constituted no more than a metatheory *per se*. I will make more of this point below. The immediate issue for him was to clarify the epistemological nature and status of the concepts he thought it appropriate to use in theoretical understanding and explanation if they were to be other than ideal types.

7.2.4 Philosophical outcomes

What are we to make of these various and sometimes contrasting readings of Mises's ontological pemisses and epistemological connections? As will become apparent below, there is clear evidence that at certain points in his work, Mises thought of the concepts and arguments of praxeology in epistemological terms as analytical and thus isolated from and prior to any ontology of observed human action. Somehow, from this perspective, purely rational action was a conceptual form that had an unreal existence. In this respect, my reading suggests that the 'impositionist' position on *a priori* knowledge was an integral part of his many Kantian and neo-Kantian moments in applying the concept of rational action. As conceptual forms, Mises frequently inferred that the axioms of human action are, in and of themselves, ontologically empty.

But, as already suggested, there is juxtaposed and contrasting evidence of equal cogency that at other points, he thought of the praxeological axioms as existentially present in observed action. This facilitated his 'reflectionist' and realist references to the ontology of human action and phenomena. He made many explicit claims that the axiom of rational action could be identified within the phenomena of reality. Such claims render it unnecessary to pursue Mises's 'practice' to elicit that it was a 'reflectionist' realism that gave his praxeology its epistemological grounding and that gave the essential shape to his subjectivist economics.

The potential difficulty in such intellectual ecumenicism, consciously or unconsciously espoused, is that the Austrian and German philosophical traditions were fundamentally incompatible in their ontologies and related epistemologies. Ultimately, Mises was left with a chronic ambivalence that continued throughout his career to impair the precision of his metatheoretical writings and of the interpretations that may reasonably be given to them. This dilemma can only be addressed by identifying some rationale in his work for giving dominant weight to one or the other of these alternative orientations.

7.3 Praxeology: Kantian and realist perspectives

Mises revealed a fundamentally Kantian orientation in grounding his metatheory when he wrote that 'the human mind is not a tabula rasa on which external events write their own history. It is equipped with a set of tools for grasping reality' (1966, p. 35). Elsewhere he reiterated that the mind is not 'a Lockian paper upon which reality writes its own story'. Rather, the mind has:

> a special quality that enables man to transform the raw material of sensation into perception and the perceptual data into an image of reality. It is precisely this specific quality or power of his intellect – the logical structure of his mind – that provides man with the faculty of seeing more in the world than nonhuman beings see. (1990, p. 48)

That is to say while 'all those objects which are the substratum of human sensation, perception, and observation also pass before the senses of animals', it is the human being alone who 'has the faculty of *transforming* sensuous stimuli into observation and experience . . . [and] can *arrange* his various observations and experiences into a coherent system' (1966, p. 177, emphasis added; cf. 1962, p. 71). So, although 'life and reality are neither logical nor illogical, they are simply given', it is logic that is 'the only tool available to man for the comprehension of both'. And, 'as far as man is able to attain any knowledge, however limited, he can use only one avenue of approach, that opened by reason' (1966, pp. 67f, cf. 1990, p. 48). More generally expressed, 'what we know is what the nature or structure of our senses and of our mind makes comprehensible to us. We see reality, not as it "is" and may appear to a perfect being, but only as the quality of our mind and of our senses enables us to see it' (1962, p. 18). In this respect, Mises stressed that 'we must never forget that our representation of the reality of the universe is conditioned by the structure of our mind as well as of our senses' (1962, p. 19).

Particularly in the case of praxeology, 'its concepts and theorems are mental tools opening the approach to a complete grasp of reality . . .' (1966, p. 38). Here Mises's position was that 'all experience concerning human action is conditioned by the praxeological categories and becomes possible only through their application. If we *had not in our mind* the schemes provided by praxeological reasoning, we should never be in a position to discern and to grasp any action' (1966, p. 40, emphasis added; cf. 1962, p. 16). Most important here were the matters of the origin and status of these tools and the meaning attributed to the 'reality' that is to be grasped. The tools, he wrote, comprise 'the logical structure' of the mind and are acquired by the human being 'in the course of his evolution from an amoeba to his present state' (1966, p. 35). Mises's claim was, then, that human science is grounded in a praxeology that is not dependent on discovering the ontological realities of human conduct, ordered and coherent or otherwise, for praxeology 'is not derived from experience; it is prior to experience. It is, as it were, the logic of action and deed' (1960, pp. 12f). He reiterated his belief that its categories emanate from the logical structure of the human mind. In this sense they are, in a clearly 'impositionist' sense, 'the necessary mental tool to arrange sense data in a systematic way, to transform them into facts of experience . . .' (1962, p. 16). In this respect, Mises stressed that 'we must never forget that our representation of the reality of the universe is conditioned by the structure of our mind as well as of our senses' (1962, p. 19).

Consistently with such Kantian fundamentals in their neo-Kantian guise, Mises also held that in cognition and mental representations, the concepts involved 'are never and nowhere to be found in reality; they belong rather to the province of thought' (1960, p. 78). And, even more unequivocally expressing the 'impositionist' requirement, 'it is true . . . that between reality and the knowledge that science can convey to us there is an unbridgeable gulf. Science cannot grasp life directly. What it captures in its system of concepts is always of a different character from the living whole' (1960, p. 46). On another occasion he expressed the same strongly neo-Kantian sentiments: 'The imaginary constructions that are the main – or, as some people would rather say, the only – mental tool of praxeology describe conditions *that can never be present in the reality of action*. Yet they are indispensable for conceiving what is going on in this reality' (1962, p. 41, emphasis added). This preserved a neo-Kantian void between conceptual forms and the experiential sensations of reality that led the mind to form them.

Read in isolation, the implication of these arguments is that the order and coherence of the agents' cognitive grasp of the world around them is a product of some capacity of the mind itself. Mises thus reinforced his neo-Kantian views by rejecting as pointless speculation about the issue of whether human beings have the capacity to grasp an ultimate reality-in-itself. 'It is idle to ask whether things-in-themselves are different from what they appear to us, and whether there are worlds which we cannot devine and ideas which we cannot comprehend. These problems are beyond the scope of human cognition' (1966, p. 36). Most especially from this perspective, then, Mises argued that 'there can be no theory other than an aprioristic and universally valid theory . . ., because human reasoning is unable to derive theoretical propositions from historical experience' (1960, p. xixn.2). His claim was that human science is not dependent on discovering the ontological realities of human conduct, ordered and coherent or otherwise. Any theory that grasps human action 'is not derived from experience; it is prior to experience. It is, as it were, the logic of action and deed' (1960, pp. 12f). However, the inferred isolation of such logic from any realities of action needs to be interpreted with some care if Mises's intention is to be correctly understood. It is reasonable on the above evidence to interpret his epistemology as Kantian and his *a priori* as 'impositionist' in the particular sense that knowledge of the world of reality is the combined product of sensory experience and the synthetic *a priori* structures and judgements that pre-exist in the individual human mind. *A priori* knowledge is combined with immediately observed instances of human action as the means for generating empirico-historical knowledge. However, he was no committed Neo-Kantian and often shifted ground towards a realist perspective in which it was claimed that the ordered and coherent conceptual form is immediately the abstracted form of the observed reality-in-itself.

If the Aristotelian realist perspective is to be identified in Mises's work, it is fundamental that his ideas be shown to be consistent with a number of particular ontological theses (Smith, 1990a, pp. 266ff). First, that an inherent order and coherence can be discovered in the real world of the phenomena of human action. This takes the form of structured relationships between essential constituent elements that have universal status. Secondly, while the existential nature of this reality is considered to be independent of human cognition, that cognition is capable of grasping its essentially pre-ordered constitution. Thirdly, experience and cognition of the object world comprise a mix of universal elements and other individual characteristics.[8] My position here is that there are in Mises's writings some very definite statements that conform to this realist orientation and its required ontological premisses.

First of all, it was Mises's expressed view in this connection that human agents can only grasp the reality around them if the ontological presumption is made that it has an innately and essentially coherent form to which they can gain cognitive access (1962, pp. 19ff). He wrote of the idea that 'no thinking and no acting would be possible to man if the universe were chaotic, i.e., if there were no regularity whatever in the succession and concatenation of events' (1962, p. 19, cf. pp. 21f). Moreover, 'in a world without causality and regularity of phenomena there would be no field for human reasoning and human action. Such a world would be a chaos in which man would be at a loss to find any orientation and guidance. Man is not even capable of imagining the conditions of such a chaotic universe' (1966, p. 22). The potential for such a paralysing state of humankind is overcome by the fact that 'the first and basic achievement of thinking is the awareness of constant relations among the external phenomena that affect our senses' (1962, p. 20). This means that in the human sciences, conceptual forms must, as a first principle, immediately grasp and express in discursively rational arguments the irreducible existential 'essentials' of human action that are present within the superficial disorder of human affairs. Most importantly in the present context, Mises expressed his 'reflectionist' belief that praxeology is 'not arbitrarily made, but *imposed upon us by the world in which we live and act and which we want to study.* ... [It is] not empty, not meaningless, and not merely verbal. ... [It comprises] – for man – the most general laws of the universe, and without them no knowledge would be accessible to man' (1962, p. 14, emphasis added).

For Mises, we know that a subjectivist interpretation and understanding of the world of human phenomena meant recognizing first and foremost that the human being perceives action as 'the essence of his nature and existence' (1966, pp. 18f). As 'the characteristic feature of man is action', he reasoned that 'the study of man, as far as it is not

biology, begins and ends with the study of action' (1962, p. 34). Praxeology is, he argued, a theory in which human reason manifested as action
in pursuit of particular ends is ontologically causal. And, because active
human agents, taking a perspective from their current life-world situation, self-consciously seek to better their condition, the causality is
teleological (1966, pp. 23, 25; cf. 1962, pp. 7f). They can only achieve
this generalized objective by choosing means they individually believe
will achieve the ends envisaged. On this basis, Mises concluded that
action and its observed results cannot be anything but the existential
manifestations of reason applied to problematic circumstances.

What we find here is the suggestion that Mises intended to preserve
the immediately ontological content and context of his concepts: thus
praxeological propositions refer 'with the full rigidity of their apodictic
certainty and incontestability to the reality of action as it appears in
life and history. Praxeology conveys exact and precise knowledge of
real things' (1966, p. 39; cf. 1990, p. 15). And, with an even more
apparent realist and 'reflectionist' orientation, Mises continued with the
argument that 'the starting point of praxeology is not a choice of axioms
and a decision about methods of procedure, but reflection about the
essence of action. *There is no action in which the praxeological categories
do not appear fully and perfectly*' (1966, pp. 39f; emphasis added). Since
the categories of praxeology 'have enabled man to develop theories the
practical application of which has aided him in his endeavours to hold
his own in the struggle for survival and to attain various ends that he
wanted to attain, *these categories provide some information about the
reality of the universe*' (1962, p. 16; emphasis added). So, as a means of
understanding individual agency, praxeology 'does not deal in vague
terms with human action in general, but with concrete action which a
definite man has performed at a definite date and at a definite place.
But, of course, it does not concern itself with the accidental and environmental features of this action and with what distinguishes it from all
other actions, but only with what is necessary and universal in its
performance' (1966, p. 44). It was, then, Mises's belief that the *a priori*
categories of praxeology in some sense manifest a universal reality of
human action that exists imbedded in the complex, individual empirico-
historical phenomena of economics. The evidence for this belief was
compounded by his methodology of separately identifying, but then
arguing the necessary integration of the *a priori* of praxeology and the
investigation of actual economic phenomena.

7.4 Human action and human agency

For Mises, understanding the world of human phenomena meant recognizing first and foremost that the human being perceives action as 'the essence of his nature and existence, his means of preserving his life and raising himself above the level of animals and plants. However perishable and evanescent all human efforts may be, for man and for human science they are of primary importance' (1966, pp. 18f). As 'the characteristic feature of man is action', Mises reasoned that 'the study of man, as far as it is not biology, begins and ends with the study of action' (1962, p. 34). He summarized his position regarding the priority and scope of human action in the following passages:

> Human action is purposeful behavior. Or we may say: Action is will put into operation and transformed into agency, [it] is aiming at ends and goals, [it] is the ego's meaningful response to stimuli and to the conditions of its environment, [it] is a person's conscious adjustment to the state of the universe that determines his life. (1966, p. 11)

Thus, he continued, 'we may say that action is the manifestation of man's will . . . [which] means nothing else than man's faculty to choose between different states of affairs, to prefer one, to set aside the other, and to behave according to the decision made in aiming at the chosen state and forsaking the other' (1966, p. 13).

> The category of action is the fundamental category of human knowledge. It implies all the categories of logic and the category of regularity and causality. It implies the category of time and that of value . . . In acting, the mind of the individual sees itself as different from its environment, the external world, and tries to study this environment in order to influence the course of the events happening in it. (1962, pp. 35f)

All of the facets of human action cited here will become apparent in the discussions below.

At this point, Mises had to confront the fact that the idea of actions being the result of choice begs the question of what is the ontological nature and origin of the range of ends available to the deliberating mind that makes such a choice? He gave us some clues as to his belief here when he set out three 'general conditions of human action': 'Man is the being that lives under these conditions. He is not only *homo sapiens*, but no less *homo agens* . . . [as] the essential feature of humanity' (1966, p. 14). That is, man as the only extant member of the species *homo* has not only the capacity for wisdom (as implied by *sapiens*), but also the capacity to act in the light of it (as implied by *agens*). First, 'acting man is eager to substitute a more satisfactory state of affairs for a less satisfactory. . . . The incentive that impels man to act is always some uneasiness' (1966, p. 13). Secondly, the actor '*imagines* conditions that suit him better, and his action aims at bringing about this desired state' (1966, p. 13, emphasis added). This was the most contentious step in relation to Mises's claim that all action is rational. For by recognizing the future orientation of deliberations, together with the necessary resort to imagination in the process, it introduced an extreme subjectivism into the idea of choice. The third condition then compounded the matter further. It was that the actor formed 'the expectation that purposeful behavior has the power to remove or at least to alleviate the felt uneasiness' (1966, p. 14). The issue not addressed by Mises was how agents form the ends they deem to be realizable under a set of perceived circumstances, where such circumstances include the means available to them. Because the end state aimed at does not exist *ex ante*, and must therefore be a product of the individual's imagination, the choice of the end as it drives any action is wholly subjective. The precise meaning to be attributed to the pure logic of choice and action in the face of such subjectivism was left unclear as a result.

Mises posed the Kantian question: 'How can the human mind, by aprioristic thinking, deal with the reality of the external world?' (1962, p. 42). His response was that the connection between the processes of the mind and manifested action is their common referent, the immutable logical structure of human thought and reason: 'Thinking and acting are the specific human features of man. They are peculiar to all human beings' (1966, p. 25). To this he added that 'the characteristic feature of man is precisely that he consciously acts. Man is Homo agens, the acting animal' (1962, p. 4). Furthermore, it is reason that is 'man's particular and characteristic feature' (1966, p. 177). Bringing these ideas together, Mises argued that 'a priori thinking and reasoning on the one hand and human action on the other, are manifestations of the human mind. The logical structure of the human mind creates the reality of action. Reason and action are congeneric and homogeneous, two aspects of the same phenomenon' (1962, p. 42, cf. p. 64). In sum, then:

> human action which is inextricably linked with human thought is conditioned by logical necessity. It is impossible for the human mind to conceive logical relations at variance with the logical structure of our mind. It is impossible for the human mind to conceive a mode of action whose categories would differ from the categories which determine our own actions. (1966, p. 25)

It was his belief, then, that 'the categories of value and action are primary and aprioristic elements present to [sic] every human mind' (1958, p. 283). And, he continued, 'being himself a valuing and acting ego, every man knows the meaning of valuing and acting.... It is impossible to imagine a sane human being who lacks this insight. It is no less impossible to conceive how a being lacking this insight could acquire it by means of any experience or instruction' (1958, p. 283). This existential referent common to all human agents that have ever lived brought real ontological content to the apparently isolated concepts of praxeology. In relation to the phenomenology of the life-world, he made the self-evident observation that 'both human thought and human action stem from the same root in that they are both products of the human mind' (1990, p. 11).

The science of human action was strongly subjectivist in this sense, for as Mises conceived it, 'praxeology does not deal with the external world, but with man's conduct with regard to it. Praxeological reality is not the physical universe, but man's conscious reaction to the given state of the universe. Economics is not about things and tangible material objects; it is about men, their meanings and actions' (1966, p. 92). His argument was that thought and reason are prior to and direct human action: 'Action is preceded by thinking. Thinking is to deliberate beforehand over future action and to reflect afterwards upon past action. Thinking and action are inseparable. ... Action without thinking, practice without theory are unimaginable. The reasoning may be faulty and the theory incorrect; but thinking and theorizing are not lacking in any action' (1966, p. 177; cf. 1960, p. 13). Moreover, human action in the real world is the product of reason applied to the situational conditions confronted by the agent:

> Acting man is faced with a definite situation. His action is a response to the challenge offered by this situation; it is his re-action. He appraises the effects the situation may have upon himself, i.e., he tries to establish what it means to him. He then chooses and acts in order to attain the end chosen. (1958, p. 286)

To some extent the situation will comprise conditions and aspects of the natural world and this can be grasped by agents through applied natural science. Other dimensions of the situation will be of human origin and require agents to interpret the legacies of the past that surround them (1958, p. 287). As a practical concept, Mises's idea was that 'in speaking of human action, we have in mind conduct that, in the opinion of the actor, is best fitted to attain an end he wants to attain, whether or not this opinion is also held by a better informed spectator or historian' (1990, p. 45). The qualification about an observer here referred to the belief that incorrect action, for whatever reason, is still rational. Thus, 'to make mistakes in pursuing one's ends is a widespread human weakness. Some err less often than others, but no mortal man is omniscient and infallible. Error, inefficiency, and failure must not be confused with irrationality' (1958, p. 268). As far as Mises was concerned, then:

> it is a fact that human reason is not infallible and that man very often errs in selecting and applying means. An action unsuited to the end sought falls short of expectation. It is contrary to purpose, but it is rational, i.e., the outcome of a reasonable – though faulty – deliberation and an attempt – although an ineffectual attempt – to attain a definite goal. (1966, p. 20)

Be this as it may, it was integral to Mises's argument that 'action, if successful, attains the end sought. It produces the product' that was its intended result (1966, p. 140). The idea of a direct link between action and its product expressed here enabled him to amplify his views about the nature of action and our capacity to understand it. As a practical matter, as it is manifested in reality, what action achieves is 'a transformation of given elements through arrangement and combination' (1966, p. 140). The human agent is not a creator of anything material. But the agent is creative in the sense that production is grounded on and directed by human reason. It is a creative act of the mind that imagines before the fact that the action decided upon will produce the result expected. And, the expected material result of production is driven by the anticipation of a more fundamental, subjective result that is 'spiritual and intellectual'. Action has the human objective of removing a mental state of uneasiness about the agent's existing condition and replacing it by another, more satisfying condition. In this sense, 'human action is a manifestation of the mind' and 'production is alteration of the given according to the designs of reason' (1966, p. 142). What this leaves us with, according to Mises, is a non-material understanding of economics, for to presume that it 'deals with the material conditions of human life is entirely mistaken' (1966, p. 142). The most apt response to this claim is to say that it exaggerates the separation between the material and psychic dimensions of economic actions. Economics should give due emphasis to the mental origins of action in all their complexity. But the fact remains that the deliberations that precede action must be cognizant of material situation in and through which any action must be carried out. In Mises's own words here, in undertaking production all the agent can accomplish 'is to combine the means available in such a way that according to the laws of nature the result aimed at is bound to emerge' (1966, p. 140). The creative and spiritual dimension are ultimately materially bounded if the action is to be successful. Indeed, at one point Mises defined the external world confronting the acting agent as 'the totality of all those things and events that determine the feasibility or unfeasibility, the success or failure, of human action' (1962, p. 6).

It was Mises's belief that every observed human action in reality could be legitimately interpreted as grounded in a core of praxeological rationality by virtue of the sole fact that it involves the choice and application of objective means to subjectively given ends. His claim was that 'action is conduct directed by choices', and the 'mental acts that determine the content of a choice refer either to ultimate ends or to the means to attain ultimate ends' (1958, p. 12). This rationality can never be empirically apparent in its pure form, but its presence in the human phenomena of the real life-world was taken by Mises to be an indisputable existential fact. It is 'the fact that our deeds are intentional that makes them actions' (1960, p. 14). Moreover, he believed that 'there is something that is absolutely valid for all human action irrespective of time, geography, and the racial, national, and cultural characteristics of the actors' (1990, p. 49). Thus he claimed 'all action . . . is necessarily in accord with the statements of the *a priori* theory of human action. . . . Action always seeks means to realize ends, and it is in this sense always rational and mindful of its utility. It is, in a word, human' (1960, pp. 65f). More specifically, 'there is no human action that can be dealt with without reference to the categorical concepts of ends and means, of success and failure, of costs, of profit or loss' (1990, p. 49). So, praxeology accounts for action by grasping the rational essence of thought manifested as action: 'Our science, . . . disregarding the accidental, considers only the essential. Its goal is the comprehension of the universal and . . . [i]t views action and the conditions under which action takes place not in their concrete form, as we encounter them in everyday life, nor in their actual setting, . . . but as formal constructions that enable us to grasp the patterns of human action in their purity' (1960, p. 13).

For Mises, it did not matter that the active subjective agents, '*homo agens* as he really is', turn out to be 'often weak, stupid, inconsiderate, and badly instructed' (1990, p. 24). Economics, in particular, must deal with 'real man, weak and subject to error as he is, not with ideal beings, omniscient and perfect as only gods could be' (1966, p. 97). Praxeological human science's correct focus was on the fact that agents act in accordance with a reasoned logic common to them all and not on any ancillary matters that may be 'behind' or that qualify the nature of the action. Mises summarized his position in the following passage.

> Praxeology and economics do not deal with human meaning and action as they should or would be if all men were inspired by an absolutely valid philosophy and equipped with a perfect knowledge of technology. For such notions as absolute validity and omniscience there is no room in the frame of a science whose subject matter is erring man. An end is everything which men aim at. A means is everything which acting men consider as such. (1966, pp. 92f)

Action is about the choice of scarce means that agents believe under the circumstances will realize particular, subjectively chosen ends. Regarding the status of means, Mises wrote that

> means are not in the given universe; in this universe there exist only things. A thing becomes a means when human reason plans to employ it for the attainment of some end and human action really employs it for this purpose. Thinking man sees the serviceableness of things, i.e., their ability to minister to his ends, and acting man makes them means. (1966, p. 92)

Once agents settle on their respectively desired ends, then, 'choosing means is a technical problem, as it were, . . . [and] a matter of reason' (1958, pp. 14f). In this respect, 'means are judged and appreciated according to their ability to produce definite effects. . . . [J]udgements about means are essentially inferences drawn from factual propositions concerning the power of the means in question to produce definite effects' (1958, p. 14). Having said all this, there remained a subjectivist element in the choice of means. As we have seen, means are not means until chosen by the exercise of judgement. There may be a technical and an inferential logical side to the choice of means, but they are 'judged and appreciated', too, in what can only be a subjective sense. Mises put this point himself. He defined 'value' in subjectivist terms: 'Value is not intrinsic, it is not in things. It is within us; it is the way in which man reacts to the conditions of his environment' (1966, p. 96). On the very same page, he wrote that 'means are valued derivatively according to the serviceableness in contributing to the attainment of ultimate ends. Their valuation is derived from the valuation of the respective ends' (1966, p. 96). These observations serve to compound the real-world condition that even at the praxeological level of analysis, human action must rely on means that are selected on the basis of incomplete knowledge and may be less than optimal relative to the ends pursued.

A further characteristic of means according to Mises was that where conscious action is concerned, their availability is always limited relative to the demands for them: 'As far as there is scarcity of means, man behaves rationally, i.e., he acts' (1990, p. 35; cf. 1966, p. 93). Praxeology's 'fundamental insight is the incontestable fact that man is in a position to choose among different states of affairs with regard to which he is not neutral and which are incompatible with each other, i.e., which cannot be enjoyed together' (1990, p. 20). His conclusion was that 'all action is economizing with the means available for the realization of attainable ends. The fundamental law of action is the economic principle. Every action is under its sway' (1960, p. 80). In even more explicitly economic terms, Mises saw all action as having the objective of exchange and, because of the scarcity of means, there is a price to be paid, an opportunity cost to be accepted. Both exchange and its associated cost were given a strongly subjectivist construction.

> Action is an attempt to substitute a more satisfactory state of affairs for a less satisfactory one. We call such a willfully induced alteration an exchange. A less desirable condition is bartered for a more desirable. What gratifies less is abandoned in order to attain something that pleases more. That which is abandoned is called the price paid for the attainment of the end sought. The value of the price paid is called costs [sic]. (1966, p. 97)

Considerations such as these should give us cause to temper our misgivings about claims by Mises along the lines that 'we do not maintain that the theoretical science of human action should be aprioristic, but that it is and always has been so. Every attempt to reflect upon the problems raised by human action is necessarily bound to aprioristic reasoning' (1966, p. 40). Consider, too, the claim that 'correct results from our aprioristic reasoning are not only logically irrefutable, but at the same time applicable with all their apodictic certainty to reality provided that the assumptions involved are given in reality' (1990, p. 11). That is, 'whether the results obtained apply to reality can be decided only by the demonstration that the assumptions involved have or do not have any counterpart in the reality which we wish to explain' (1990, p. 11). The methodological mediation in the process of reaching sound understanding and explanation is what Mises referred to as 'the method of speculative constructions' and 'the only method available' for economic reasoning to be applied (1990, p. 11).

Mises was especially concerned that the relationship between the notions of rationality and irrationality as these were thought to apply to the understanding of human action should be properly specified. The particular point that he addressed was the claim that rational human action had been allowed to exclude efforts to account for the irrational nature of the real life-world of human agents. This was accompanied by calls for an irrationally grounded human science to be developed. There was in this a link back to Max Weber, too. Mises noted that Weber had correctly distinguished such action from unconsciously driven, instinctive functional and reactive bodily responses to stimuli that were not the subject of reason. Mises's position on this distinction was that 'conscious or purposeful behavior is in sharp contrast to unconscious behavior, i.e., the reflexes and the involuntary responses of the body's cells and nerves to stimuli' (1966, p. 11). His point was, then, that 'the opposite of [rational] action is not *irrational behavior*, but a reactive response to stimuli which cannot be controlled by the volition of the person concerned' (1966, p. 20). But as we saw above, one of the earliest problems he encountered in this area was Weber's treatment of non-instinctive human conduct as only potentially rational (Mises, 1960, pp. 82ff; cf. 1990, pp. 23, 44). Weber then made a delimited rational action concept, based on an agent's subjectively intended meaning, a cornerstone of his metatheory for the empirical human sciences. As far as Mises was concerned, Weber had understated the reach of rationality in failing to realize that all action was most appropriately conceived as necessarily and exclusively rational. There was no sense in which action needed to be investigated according to its different objectives as Weber had done. For example, 'it is quite clear', Mises thought, 'that what Weber calls "valuational" behavior cannot be fundamentally distinguished from "rational" behavior' (1960, p. 83). The same conclusion applied to his separation of conduct directed by 'tradition' and 'affective' states of emotion. Mises saw these, too, as rational actions in his sense (1960, pp. 84f). Action must be regulated by will and volition, and it must be self-consciously end-directed and meaningful to the agent. The essential character of rational action always remained independent of its purposes or ends: 'it chooses between given possibilities in order to attain the most ardently desired goal' (1960, p. 85). Mises intended the rational essence of action to have the particular sense that it is always and everywhere the product of the conscious logic of reasoned thought applied to realizing the chosen end under the circumstances known to the agent. Conscious choice not to act, habitual action, as well as incorrect or suboptimal action were all rational, too.

However complex their ultimate conditions, praxeology and economics also remain strictly unconcerned about the particular ends, purposes or goals that agents choose to pursue. As a libertarian, Mises saw these things as a subjective matter to be settled by private individual values and judgements. This meant that praxeology 'is subjectivistic and takes the value judgements of acting man as ultimate data not open to any further critical examination' (1966, p. 22, cf. p. 95). And, as 'for the evaluation of ultimate ends there is no interpersonal standard available' (1958, p. 14, cf. pp. 12, 14f), this put the process beyond the grasp of others' reason. Thus praxeology 'is neutral with regard to the ultimate ends that the individuals want to attain' (1990, p. 42), or, more strongly put, 'it is in this subjectivism that the objectivity of our science lies' (1966, p. 22). Here Mises reasoned as a result that 'any examination of ultimate ends turns out to be purely subjective and therefore arbitrary' (1966, p. 96). It is not the province of scientists to challenge the philosophies of eudaemonism, hedonism, utilitarianism or any other that are manifested in agents' choices of objectives. Rather it is their obligation to accept that all goals may exist and confine themselves to ensuring that actions are understood (1990, pp. 22f; cf. 1966, pp. 14f). Thus, Mises wrote that 'ends are irrational, i.e., they neither require nor are capable of a rational justification' (1960, pp. 92f; cf. 1958, p. 267). But, any attempt to classify an *action* as irrational and unacceptable on the basis of its goals was for Mises unwarranted censorship (1990, pp. 23f).

In spite of his focus on human action, with its necessarily mental origins, it is nonetheless certain that Mises intended to avoid any taint of psychologism. He took the trouble to separate two schools of psychology, distinguishing the naturalistic cum experimental orientation from one which pursues 'cognition of human emotions, motivations, ideas, judgements of value and volitions . . .' (1958, p. 264). To this latter, 'mundane and common-sense' version of psychological inquiry Mises ascribed the distinctive name of 'thymology' (1958, pp. 265 ff; cf. 1962, pp. 46ff). It was of relevance to the human sciences for two reasons. First, it is immanently involved in any inquiry concerned with human agency because it is directed towards comprehending 'a faculty indispensable to everybody in the conduct of daily affairs . . .' (1958, p. 264). Secondly, it is integral to the process of understanding (*Verstehen*) applied by analysts in devising their discursive accounts of empirico-historical phenomena.

It is appropriate to note that the two aspects come together, according to Mises, in the fact that all agents, not just formal analysts, apply such thymologically grounded understanding in their daily dealings with others around them (1962, p. 50). That is, such 'insight into the minds of other men' is 'a technique employed in all human relations. . . . All [agents] are eager to get information about other people's valuations and plans and to appraise them correctly' (1958, p. 265). He elaborated on the reasons for this: 'The environment in which man acts is shaped by natural events on the one hand and by human action on the other. The future for which he plans will be codetermined by the actions of people who are planning and acting like himself. If he wants to succeed, he must anticipate their conduct' (1962, p. 46). This is quite a different issue from anticipating events in nature, as Mises expressly realized and he was inevitably sceptical about the intellectual security of human anticipations: 'There is no method that would enable us to learn about a human personality all that would be needed to make such prognostications with the degree of certainty technology attains in its predictions' (1962, p. 59).

7.5 Time and human action

In all that has been said so far, Mises had failed to confront the most troublesome aspect of the applying the tenets of praxeology to the search for understanding and explanation in the realm of human phenomena. This is the fact that all actual human action takes place within the unceasing and irreversible efflux of time. He recognized this: 'It is acting that provides man with the notion of time and makes him aware of the flux of time. The idea of time is a praxeological category' (1966, p. 100). Furthermore, 'the concepts of change and of time are inseparably linked together. Action aims at change and is therefore in the temporal order. Human reason is even incapable of conceiving the ideas of timeless existence and of timeless action' (1966, p. 99). Human agents must act from an ever-moving and changing location between an irrevocable and cumulative past and an unknowable and perfidious future. Thus, 'he who acts distinguishes between the time before the action, the time absorbed by the action, and the time after the action has been finished. He cannot be neutral with regard to the lapse of time' (1966, p. 99).

In this respect, the common status of human reason in pure logic, mathematics and praxeology can no longer be sustained, as Mises was aware. Logic and mathematics comprise ratiocinative processes of the mind that are 'synchronous or ... out of time' (1966, p. 99). Time and action will be involved in discursively setting them out, but this temporality:

> must not be confused with the logical simultaneity of all parts of an aprioristic deductive system. Within such a system the notions of anteriority and consequence are metaphorical only. They do not refer to the system, but to our action of grasping it. The system itself implies neither the category of time nor that of causality. (1966, p. 99)

Praxeology was defined by Mises as an aprioristic and deductive system. But by contrast to other such systems, it explicitly argues its logic in temporal and causal terms. This is because 'change is one of its elements. The notions of sooner and later and of cause and effect are among its constituents. Anteriority and consequence are essential concepts of praxeological reasoning. So is the irreversibility of events' (1966, p. 99). Moreover, though set in time, the sequences of praxeology provide 'exact knowledge about future conditions' so that the 'predictions of praxeology are, within the range of their applicability, absolutely certain' (1962, pp. 64f).

It is evident that Mises understood much about the import of time for action and its implications for the empirico-historical human sciences. The certainties of praxeology are negated once its tenets are set in real-world human events. In simplified terms, the conditional logic of praxeology in the form if **A**, then **B**, is incomplete as an account of human conduct once we pose the question of the origin of condition **A**. He argued this condition as the value judgements of acting agents which effectively situated the logic into an historical context. In such a context, 'whether our anticipations of – our own or other people's – future value judgements and of the means that will be resorted to for adjusting action to these value judgements will be correct or not cannot be known in advance' (1962, p. 65). Here Mises demonstrated his awareness of the significance of the fact that individual active agents must act in the face of time yet to come: 'No action can be planned and executed without understanding of the future. . . . Every action is a speculation, i.e., guided by a definite opinion concerning the uncertain conditions of the future. Even in short-run activities this uncertainty prevails. Nobody can know whether some unexpected fact will not render vain all that he has provided for the next day or the next hour' (1962, pp. 50f). This is because in pursuing a chosen course of action, 'man is at the mercy of forces and powers beyond his control' (1962, p. 65). As a consequence, the agent faces true uncertainty because 'to acting man the future is hidden' (1966, p. 105). It is 'one of the fundamental conditions of man's existence and action . . . that he does not know what will happen in the future' (1958, p. 180). Mises saw clearly that 'the uncertainty of the future is already implied in the very notion of action. That man acts and the future is uncertain are by no means two independent matters. They are only two different modes of establishing one thing' (1966, p. 105).

In this respect, the idea that an acting agent is aware of 'the time after the action has been finished' takes on a dual meaning. This period will be in focus, as far as it can be imagined, before the action proceeds.

The time to come must be the subject of planning and envisaged change for the better. In Mises's words, 'action is always directed toward the future; it is essentially and necessarily always a planning and acting for a better future' (1966, p. 100). The very driving force for action depends upon an agent's 'dissatisfaction with expected future conditions as they would probably develop if nothing were done to alter them' and the agent 'becomes conscious of time when he plans to convert a less satisfactory present state into a more satisfactory future state' (1966, p. 100). The end state towards which the action is to be directed must be conceived of *ex ante* in the imagination in order to establish the subjective belief that it will make the agent better off in the sense and to the degree desired. This state can have no other content than that which comes from forming expectations. In addition, the time after the action will be a period of *ex post* monitoring and reflecting upon the result of the action (1966, pp. 100f). At that time, the point is for the agent to assess the results of the action relative to what had been anticipated *ex ante*. In particular, as Mises put it, the agent 'can never know beforehand to what extent his acting will attain the end sought and, if it attains it, whether this action will in retrospect appear – to himself or to the other people looking upon it – as the best choice among those that were open to him at the instant he embarked upon it' (1962, p. 65). In what follows, we will need to ascertain the extent to which Mises took account of this important duality.

As we have seen, he was aware that individual active agents as well as analysts, each for their own purposes, had to try to anticipate the future actions of relevant others. It is to be noted, though, that he devoted considerably more attention to the perspective of the observer-analyst than to the active subjective agent in this context. Of course, the substance of what the observer seeks to know is none other than the manner in which the active agent copes with uncertainty, but Mises chose not to make the latter an explicit issue. His choice was a result of the praxeological abstraction that axiomatic human action could be conceived of without any time referent. In turn, this was the result of its logical rather than immediately ontological status, for as was noted above, there could be no claim that human action in its axiomatic form could have an empirical existence.

As active agents or as analysts, we are bounded by the limitation of current knowledge that there is simply no way that observed actions of agents can be completely and reliably linked to the internalized human character and conditions which are prior to them. Individual conduct is the product of human mental processes and the ideas and judgements of value that direct the individual's actions. However, they cannot be traced back to their ultimate causes because we know so little about these processes that produce within a human being the thoughts that precede responses to the state of his physical and ideological environment. This means recognizing that when trying to predict the future pattern of another individual's actions, the chance and contingency we find in agents' conduct, together with the apparent unreliability of human responses to situational change that we notice, cannot legitimately be ascribed to conditions of reality-in-itself. It is likely that these characteristics are rather the product of our *ex ante* ignorance as observers, our inability to get at the cause and effect relationship between human ideas and actions (1958, pp. 90, 93).

The result is that uncertainty about the future states of affairs to be realized defies reliable quantification. Because they are based on individual human experiences of the past, no expectations and predictions can be apodictic according to Mises: 'Apodictic certainty is only within the orbit of the deductive system of aprioristic theory' (1966, p. 105; cf. 1958, pp. 303f). This uncertainty of predictions included those made with respect to the world of nature, although in that world, the reliability of extrapolation of past regularities into the expected future is generally quite high. High enough, at least, for agents continuously to rely upon relevant physical and quantitative temporal patterns of their natural and technological surroundings. So, Mises observed, although 'there is no way mortal man can acquire *certain* knowledge about the future' (1958, p. 304), it is an analysts confronting human agents in managing their future that the ontology of human action in this respect is distinct from that of sequences of events in the natural world (1958, p. 273). Consequently, while observers as human themselves may 'know something' about the workings of human action, their 'knowledge of them and about them is *categorically* different from the kind of knowledge the experimental natural sciences provide about natural events' (1958, p. 307). The 'most important use' for this knowledge derived from experiences of the past is nonetheless 'the service it renders to the anticipation of future conditions and to the designing of action that necessarily always aims at affecting future conditions' (1958, p. 307). For as Mises observed, 'the task with which acting man, that is, everybody, is faced in all relations with his fellows does not refer to the past; it refers to the future. To know the future reactions of other people is the first task of acting man' (1958, p. 311). For observers, the crucial problem of understanding the human activities around them is 'how can man have any knowledge of the future value judgements and actions of other people?' (1958, p. 311). However, Mises emphasized that while in our relations with other agents, 'we try to form an opinion about their future conduct', it is readily seen 'in what the fundamental difference consists between this kind of anticipation and that of an engineer designing the plan for the construction of a bridge' (1958, p. 313).

More explicitly stated, Mises saw the problem of forecasting future agents' actions as comprised of two particular aspects (1958, pp. 314f). One was establishing the specific causal factors that would be operative in the agents' decisions. The other was to establish the relevant weightings and timing to be attributed to the influence of each factor in a particular case of expected action. Mises concluded here that 'the precariousness of forecasting is mainly due to the intricacy of this second problem', for the observer's insight in the former identification process is likely to be greater (1958, p. 314).

The sole source of any knowledge about human existence is experience of the past. In this respect, when dealing with other agents, Mises reasoned that 'all that can be asserted about their future conduct is speculative anticipation of the future based on the specific understanding of the historical branches of the sciences of human action' (1958, p. 272, cf. p. 288). And, most significantly, to these observations he added a rider: 'it is obvious that this knowledge which provides a man with the ability to anticipate to some degree other people's future attitudes is not a priori knowledge' (1958, p. 311). Rather it relies on the thymological principle that 'what we know about the actual content of judgements of value can be derived only from experience', that is, from the interpreted past (1958, p. 311). We have experience of other people's past value judgements and actions which we obtain 'from intercourse with other men, from our acting in various human relations' (1958, p. 312); and we have experience of our own value judgements and actions that we recognize through introspection.

So it has to be, Mises concluded, that 'for lack of any better tool, we must take recourse to thymology if we want to anticipate other people's future attitudes and actions' (1958, p. 313). However, he added the caveat that 'it is impossible to deduce with certainty from thymological experience the future conduct of men, whether individuals or groups of individuals. All prognostications based on thymological knowledge are specific understanding of the future as practised daily by everyone in their actions . . .' (1958, pp. 273f). All that thymology can achieve is 'the elaboration of a catalogue of human traits. It can, moreover, establish the fact that certain traits appeared in the past as a rule in connection with certain other traits'. However, it can never enable observers to 'know in advance with what weight the various factors will be operative in a definite future event' (1958, p. 274).

7.6 From praxeology to the realities of human agency

In confronting the real world of human action, Mises argued that scientists and active agents must accept that 'life and reality are not logical' (1966, p. 67). The situation, he continued, was rather that:

> life and reality are neither logical nor illogical, they are simply given. But logic is the only tool available to man for the comprehension of both. It is vain to object that life and history are inscrutable and are ineffable and that human reason can never penetrate to their inner core.... There are many things beyond the reach of the human mind. But as far as man is able to attain any knowledge, however limited, he can use only one avenue of approach, that opened by reason. (1966, pp. 67f, cf. p. 89)

As exercises in applied reason and logic, whatever the limitations of these capacities dictated by the intractabilities of the real world, Mises identified what he called 'two main branches of the sciences of human action' as praxeology and history (1966, p. 30; cf. 1962, p. 41ff). In interpreting him, therefore, we should maintain a clear separation between praxeology and the manifestation of its axioms in humanly generated phenomena of experience. That is, between praxeology as the *a priori* science of human action and its application to the empirico-historical sciences of human phenomena. Most significant, and yet potentially confusing to readers, was his identification of the term *economics* exclusively with *praxeology*. The result was that *this economics* was never intended to have any immediately empirico-historical status. Thus, care is needed when dealing with what is often loosely referred to as 'Mises's economics' without giving due attention to this crucial distinction.

The general objective of both praxeology and history 'is the comprehension of the meaning and relevance of human action', but they apply for their respective purposes to 'two different epistemological procedures: conception and understanding. Conception is the mental tool of praxeology; understanding is the specific mental tool of history' (1966, p. 51). More specifically, Mises argued that 'the cognition of history refers to what is unique and individual in each event or class of events' (1966, p. 51). He conceived of history as comprising a study of the full range of events generated by human action. Baldly put, 'history in the broadest sense of the term is the totality of human experience. History is experience, and all experience is historical' (1962, p. 45). History 'deals with the concrete content of human action. It studies all human endeavours in their infinite multiplicity and variety and all the individual actions with all their accidental, special, and particular implications. It scrutinizes the ideas guiding acting men and the outcome of the actions performed' (1966, p. 30). For the purpose of comparison, Mises reminded us that praxeology with its cognition confined to conception in the form of universals and general categories is 'a theoretical and systematic, not a historical, science. Its scope is human action as such, irrespective of all environmental, accidental, and individual circumstances of . . . concrete acts' (1966, p. 32, cf. p. 51). In the case of the study of the economic realm, he phrased these insights this way: 'There are no such things as a historical method in economics or a discipline of institutional economics. There is economics and there is economic history. The two must never be confused' (1966, p. 66). For as he elaborated elsewhere, 'economics is not history. Economics is a branch of praxeology . . .' and it is 'economic history that needs to be interpreted with the aid of the theories developed by economics' (1962, p. 73).

The import of the metatheoretical beliefs that have been attributed to Mises above was to be found in his emphasis that while praxeology is an *a priori*, and purely general science of human action, its rationale and utility could only be in its application to the understanding and explanation of empirico-historical phenomena (cf. Ebeling, 1990a, p. xvi). He was not a builder of a system of theoretical concepts for its own sake and was, at times, very careful to explain the intentions and meaning of his metatheory and the distinctive view of theoretical conception to which it led him. It is important to reiterate first of all that his *a priori* axioms about human conduct, and the so-called economic theory *qua* praxeology that he constructed from them, were never intended to be ends in themselves for economists. The scope of the conceptual insights into human action claimed by the axioms was very restricted and limited to what all of us as human beings know to be always and everywhere correct. There was, then, no sense in which these essentials of human action could be, or needed to be, subjected to independent empirically oriented tests of veracity. Mises observed pithily: 'some authors have raised the rather shallow question how a praxeologist would react to an experience contradicting theorems of his apriorist doctrine. The answer is: in the same way in which a mathematician will react to the "experience" that there is no difference between two apples and seven apples or a logician to the "experience" that A and non-A are identical' (1962, p. 42). The essentials are nowhere manifested in their 'raw' form to be tested, anyway, for they are conceptual forms that represent merely the consistent ontological core of an infinite range of empirically determined actions.

Mises stressed that 'the end of science is to know reality. It is not mental gymnastics or a logical pastime. Therefore praxeology restricts its inquiries to the study of acting under those conditions and presuppositions which are given in reality' (1966, p. 65). Empirically, 'the experience with which the sciences of human action have to deal is always an experience of complex phenomena. Historical experience as an experience of complex phenomena does not provide us with facts . . .' for the reason that every such experience 'is open to various interpretations, and is in fact interpreted in different ways' (1966, p. 31; cf. 1990, pp. 10, 18, 40). The ultimate challenge for praxeological theory is to serve as the foundation for the understanding and explanation of empirico-historical economic phenomena whose constitution extends well beyond the axiomatics of rational agents' actions. Therefore, argued Mises, references to experience as the context of theory 'does not impair the aprioristic character of praxeology. Experience merely directs our curiosity toward certain problems and diverts it from other problems. It tells us what we should explore, but it does not tell us how we could proceed in our search for knowledge' (1966, p. 65, cf. p. 66). In this respect, then, 'theory and the comprehension of living and changing reality are not in opposition to one another. Without theory, the general aprioristic science of human action, there is no comprehension of the reality of human action' (1966, pp. 38f). He reinforced this idea by stating the principle that economic inquiry 'adopts for the organized presentation of its results a form in which aprioristic theory and the interpretation of historical phenomena are intertwined' (1966, p. 66).

In his strategy for the pursuit of empirico-historical knowledge in the human sciences, Mises adopted the definition and use of ideal types much as they had been espoused by Max Weber. The need for ideal types arose in Mises's metatheoretical inquiries because of the ontological origin and nature of historical events as products of situationally conditioned human action. He wrote that history 'deals with unique and unrepeatable events, with the irreversible flux of human affairs. A historical event cannot be described without reference to the persons involved and to the place and date of its occurrence'. Thus, 'although unique and unrepeatable, historical events have one common feature: they are human action. . . . What counts for history is always the meaning of the men concerned: the meaning that they attach to the state of affairs they want to alter, the meaning they attach to the effects produced by the actions' (1966, p. 59). Now the demands that such objects of knowledge place on scientific inquiry can only be coped with by means of the common thread of the agents' meaning that can be attributed to each event. Mises summarized his approach in the argument that 'the aspect from which history arranges and assorts the infinite multiplicity of events is their meaning. The only principle which it applies for the systemization of its objects – men, ideas, institutions, social entities, and artifacts – is meaning affinity' (1966, p. 59). It was this 'meaning affinity' that for Mises provided the grounds for constructing ideal types.

Mises gave emphasis to two characteristics of ideal types that assist in understanding their role in the human sciences. First, with their empirico-historical orientation, ideal types are theoretical constructs that reach beyond the substantive scope of praxeological and scientific concepts, even though all such concepts may appear as elements in their construction. In particular, there is one human trait that must be imbedded in any action as its essential and determining motivation: 'to remove, directly or indirectly, as much as possible any uneasiness felt' (1962, p. 76). Thus 'ideal types are constructed with the use of ideas and concepts developed by all nonhistorical branches of knowledge. . . . This is valid . . . with regard to praxeological categories and concepts. They provide, to be sure, the indispensable mental tools for the study of history. However, they do not refer to the understanding of the unique and individual events which are the subject matter of history'. For this reason, an ideal type can 'never be a simple adoption of a praxeological concept' (1966, p. 61). And Mises emphasized that in the case of particular conceptual forms, those comprising 'type-concepts . . . ought not to be confused with praxeological concepts used for the conceiving of the categories of human action', even though they may carry the same name (1990, p. 14; cf. 1966, p. 61).

The example he used to indicate the distinction was the concept of the *entrepreneur*. Entrepreneur in praxeology can only refer to a distinct function that is integral to the axiom of human action. It gives the axiom an immediate ontological status because the action has a particular character attributed to it that is recognizable in the reality of action. Mises saw this function as reason applied to 'provision for an uncertain future', and the concept is the 'personification of the function which results in profit or loss' (1990, p. 14). Thus he posited the praxeological concept as different from the empirico-historically relevant ideal type of the entrepreneur who appears in 'current economic problems . . . [as] a class of men who are engaged in business . . .'. The type immediate to reality of economic activity 'can never have the conceptual exactitude which the praxeological concept entrepreneur has. You never meet in life men who are nothing else than the personification of one function only' (1990, p. 14; cf. 1966, pp. 61f). However, what Mises has prescribed here is a distinction that is one of degree only with the implication that by compounding functions we can move from the concepts of the praxeology to ideal types.

These references to two categories of entrepreneur is indicative of the second particular characteristic of ideal types cited by Mises: namely, they are not general class categories. As always, in the case of the entrepreneur, the praxeological concept is logically prior to, and more specifically defined as a class of economic agent than the ideal type of entrepreneur. It is in this sense that the ideal type:

> is not a class concept, because its description does not indicate the marks whose presence definitely and unambiguously determines class membership. An ideal type cannot be defined; it must be characterized by an enumeration of those features whose presence by and large decides whether in a concrete instance we are or are not faced with a specimen belonging to the ideal type in question. (1966, p. 60)

Ideal types are to be constructed *ad hoc* in the process of their use in devising an understanding of particular empirico-historical phenomena. They cannot be set up prior to their application. Here Mises made reference to the sometimes expressed idea that the classical concept of economic man as *homo oeconomicus* constituted an ideal type. He rejected this on the grounds that an ideal type cannot be such 'an embodiment of one side or aspect of man's various aims and desires' and that it would be pointless 'to refer to such an illusory homunculus in dealing with life and history' (1966, p. 62; cf. 1962, pp. 75f). If empirico-historical economic phenomena are to be comprehended, the relevant categories of agents need to be drawn with an adequately meaningful set of characteristics. In any inquiry, then, the required content of pertinent ideal types will be determined by the pragmatics of conveying understanding. The content of an ideal type will indicate that it is a case of a previously established category, but 'not all its [potential] characteristics need to be present in any one example' (1966, p. 60). Most importantly, Mises noted that 'it is not the ideal type that determines the mode of understanding; it is the mode of understanding that requires the construction and use of corresponding ideal types' (1966, p. 61).

In Weber's case, ideal types were employed by analysts to bring theoretical concepts and constructs to bear in the endeavour to understand specific empirico-historical phenomena. Mises concurred, emphasizing that 'no historical problem can be treated without the aid of ideal types' (1966, p. 60). He viewed ideal types as 'specific notions employed in historical research and in the representation of its results. They are concepts of understanding' (1966, p. 59). They 'are constructed and employed on the basis of a definite mode of understanding the course of events, whether in order to forecast the future or to analyse the past. . . . An ideal type is a conceptual tool of understanding and the service that it renders depends entirely on the serviceableness of the definite mode of understanding' (1958, pp. 316f, cf. p. 319). As Mises also agreed, the purpose of constructed ideal types was to help to overcome the complex of difficulties analysts meet in their efforts to bring some coherence to accounts of how human events are caused. Analysts confront 'the opposition of mind and matter, . . . freedom of the will, and . . . individuality' when dealing with human agency. In this context, 'ideal types are expedients to simplify the treatment of the puzzling multiplicity and variety of human affairs' (1958, p. 320). It was Mises's conclusion that the ideal type 'is always the representation of complex phenomena of reality, either of men, of institutions, or of ideologies' (1966, p. 62). But he hastened to add the qualification that such complexities of human life and action cannot be fully grasped by any constructed concepts and definitions. As a result, there would always exist in explanations of human phenomena some residue of unanswered or even unanswerable questions (1958, p. 320).

As a practical matter of doing human science, however, it was the comparison of the typical with the reality that was supposed to allow a causal explanation of human events. It could do so by means of compounding the ideal type constructs of theory with the additional qualities that gave the real-world object phenomenon the particular characteristics that brought about the deviations from those constructs. Following Max Weber, Mises viewed the constructions comprising economic theory as images of 'non-existent states of things' built up 'from an insight into the conditions of human action' (1990, p. 11; cf. 1966, p. 65). These conditions are captured in ideal types of agents who 'are valuing and acting in a uniform or similar way' (1958, p. 316). As mediations in inquiry, whether or not the state of things depicted 'corresponds or could correspond to reality is irrelevant for their instrumental efficiency. Even unrealizable constructions can render valuable service in giving us the opportunity to conceive what makes them unrealizable and in what respect they differ from reality' (1990, p. 11). Using the example of a static equilibrium state of a market, Mises was able to suggest how, even though such a state is speculative and could never be realized empirically, it did allow the analyst insight into particular deviant effects observable in real-world disequilibrium states. One outcome so observed may be the entrepreneurial profits (or losses) that he argued are disequilibrium phenomena (1990, p. 11).

Mises continued by reminding us that every extant economic phenomenon that is the object of theoretical investigation is a unique piece of historical experience. It is, therefore, appropriate to identify object economic phenomena as included under the rubric of individualizing moral or historical sciences (for which he used the term *Geisteswissenschaften*). Economic theory *qua* praxeology when brought to such phenomena is 'the indispensable tool for the grasp of economic history. Economic history can neither prove nor disprove the teachings of economic theory. It is on the contrary economic theory which makes it possible for us to conceive the economic facts of the past' (1990, pp. 11f; cf. 1960, pp. 101f). At the level of empirico-historical investigations, analysts have 'to study the individual and unique conditions of the case in question' (1990, p. 12). In relation to understanding human actions, they must recognize that:

> every individual is born into a definite social and natural milieu. An individual is not simply man in general, whom history can regard in the abstract. An individual is at any instant of his life the product of all the experiences to which his ancestors were exposed plus those to which he himself has so far been exposed. (1958, p. 159)

At this point, it is appropriate to stress Mises's singularist and individualist orientation with respect to understanding human action and agency. He emphasised the fact that although each action by each individual can only be a singular act, as 'human life is an unceasing sequence of single actions ... the single action is by no means isolated' (1966, p. 45). Human action can, therefore, only be fully understood if it is realized that it 'has two aspects. It is on the one hand a partial action in the framework of a further-stretching action, the performance of a fraction of the aims set by a more far-reaching action. It is on the other hand itself a whole with regard to the actions aimed at by the performance of its own parts' (1966, p. 45). He provided a definition of individualism that probed the significance it has for human science by explicating the concept of the individual to which it referred:

> Individualism as a principle of the philosophical, praxeological, and historical analysis of human action means the establishment of the facts that all actions can be traced back to individuals and that no scientific method can succeed in determining how definite external events, liable to a description by the methods of the natural sciences, produce within the human mind definite ideas, value judgements, and volitions. In this sense the individual that cannot be dissolved into components is both the starting point and the ultimate given of all endeavours to deal with human action. (1962, p. 82)

As an individualist, Mises was categorical that always and everywhere 'praxeology deals with the actions of individual men' (1966, p. 41), so that 'no sensible proposition concerning human action can be asserted without reference to what the acting individuals are aiming at and what they consider as success or failure, as profit or loss' (1962, p. 80). For as he put it, the singular '*Ego* is the unity of the acting being. ... No matter what a man was and what he may become later, in the very act of choosing and acting he is an *Ego*' (1966, p. 44). As individuals, human agents are the joint products of their genetico-physiological inheritance and the cumulative influences of the social and other situational conditions they experience over their lifetime. 'The content of human action ... is determined by the personal qualities of every acting man' (1966, p. 46). These qualities of an individual agent are a compound of 'the innate and inherited biological qualities and all that life has worked upon him [to] make a man what he is at any instant of his pilgrimage. They are his fate and destiny' (1966, p. 46). In this primary respect, Mises recognized that an agent's 'will is not "free" in the metaphysical sense of this term. It is determined by his background and all the influences to which he himself and his ancestors were exposed' (1966, p. 46). On the most general, cosmic level, he stressed that the conception of agents' freedom to choose their existence must be tempered:

> [I]t is not permissible to interpret this freedom as independence of the universe and its laws. Man too is an element of the universe, descended from the original X out of which everything developed. ... He is at any instant of his life ... a product of the whole history of the universe. All his actions are the inevitable result of his individuality as shaped by all that preceded. (1962, p. 57)

More specifically put, 'actions are directed by ideas, and ideas are products of the human mind, which is definitely a part of the universe and of which the power is strictly determined by the whole structure of the universe' (1962, p. 57). He recognized, too, that on a more pragmatic level, human agents are social beings. Each is 'born into a socially organized environment ... [and] lives and acts within society' (1966, p. 143). In reality individuals are to some extent contained in their actions by virtue of their social and structural situations. They can only act *qua* individuals with given innate and learned characteristics, but 'the social or societal element is a certain orientation of the actions of individual men' (1966, p. 143). That is, it is both:

> inheritance and environment [that] direct a man's actions. They suggest to him both the ends and the means. He lives not simply as man *in abstracto*; he lives as a son of his family, his race, his people, and his age; as a citizen of his country; as a member of a definite social group; as a practitioner of a certain vocation; as a follower of definite religious, metaphysical, philosophical, and political ideas ... (1966, p. 46)

And, 'seen from the point of view of the individual, society is the great means for the attainment of all his ends' (1966, p. 165). It is with respect to these situated qualities of action that we should consider society as 'logically or historically . . . antecedent to the individual' (1966, p. 143).

Mises believed, therefore, that individualism must be accepted as 'a philosophy of social cooperation and the progressive intensification of the social nexus' (1966, p. 152). The foundation for this is that 'in striving after his own – rightly understood – interests the individual works toward an intensification of social cooperation and peaceful intercourse' (1966, p. 146). Thus, 'society and the state are . . . the primary means for all people to attain the ends they aim at of their own accord. They are created by human effort and their maintenance and most suitable organization are tasks not essentially different from all other concerns of human action' (1966, p. 148).

It is in this respect that individual agents are prepared to exercise their existential freedom of will and to curb its potentially contingent effects within the constraints imposed by the social structures they must confront and work through. *In situ* then, even though 'the adjustment of the individual to the requirements of social cooperation demands sacrifices', they are 'only temporary and apparent sacrifices as they are more than compensated for by the incomparably greater advantages which living within society provides' (1966, p. 148). The general principle that Mises established here with respect to the situated nature of individual actions was summarized as it applies to government. 'Whatever the system of government may be, the foundation upon which it is built and rests is always the opinion of those ruled that to obey and to be loyal to this government better serves their own interests than insurrection and the establishment of another regime' (1966, p. 149). The relationship of individuals to their government expressed in this passage was that which could be extrapolated to individuals' participation in any structured situational entity that demands their conformity. Mises's view was that the vast majority of active agents channel their subjectively devised actions through, and are prepared to accede to the authority and demands of, their inherited environmental situations to the best of their ability and knowledge. For the most part, as a consequence, agents' day-to-day actions are characterized by an apparent 'intellectual inertia' and take on a routine and habitual quality (1966, pp. 46f). However, he hastened to add a crucial rider: 'The fact that an action is in the regular course of affairs performed spontaneously, as it were, does not mean that it is not due to conscious volition and to a deliberate choice. Indulgence in a routine which possibly could be changed is action' (1966, p. 47). In such cases of action, real choice is still involved, for the agent 'chooses to adopt traditional patterns or patterns adopted by other people because he is convinced that this procedure is best fitted to achieve his own welfare. And he is ready to change his ideology and consequently his mode of action whenever he becomes convinced that this would better serve his own interests' (1966, p. 46).

Such observations raise the issue of how Mises perceived the relationship of collectivism to the primary individualist mode of interpreting human agency. That is, what are the implications of recognizing that, as a matter of observed fact, individuals exist only in collectives and that, therefore, they can have no meaningful existence as isolated individual actors *per se*. While he believed it correct to see individuals and collectives as enjoying a correlative and inseparable existence in reality, he maintained that active individuals are ontologically prior to any collectives of which they may be part. As a matter of first principle, 'the *We* cannot act otherwise than each of them acting on his own behalf. They can either all act together in accord, or one of them may act for them all. In the latter case the cooperation of the others consists in their bringing about the situation which makes one man's action effective for them too' (1966, p. 44; original emphasis). That is, as 'all actions are performed by individuals', a collective 'operates always through the intermediary of one or several individuals whose actions are related to the collective as a secondary source ... [and] has no existence and reality outside of the individual member's actions' (1966, p. 42). For Mises it followed that 'the way to a cognition of collective wholes is through an analysis of the individuals' actions', for 'if we scrutinize the meaning of the various actions performed by individuals we must necessarily learn everything about the actions of collective wholes' (1966, p. 42). Therefore, he concluded, 'it is illusory to believe that it is possible to visualize collective wholes. They are never visible; their cognition is always the outcome of the understanding of the meaning which acting men attribute to their acts' (1966, p. 43; cf. 1962, pp. 78ff).

Applied theoretical inquiry is intended to enable observers to understand (Mises used *verstehen* in some contexts) the situationally conditioned actions that result in an individual object phenomenon of human science. It was at this empirico-historical level of scientific inquiry that thymology became directly relevant. Baldly put by Mises, 'psychology in the sense of thymology is a branch of history. It derives its knowledge from historical experience. . . . All that thymology can tell us is that in the past definite men or groups of men were valuing and acting in a definite way' (1958, p. 272, cf. p. 280). In this connection, he attributed a twofold function to the process of *a posteriori* understanding in the historical sciences of human action. First, 'it establishes ... the fact that, motivated by definite value judgements, people have engaged in definite actions and applied definite means to attain the ends they seek' (1958, pp. 264f). Secondly, 'it tries ... to evaluate the effects and the intensity of the effects of an action, its bearing upon the further course of events' (1958, p. 265).

For Mises, these insights were fundamental to the metatheory of the empirico-historical human sciences in that they orient inquiry towards the central role of agency based on the meaning agents as individuals attribute to their circumstances: 'As a rule, the situation to which man consciously reacts can be analyzed only with concepts that make reference to meaning'. The important implication is then that 'if one chooses to analyze the situation without entering into the meaning that acting man sees in it, the analysis will not be successful in bringing into relief what is essential in the situation and decisive of [sic] the nature of the reaction to it' (1960, p. 131). So it is that 'if the historian refers to the meaning of a fact, he always refers either to the interpretation acting men gave to the situation in which they had to live and to act, and to the outcome of their ensuing actions ...' (1958, p. 161; cf. 1966, p. 26).

The process of reaching *Verstehen* for Mises was 'not a privilege of the historians. It is everybody's business' (1966, p. 58). It is a process 'all historians and all other people always apply in commenting upon social events of the past and in forecasting future events' (1990, p. 26). Thus 'in observing the conditions of his environment everybody is a historian. Everybody uses understanding in dealing with the uncertainty of future events to which he must adjust his own actions' (1966, p. 58). Elsewhere he elaborated that 'this specific understanding of human action as it is practised by everybody in all his interhuman relations and actions is a mental procedure that must not be confused with any of the logical schemes resorted to by the natural sciences ...' (1958, p. 310). As such, it 'aims at the cognition of other people's actions. It asks in retrospect: What was he doing, what was he aiming at? What did he mean in choosing this definite end? What was the outcome of his action?' (1958, p. 310). Its objects have an 'ultimate datum' comprising 'the uniqueness and individuality which remains at the bottom of every historical fact when all the means for its interpretation provided by logic, praxeology, and the natural sciences have been exhausted ...' (1990, p. 26).

In this desire to understand their phenomena, analysts in the human sciences face a profound challenge. Mises was quite frank about the metatheoretical import of this. The conceptual forms of praxeology were readily defended and proven on the objective grounds of their logical consistency. Their application in the search for understanding in the domain of complex reality in which the origins of human action transcend the purely rational, however, could not be defended with any objective certainty. Mises explicitly realized that 'understanding does not explain the individual, the personal, or the values given in experience, because it does not grasp their meaning by way of conception. It merely beholds them' (1960, p. 137). That is, while the process of conception in praxeology expresses meaning by formal reasoning, 'understanding seeks the meaning of action in empathetic intuition of a whole' (1960, p. 133). So, regarding its 'validity', 'there can be no discussion concerning understanding because it is always subjectively conditioned' (1960, p. 134). Included in this complete situational whole faced by an agent are 'fellow men acting on their own behalf as he himself acts. The necessity to adjust his actions to other people's actions makes him a speculator for whom success and failure depend on his greater or lesser ability to understand the future' (1966, p. 113). There is in this respect an intersubjective dimension of human action in the real world that further compounds the problem of understanding it.

At the empirico-historical level of inquiry in the human sciences, the results may well be considered 'irrational' because they are based on 'individual judgements not amenable to criticism by purely rational methods' (1990, p. 30). This is because 'specific understanding cannot be separated from the philosophy of the interpreter. The degree of scientific objectivity which can be reached in the natural sciences and in the aprioristic sciences of logic and praxeology can never be attained by the moral or historical sciences ... in the field of specific understanding. You can understand in different ways' (1990, p. 12; cf. 1960, p. 137). Thus, 'where understanding enters, the realm of subjectivity begins' and, in this respect, 'understanding suffers from the same insufficiency as all other efforts – artistic, metaphysical, or mystical – to reproduce the intuition of a whole' (1960, p. 134). Here we are back with the very problem of the intrusion of values into the empirical human sciences that dogged the Baden Neo-Kantians and Weber.

Ultimately, Mises expressed a deep scepticism about the potential for establishing any soundly grounded, formally reasoned knowledge of the irrational world of empirico-historical phenomena. Praxeology 'cannot grasp human action in its fullness. It must take the actions of individuals as ultimately given' and accept that 'the value judgements that are made in human action are ultimate data' (1960, p. 116). In sum:

> understanding is always based on incomplete knowledge. We may believe

we know the motives of the acting men, the ends they are aiming at, and the means they plan to apply for the attainment of these ends. We have a definite opinion with regard to the effects to be expected from the operation of these factors. But this knowledge is defective. We cannot exclude beforehand the possibility that we have erred in the appraisal of their influence or have failed to take into consideration some factors whose interference we did not foresee at all, or not in the correct way. (1966, p. 112)

Elsewhere, he returned to the problematic of reason in the face of an irrational world.'

Science belongs completely to the domain of rationality. . . . The irrational lies outside the domain of human reasoning and science. When confronted with the irrational, reasoning and science can only record and classify. They are unable to penetrate more 'deeply', not even with the aid of 'understanding'. Indeed, the criterion of the irrational is precisely that it cannot be fully comprehended by reasoning. That which we are able to master completely by reasoning is no longer irrational. (1960, p. 135)

Human agency, whatever the degree of constraint and containment that its situation dictates, always retains the prospect of contingency. The fact is, as Mises stated it, 'we do not know how out of the encounter of a human individuality, i.e., a man as he has been formed by all he has inherited and by all he has experienced, and a new experience definite ideas result and determine the individual's conduct. We do not even have any surmise how such knowledge could be acquired' (1962, p. 58). The bottom line is that after all that can be reasonably known about situated human agents by an observer is allowed for, 'something remains that defies any attempts at further interpretation, namely, the personality or individuality of the actor. When all is said about the case, there is finally no other answer to the question why Caesar crossed the Rubicon than: because he was Caesar. We cannot eliminate in dealing with human action reference to the actor's personality' (1962, p. 59). The ultimate ontological determinates of conduct, however determinate they may in reality be, just cannot be known to us as human observers.

7.7 Concluding observations

The exegetical revelations of the previous sections leave us with mixed results to apply in assessing Mises's most fundamental contributions to subjectivist economics. The intended nature and point of praxeology as the existential foundation for understanding observed economic actions and phenomena seem clear. The ontological and epistemological status to be ascribed to its logical arguments is much less definite when the totality of Mises's thought is taken at its face value. There is no denying his ambivalence between the unreal conceptual forms of Neo-Kantianism and the realism of Aristotelian epistemology. Consciously or unconsciously, he simply left in place an incompatible mix of arguments in which the concepts of praxeology were sometimes ontologically sterile and sometimes replications of essential living forms claimed to be actually discoverable in empirical phenomena. A reasonable response to this overall dilemma is to give priority to Mises's realist inclinations in understanding his ontology and epistemology. This would require us to agree that maximum sense of his praxeology is made if it is perceived as expressing a core rationality that active agents actually can and do universally exercise, albeit always in some imperfect but purposeful empirically manifested form. But as we have seen, Mises himself had a vision of human agents that included facets that negate any realistic ontology of rational action even at the most essential level.

One by-product of my discussions in this chapter has been to provide some counterweight to the extremely narrow image of Mises's methodology that has been painted in the desultory and vituperative critiques of Mark Blaug (1980, pp. 92f) and Terence Hutchison (1981, pp. 207ff). In a recent book, Hutchison has renewed his withering attack on Mises and those recent disciples he labels as 'Modern Austrians' (1994, pp. 189ff). There he reads Mises as an extreme and unqualified adherent of an *a priorist* epistemology that led to claims of infallibilism for economic analysis (pp. 193, 215, 217, 219, 220). The effect, Hutchison claims, was that Mises aligned himself with the Classicals and the Neoclassicals who assumed perfect agent knowledge and omniscience (1994, pp. 209n.7 and n.8, pp. 227f). His reading in the same book also cites Mises's espousal of a dogmatic praxeology and this leads him to reject Mises's subjectivist bona fides altogether (pp. 201, 205, 206). This is compounded when he goes on to dismiss Mises as an extreme rationalist whose individualism was, as a consequence, of a kind that Friedrich von Hayek called 'false' because it failed to make due allowance for human agents as irrational and fallible in their actions (pp. 223, 224, 229). Not unexpectedly, Hutchison then makes critical reference to Mises's antiempirical vision of economics (pp. 207f, 227f, 232n.5, 233n.7, 234n.9). In sum, Hutchison concludes that Mises 'could, as regards his very emphatic and dogmatic methodological ideas, hardly be described even as "an inconsistent subjectivist"' (p. 205). And, 'what Misesian, or "Modern Austrian" praxeology succeeds in achieving is a quite unacceptable combination of dogmatic, "apodictic certainties" with total empirical vacuity' (p. 228). At one point, nevertheless, Hutchison quotes

Hayek to the effect that it was 'greatly to Mises's credit that he largely emancipated himself from that rationalist–constructivist starting-point. . . .' But, he questions the legitimacy of the claim, for 'Hayek does not indicate where the evidence for this emancipation of Mises is to be found' (1994, p. 235n.14). I suggest that some of the evidence in support of Hayek's conclusion and that stacks up against Hutchison's reading of Mises in general is to be found in the arguments of this chapter.

Mark Blaug's criticism of Mises on this point simply misconceives its target and thereby reveals a failure properly to comprehend the thesis being argued (Blaug, 1980, pp. 92f). For Mises, what he calls praxeology and identifies with economic theory was never intended to provide a sufficient theoretical understanding or explanation of any phenomenon, either generalized or empirical. As I have established here, Mises was not anti-empirical and went to some lengths to defend his negative views about quantitative theory and predictions on soundly ontological bases. Blaug asserts without much supporting argument that Mises's writings on metatheoretical principles 'smack of an antiempirical undertone in the history of continental economics that is wholly alien to the very spirit of science' and 'are so cranky and idiosyncratic that we can only wonder that they have been taken seriously by anyone' (p. 93). Such commentary tells us more about the narrowness of Blaug's vision of economics than it does about Mises's failings.

In the end, however, it is quite apparent from my analyses that Mises's work was beset by certain limitations. The subjectivist metatheoretical insights that comprise his legacy are confined to a compendium of observations concerning the problematic at issue. Beyond that, he left much to be done to provide a complete and cogent alternative to the established foundations of orthodox economics. In this sense his work became a further piece in the subjectivist and individualist metatheoretical jigsaw that has been assembled in the foregoing chapters. In the final chapter to follow, I will assemble the pieces and indicate the ambiguities and limitations that remained for those who were later to align themselves with the Austrian heritage and take up subjectivism as the foundation for their economics research programme.

Notes

1. S. Parsons (1990, p. 296) has listed some of these suggestions, but his list is incomplete. There is, first of all, the connection to certain of the classical economists whose

methodological contributions were admired by Mises. Most often cited are Senior and Cairnes (e.g. by Ebeling, 1988, p. 13; cf. Rothbard, 1973, pp. 327ff; 1976a, pp. 26ff). J. Patrick Gunning (1989, p. 165) suggests a Cartesian influence, while Emil Kauder (1957, pp. 418n., 419) has Leibniz as one of the links back to Aristotle's influence. Johnston's (1972, pp. 86f) denial of the Leibnizian connection is firm. It is Barry Smith (1990a, 1990c) who has taken up the Aristotelian filiation and defined its significance in detail and with some cogency. In this he has followed Kauder's earlier (1957, *passim*), but more unqualified insights and has had support from the doyen of the Mises disciples, Murray Rothbard (1976a, pp. 24, 28), at least as far as concerns the doctrine of praxeology itself. Rothbard also cites Kauder's Aristotelian reference to Mises without critical comment, suggesting assent (1973, p. 331; cf. 1976b, pp. 68ff). At the same time, though, both Rothbard and Barry Smith read Mises the praxeologist as an adherent of Kantian epistemology (Rothbard, 1973, p. 315; 1976a, p. 24 and Smith, 1986b, pp. 8, 18). Others also pick up the Kantian link, including Don Lavoie (1986, p. 200) and Jochen Runde (1988, p. 103). Lavoie also refers to Wilhelm Dilthey as a potential influence (1986, pp. 197, 205). The neo-Kantian connection is argued to be an important one, with S. Parsons (1990, *passim*) elaborating this thesis in some detail. It is to the Southwest German (Baden) Neo-Kantians that he refers mainly, but he brings in the Marburg Neo-Kantian School alternative as an influence at one point. Bruce Caldwell (1984, p. 365) notes the neo-Kantian link, but the effect was to have Eugene Rotwein respond that such adherence would negate the link back to Kant (1986, p. 670n. 4). That the Baden neo-Kantian influence reached Mises to a significant extent through the work of Max Weber is noticed by Ludwig Lachmann (1976, p. 56; 1977, p. 95; 1982a, p. 35), as well as by Richard Ebeling (1987, p. 22; 1988, pp. 13ff) and Jeremy Shearmur (1992, pp. 104, 113, 117f). There is, in this case, the supporting evidence that the Weber connection was reinforced through the frequent discussion of his work in Mises's *Privatseminar* in Vienna (Haberler, 1981, p. 123). For the most part, it has been the fate of Mises's praxeology to be widely interpreted as having a strongly Euclidean tenor. This summary point is made by Lavoie (1986, *passim*). But he goes on to defend with enthusiasm an alternative hermeneutical connection, subsequently rejected with even more enthusiasm (and a touch of irritation and vituperation) by Rothbard (1989, *passim*). Barry Smith joins in here, too, finding the hermeneutical suggestion un-Austrian (1990c, pp. 229ff). An Alfred Schutz connection is also part of Lavoie's picture of Mises as an hermeneutist (1986, pp. 205, 206f). Ebeling joins Lavoie towards this hermeneutical end of the spectrum by citing a connection to Edmund Husserl's phenomenology (1987, pp. 21f; 1988, p. 13).

2.　In this chapter, the references cited in parentheses are to the writings of Mises listed in the bibliography, and the emphases are in the original, unless otherwise indicated.

3.　Smith added some mitigation at this point, noting that 'this is hardly surprising, given that . . . the special nature of Austrian Aristotelian apriorism was appreciated by very few at the time when Mises was working out the philosophical foundations of his praxeology' (1990a, pp. 279f).

4.　Some examples of such references are included in note 1 above.

5.　Parsons's paper consists of a complex of philosophical inquiry that has relevance to our understanding of Mises's and George Shackle's contribution to Austrian economic thought. I do not pretend to have dealt with the paper as a whole in any detail. My intention is only to nominate some key points where I think Parsons fails to pursue and interpret Mises's ideas completely.

6.　Lachmann referred here to Weber's *Wirtschaft und Gesellschaft (Economy and Society*, 1964, 1968) as having been especially influential, but it is apparent from Mises's essays that he also found much of relevance in the collection of Weber's methodological contributions *Gesammelte Aufsätze zur Wissenschaftslehre* (1973a). Both were posthumously published in the early 1920s.

7.　The substance of the Weber connection for Jeremy Shearmur is not one of complementarity, but rather has been expressed as representing instead a duality in the conception of subjectivism (1992, pp. 104, 113). This involves setting the praxeological subjectivism of Mises, with its axiomatics of human action, against the historical or institutional subjectivism of Weber, with its depiction of human agency as ideal types tied to the historical situation. This is an appropriate interpretation as far as it goes. It captures just the distinction that I will pursue here. What I am about to show, though, is that while the divergence between the two authors applies to the *foundation* of their subjectivism, Mises ended up qualifying his version in just the empirico-historical direction that Weber took from the outset.

8. Barry Smith (1990a) provides an extended and detailed listing of the theses that constitute Austrian Aristotelianism. I have emphasized here only those most pertinent to my understanding of Mises's metatheory.

8. A retrospective summary

The retrospective inquiry contained in the above chapters has critically examined the various themes and theses that developed in subjectivist and individualist human science during the period between the work of Menger and its revival in the contributions of Mises. Each writer on whom I have focused has, in his own way, attempted to confront and resolve the epistemological and methodological issues raised by treating human sciences, and in some cases economics in particular, as separately identifiable on ontological grounds.

The essence of this ontological distinction has been seen to reside in the fact that these sciences intend to understand and explain phenomena that are the creative and original products of human action. For subjectivists, the notion of causality in accounting for human action and its observed consequences is not identifiable with causality in the physical world. Whereas the apt questions to be asked about a physical event are concerned with *how* it happened, the appropriate inquiry for the human realm is *why* an event occurred in the sense of for what humanly attributable reason? Except in theology, such ontologically oriented 'why' questions that ask for reasons have no place in the physical realm. The dimensions of cognition peculiar to the human sciences that follow from these observations are usually summarized under the objective of *Verstehen*. Inquiry about human phenomena, including those of economics, demands an understanding that confronts contingent characteristics stemming from exigencies of human nature that are not found in physical explanations. All science has a place for observation in establishing what is *there* to be explained. And, the rules of logic and consistency of argument are fundamental to all scientific exposition. Nevertheless, in the case of the human sciences, the ontology of its phenomena interpreted subjectively is so distinctive as to require an independent effort to devise suitable methodological principles and realistic epistemological expectations.

In this connection, there can be no avoiding the need for analysts to apply introspectively derived insight to the process of achieving *Verstehen*. As we have seen, the real challenge for subjectivists, including Menger and Mises, was to keep the role of introspection, and psychology more generally, in perspective by understanding their important functions and, at the same time, recognizing their limitations as means of eliciting knowledge about why particular human events occur. There can be no doubt that in order to understand human action and its products, we can and must go beyond any natural status and connections that may be attributable to human agency. Subjectivism and individualism thus focus our attention on the need to penetrate to the 'internal' characteristics of the agent that direct the form of action and give meaning to human phenomena. By contrast, the realm of nature lacks the dimensions of creativity, change and constant renewal that it implies. Nature is mostly comprised of permanent elements and relationships that are subject to laws. Most significantly, change, where it is at issue at all, is of a gradual, long-term and evolutionary character. Repetition of pre-defined phenomena is anticipated and ostensibly replicated in experimental situations. Methodologies that depend on universalism and generalization in argument make immediate sense on ontological grounds in dealing scientifically with the natural world. They do not do so in the world of human phenomena for reasons that all of our subjectivists well understood.

The nature and challenge of subjectivism and individualism in the sense just outlined have been central to my critical assessment of these writers' contributions to the foundations of the human sciences. As I indicated at the outset, there are two fundamental dimensions to the definition of subjectivism as it has guided my inquiries. One is that the intended focus of subjectivism is on the mental and cognitive processes of the human subject that mediate in giving meaning to external objects. Perception and knowledge about, and value assessments of, the object world are thus limited by and relative to the human self. Real objects, including 'goods' in economics, have a resulting dual existence for subjectivism: they have particular independent and existential qualities and quantitative dimensions, and they have a dependent and evaluated meaning for human beings who perceive them. The other and consequent tenet of subjectivism is that such a perspective leads us to consider human subjects primarily as particular individuals with a certain given mental and cognitive constitution. Subjectivism, then, relates directly to human beings in their capacity to apply wisdom, experience and reason to their life-world circumstances. In doing so, they reveal their capacity to act with self-interest and purpose towards their situational environment. It is this innate quality of human beings that is so significant in defining subjectivism in economics because it directs our attention to those particular categories of action that have deliberated and purposeful character and that originate in self-conscious, reasoned decisions and choices. Only actions of this character constitute the origin of phenomena of concern to economics. With its direct focus on the deliberated and creative actions of individual but specifically situated agents, subjectivism proceeds to give priority to the fact that economic phenomena, the objects of investigation, are the products of such actions.

In confronting the objective of understanding human action, subjectivism treats it as the joint product of individual characteristics and the situational environment in which it takes place. The idea is to steer a middle course between the existential autonomy and contingent potential of human agency and the determinism that comes with extreme versions of functionalist and structuralist interpretations. The environment is envisaged as having multiple dimensions, but most importantly it has the overall quality of being shared by the agent with others. Particular problematic conditions may, as a consequence, be responded to by agents in a manner that has some delimited common and regularized pattern. This expectation is attributable to their need to utilize the facilities and recognize the constraints of the environment that they inherit and through which they are obligated to act. Otherwise contingent actions are thus directed and shaped into an essentially common form in accordance with the problem faced and the situational conditions within which it is resolved. Even the meaning agents ascribe to all the relevant outside things involved may have a common sociocultural foundation for the majority of agents. This approach enables the subjectivist economist potentially to get beyond the relativism that may appear inevitable if the analysis requires the replication of other agents' mental processes. No more is needed than the reasonable psychological assumption that there is a core sense in which all human minds, those of the observer and the observed, function in a cognitively common manner. That this exists, to some degree at least, is certified by the fact that so much of what we do as individuals in our daily lives depends upon a mutually accepted interdependence with others. This can only operate successfully because we are able sufficiently to understand and to depend upon the consistent operation of each other's psyches. It is this ontology of phenomena that is to be elicited by economic inquiry with the objective of making particular human actions and their phenomenal consequences intelligible.

The exegetically based critique that I have pursued indicates that the writings of the main founding Austrians, Carl Menger and Ludwig von Mises, have suffered to some extent from an effective endeavour to side-step what were perceived to be the more extreme and assumed destructive scientific implications of the notions of subjectivism and individualism. This can be attributed to the demands of an intellectual world that expected all science to emulate the rigours of physics. The first objective of my inquiries was to re-examine Menger's development of what he considered to be defensible subjectivist principles on which economic analyses could be grounded as a reaction to such scientistic demands. My inquiries later shifted to the contributions of Mises as the most prominent follower of Menger's subjectivist legacy. As I indicated, albeit all too briefly, Menger's immediate successors, Eugen von Böhm-Bawerk and Friedrich von Wieser found the notion and implications of subjectivism ill-suited to their vision of economics and, for the most part, preferred not to adopt it. It was left to Mises to take the responsibility for carrying Menger's seminal Austrian subjectivism into the twentieth century as the foundations for the subsequent critical evolution of neo-Austrian economics and the divergent strands of its revival in the 1970s and beyond. The various groups of emergent Neo-Austrians have all had to wrestle with what we have seen is a rather complex and ambiguous Menger–Mises legacy. The result has been the continuation of a number of sometimes acrimonious controversies about what it means to be a Neo-Austrian in economics.

As a second strand of my retrospective I undertook a re-assessment of the cognate subjectivist themes that existed in the broader context of the philosophies of history and the human sciences as these developed in juxtaposition to, but largely independently of what Menger was doing from the 1870s onwards. The comparative study of these intellectual developments has enabled us to give some bases to the origins of a number of particular characteristics and limitations that became lodged in the subjectivism defended by Mises. The conclusion is that the available subjectivist legacy at the end of the period in focus here was richer and more extensive than that of the Menger–Mises heritage alone.

We have seen that the background ideas concerned included those of the Historicists who in rejecting the idealist tradition around them brought knowledge of the past 'down to earth'. It was Johann Droysen's historiography that gave priority to human ontology and led history to focus its epistemology on understanding events as the intelligible and meaningful products of human action. His work paved the way towards a subjectivist and individualist approach to the human sciences generally. It was Droysen's human ontological orientation that we find carried through into the subjectivism of Wilhelm Dilthey. However, the Southwest German (Baden) School of NeoKantians, especially Heinrich Rickert, reacted against the alleged psychologism of Dilthey. Rickert's attempts at forming an objective foundation for the human sciences on the basis of cultural values had its main influence through the critique of Max Weber. By contrast to the developments across the border, there arose in Austria a distinctive orientation towards human inquiry that developed independently of and largely in isolation from German influences. We have seen that there is evidence of the influence in Austrian academia of the scholastic tradition of Aristotelian realism. Such influence led a number of philosophers and other intellectuals to claim to understand the reality of human phenomena as the inherently coherent manifestations of pre-structured relationships between essential elements. Carl Menger's subjectivist foundations for Austrian economics were the result of his working in this Austrian philosophical tradition, but we have seen that they may be also linked to his background in German subjectivist and historicist economics.

My intention in pursuing this critico-retrospective inquiry has been to establish the existence of an image of subjectivism and individualism that emphasizes all the human vitality that was originally associated with these ideas in much of the philosophical literature of Menger's era and beyond. I have shown that his vitality can be found in the seminal contributions of Menger and that it was carried forward into the legacy of Mises. At the same time, I have made it apparent that very real contributions were available in the works of Germans who chose to pursue subjectivist metatheory. These contributions had the potential to facilitate the development of an economics that is more obviously conscious of the irreducibly human dimensions of its substantive objects than is always made clear by Menger and Mises.

The origins of subjectivism in economics in the present context has been traced to Carl Menger. As I have noted, he worked against a background of economics in Germany that was already concerned with subjective ideas about value. But Menger was also influenced by the Aristotelian realism of his Austrian intellectual milieu and this led him to probe rather more deeply into the human ontology of economics than any of his antecedents. He brought human agents as individuals into prominence as the consciously reasoning and active generators of a *selected* range of economic phenomena. His contributions emphasized the subjective nature and origin of these particular economic phenomena as the products of human decisions, choices and action. He was primarily concerned to understand the *telos* of human agency as it involves the satisfaction of needs and wants and as it concerns the consequent subjective nature of the value of goods and services. He also adapted his subjectivist vision of economics to the future oriented problematic of goods production, including the valuation of inputs. Menger's epistemological and methodological intentions, as they emerged in the construction of his ontologically grounded economic theory, consisted of an attempt to defend a mixture of formally exact and realistic-empirical methodological principles. This I have argued to be an outcome demanded by his subjectivist and individualist understanding of economic phenomena. More directly put, endeavours to interpret Menger's epistemology and methodology that omit ontological inquiries concerning the sort of phenomena on which he focused cannot be considered complete.

In representing economic agents in much of his theoretical argument, it remained the case that Menger's adoption of subjectivism was more ostensible than real. His individualist conception of the human agent was constricted by the very narrow set of substantive economic concerns upon which he focused formally. In choosing an analytical vision confined to the market economy operating in accordance with universal and reliable laws, the most elementary and least consequential subjective perceptions and calculations by human agents were sufficient to encompass their involvement. Such choice mitigated against the inclusion of many of his deeper insights into the highly subjective and contingent facets of situated human conduct that he had explicitly recognized. By emphasizing the role of human agents in valuation, exchange and consumption, Menger confined his attention to the processes of which the most passive and predictable characteristics of agents are prominent and in which they act much in accordance with slowly changing habits and traditions. Moreover, since most consumer decisions are of limited economic significance, there is minimal potential for agents to exercise their free will or caprice. Also, they are most likely to appear as omniscient and as acting consistently, reliably and rationally with full information and certainty. The deliberative demands made upon them in their decision-making is minimized. As consumers, human agents are for these reasons most readily dealt with in formal analysis.

At the same time, though, we have seen that Menger was able to grasp the ontological significance of shifting his perspective to bring in other categories of human agency. His seminal subjectivism included some more penetrating elements, but these were cited only in passing and then left aside without disturbing his pursuit of theoretical precision. In particular, he referred to agents other than consumers whose deliberations involve most personal initiative and creativity, demand the most detailed profiles of knowledge and information and require the greatest talent for complex calculations. It is these agents who are most concerned with the effects of uncertainty and expectations in their deliberations and decisions, and for whom errors are most probable and most economically significant. Such agents make decisions about such matters as the production of commodities and investment in new means of production, often embodying new technology. They are required to conjure up views of the future with imagination and creativity, to perceive and pursue apparent economic opportunities and to make forecasts and plans over extended time horizons. His subjectivism takes us well beyond the most elementary role of individual agents' decision-making and problem-solving. He appreciated the relevance of knowledge and information, together with the significance of varying profiles of agents' abilities and ignorance, of institutional formations and of real time in the constituent processes of a capitalist system. He realized that agents had to contend with uncertainty in their economic choices and actions, especially those to be undertaken by the entrepreneurs who put in a brief appearance in the context of his limited treatment of production. The intractabilities of time were related to often imperfect information and knowledge to enable him expressly to recognize as fallible agents' expectations, deliberations and calculations, and their consequent decisions to act. Such difficulties ensure that agents' best efforts to carry through their deliberated intentions can rarely meet with complete success. In an ever changing environment, it was also the case that the potential for agents effectively to learn from failure and thus to improve their decision-making is severely limited.

Menger avoided explicating the full complexity of his subjectivism and individualism for these vital but intractable processes of economic agency. I have concluded, then, that in spite of his awareness of a significant number of the deeper contingent elements afflicting human agency, such as the exercise of free will and caprice, uncertainty, expectations, calculation errors and lack of information, the substantive scope of his economics allowed him to assume many of them away. He chose not to allow the subjectivist detail of human agency that he was so clearly aware of to have full and consistent representation in the construction of his formal economic argument as far as he chose to take it. In the process of my inquiries, I have posed some unresolved issues concerning his subjectivism which suggest that his main legacy was to have pursued the right issues and to have been conscious of the need for some philosophical investigations in order properly to ground economics as a definitely human science. But he failed to elicit the full potential of his ideas for revising economics. It was to be the inconclusive and truncated treatment of his ontological insights into the nature and role of subjectivism and individualism that led these principles to be left only as guideposts for those who were to follow him.

In the evolution of subjectivism, I have established that Menger's German contemporary Wilhelm Dilthey was a major contributor. He has been seen to be perhaps the most significant and original of the early subjectivist philosophers of the human sciences. Following on from the work of Droysen, he extended and made more explicit the notion that the phenomena of the human sciences are the manifested expressions of the lived experiences and actions of individual human agents and can be understood only from this perspective. His demand for the human sciences was that due recognition should be given to all the subjective characteristics of agents, along with the ontology of the life-world processes in which they engage and the phenomena they generate. Dilthey took the crucial experiential preconditioning of the cognitive processes of human agents that precede action to originate in their cumulative biographies and their contemporary situations. He believed that no relevant subjectivism depicts the conduct of human agents other than as bounded and contained by a variety of internal limitations and external situational conditions. Human scientists were challenged by Dilthey expressly to strive for genuine understanding of the origins of human phenomena: the objective of *Verstehen* was to be transformed from the focus of historiography into the methodological foundation for inquiries concerned with the theory of human phenomena in general. His descriptive psychology of individuals was devised to 'get behind' the evidence of observed conduct and its empirico-phenomenal consequences in an effort more fully to understand their mental and cognitive origins. He recognized that agents' conduct most interests and concerns human science when it is purposeful and directed at particular objectives. By focusing on their expressions of life, and on the situationally conditioned conduct of agents that generates them, Dilthey was led to shift away from his directly psychological inquiries towards an hermeneutically oriented metatheory. Here we were brought face to face with his less than fully successful attempt to formulate and ontologically to legitimate subjectivist foundations for understanding and representing human agency. It was his awareness of this shortfall that led to a profound tension and insecurity in his work.

We have seen that Dilthey made an effort to get beyond the limits of a subjectivist interpretation by recognizing that active subjective agents are always strategically situated and that their conduct cannot be understood without explicit cognizance of this fact. In a subjective sense, human agents and their external world are existentially interdependent. He understood these situational conditions to play a dominant role in forming their psychic constitutions and in directing their observed conduct. It followed for Dilthey that the influence of situational conditioning is of primary concern in any attempt to account for phenomena that are pervasive and regular enough to be objects of human science inquiry. Such phenomena, he believed, are open to interpretation as reflecting typical aspects of the human life-world. The effect is to render *in situ* typical conduct as universal in its character-istics. Indeed, we have seen that Dilthey confined the capacity of *Verstehen* to the systemically situated, typical and purposeful conduct of agents. On this basis he believed it is possible to identify sufficient coherence and regularity in the production of individual human expressions to warrant their treatment as intelligible in a qualified formal sense. That is, they exhibit patterns of structures and formations, of meanings and types, but such patterns do not reflect a strict necessity of causation and thus cannot be expected to have the perma-nence and reliability of laws in the natural sciences. Rather, the human sciences should expect to settle for the derivation of functionally empirical laws. The resulting analyses should thus be presented as rea-soned and formalized pieces of discursive argument which expresses an understanding of relevant phenomena as types. Such understanding will be subject to constant critical revision as a reflection of ever changing circumstances. This having been said, however, he did not go on to explore fully the significance of physical and virtual, natural and social—institutional situations for regularizing the contingency of inherently volitional and creative agent conduct. Most especially he failed to see the need to inquire into and to understand the balance of facility and constraint that agents find in their situations. What needed further development in Dilthey's exposition was the extent to which typification procedures in conjunction with the regularizing influences of situational containments and conditioning can bring the desired degree of reliability to the relevant categories of human agents' conduct. That is, sufficient reliability effectively to allow analysts to form generalized discursive representations of human phenomena.

Dilthey's critics, especially the Baden Neo-Kantians, were intent upon defending an epistemological objectivity in the human sciences. For them, the aim for these sciences should be to overcome what appeared to be his open-ended ontology of subjectivism and psychologism. As I have argued, the work of the Neo-Kantians was a digression from our theme in the sense that it attempted to compromise the way ahead for subjectivism as a cogent ontological foundation for the human sciences. Only the genius of Max Weber and of Ludwig von Mises was ultimately able to sort out and bring some critical modifications to their confusing legacy.

The Baden Neo-Kantians, especially Heinrich Rickert, developed a very different approach to the human sciences which they presumed to be the product of a generalized historical perspective on the real-world of human events. They emphasized the historical character and understanding of the human life-world and all its phenomena, and they reasserted the role of human consciousness in the historical process. But it is apparent that at the same time, they intended to establish a distinctive metatheory for the human sciences on objective grounds that did not depend on ontological analyses. Rickert rejected any notion that the identifying criteria for the demarcation between the natural and the human sciences could be linked back to the immanently structured ontology of human agency. In their return to Kant's philosophy, they reiterated the existential independence of a reality-in-itself that could only be grasped cognitively by means of an imposed categorial structure. The latter had its origins in experience, but was not constituted by experience in the manner attributed to Dilthey's psychological subjectivism.

Rickert was intent, rather, upon providing historical science with a culturally dependent, objective foundation. He chose to accept the absolute dualism of unique historical reality and its representation as mentally imposed schemata of concepts, but he tried to formalize the understanding of that reality by objectifying the concept formation process. This concept formation procedure, so Rickert claimed, enabled the analyst to dichotomize the fields of science between the natural and the historical–cultural. This demarcation was grounded in the distinction between generalized concepts of universal meaning expressed as laws that comprise the arguments of the natural sciences, and the individualizing concepts that capture only the causal 'essentials' of particular historical–cultural phenomena. He felt that the defence of the independence of the historical–cultural sciences had not received sufficient and satisfactory attention. Such a defence could only be mounted by showing that there exists a mode of abstract concept formation in which the individual and unique character of an empirical human phenomenon is shown to be preserved in its scientific rendition. That is, the pertinent question was: can human reality be simplified in a manner which retains its individuality in the form of concepts? In achieving an affirmative response here, we have seen how Rickert combined his non-realist epistemology with individualizing concept formation to constitute empirically oriented causal explanations that made no attempt to reach reality-in-itself. In so doing, he saw himself as espousing the representation of the phenomena of reality in a way that captures all their essential and meaningful dimensions as these are dictated by the cultural values common to the analysts. Ultimately, though, his defence of this mode of dealing with the demarcation issue and the definition of human science cannot be considered successful in any rigorous sense.

The critical difficulty with Rickert's objectivist endeavours appeared in the selection criteria on which he asserted the abstracted concept formation could depend. As far as he was concerned, it simply comprised the culturally grounded values and interests that could be attributed to the observer-analysts operating in a particular realm of empirical inquiry. The unavoidable suspicion that arose as a consequence was that the selection is subjective and the resulting analyses relativistic. But, we have seen that Rickert went on to claim that an established and agreed set of value relevances will always exist in a culture or community and thereby the axiology takes on a semblance of delimited 'objectivity'. His view was finally that this was the epistemological standard achievable in the historical–cultural sciences and had to be accepted as such.

Whatever their apparent limitations, the importance of Rickert's divergent contributions here is that they were influential, nevertheless, most especially through the critical endeavours of his colleague and friend Max Weber. We have seen how it was to be Weber who critically considered and adopted some of the main principles enunciated by Rickert and made them an integral part of his search for a metatheory of the human sciences. However, he found Rickert's contributions deficient in certain crucial respects from the perspective of understanding and accounting for empirical social and economic phenomena as the products of situated human agents. For Weber as a subjectivist, the fundamental subject matter of economics was designated as human action, human action that is a product of both natural and historico-social conditions. As I have argued, these essentially human foundations for socio-economic science led Weber to pursue the objective of *Verstehen*. His efforts were devoted to discovering the methodological principles of interpretation that enable analysts to make intelligible and thereby to understand the causes of events and phenomena generated by the social actions of individual subjective agents. He was concerned that socially conscious economics should emphasize that its object phenomena originate in intentional, deliberated and meaningful human action. As Weber expressly recognized, agents are also contained within and constrained by the structured situational complex comprising their many and varied social connections with others. It is the containing and shaping influence of such social situations that he applied to developing the foundations for causally adequate explanation of social and economic objects by means of the concepts of agent rationality and the ideal type. The challenge for social science in applying an ideal–typical methodology was, according to Weber, to build the discursive causal account of an empirical phenomenon around a core model of rational ideal type categories. Then, having worked up an idealized scenario for any empirical human event in terms of the purely rational actions of agents, inquiries concerning empirically individual phenomena comprise comparing the ideal–typical with the actual course of situated action. The resulting causal explanation of the observed deviations can emphasize such factors as deficient and incorrect information, strategical errors of judgement in deliberations, personal temperament and cognitive limitations and multiple, inconsistent motivations.

My critical considerations of Weber's work confirmed a number of difficulties imbedded in these otherwise plausible principles of human scientific inquiry. First of all, he failed fully to explore the notion of agent rationality itself. He appreciated some of the crucial exigencies involved, especially concerning the fact that in the absence of agents' omniscience, it is necessary to make the highly insecure presumption that they successfully apply reason in circumstances of uncertainty by means of expectations. These matters posed problems with the conceptualization of rationality that affect our understanding of the ontology of human agency more profoundly than he chose to explicate. Weber's subjectivism and individualism just did not give adequate recognition to the sources and degree of the contingency that potentially characterize human action and render it less than fully rational. Agents' fundamental and yet complex life-world deliberations and decision-making involve them in future-oriented actions and it is in this respect that contingency is most prominent. Their subjectively rational cognitive processes are directed at choosing means and realizing preferred ends and goals. From the past they bring certain cognitive abilities, together with accumulated knowledge and experience. These processes fundamentally involve the particular inherited and learned capacities and beliefs of the agents, along with their specific motivations and intentions with respect to the problem about which they are currently deliberating. Information is required in uncertain quantities and qualities for these deliberations, and it is only available at a cost. Any deficiencies or excesses in such information gathering cannot be corrected for *ex post*. It is simply too late. Any understanding of deliberation processes must confront the need for agents to form expectations and to construct *ex ante* potential future scenarios between which some unique choice must be made. These are substitutes for non-existent knowledge of the future as inputs to the decision process.

A further difficulty in Weber's analyses to which I have given some attention concerns his treatment of the inherited contemporary situations in which agents find themselves. At issue particularly here are the constitution of such situations and how agents draw on and are conditioned by them. The natural environment, physical–technical structures, social organizations and institutions all have a potential place among the many and varied dimensions of agents' situations. Weber was most especially concerned with the situational characteristics of social life and wrote much about various forms of human association. However, we have seen that he was inclined to give more emphasis to the collective dimensions of such associations than to their role in regularizing the conduct of individual subjective agents. What required more direct consideration in his work was the fact that it is by means of judgements of relevance and priority within the characteristics of their situations that agents address their general objectives. For this reason, in successfully realizing their plans and goals, they are inclined to conform to situational demands. Such demands comprise requirements that contain and constrain what agents volitionally choose to do, mitigate difficulties and facilitate rational goal-directed and means-sensitive actions. The otherwise contingent actions of individual agents are thereby shaped and directed in particular ways that potentially have definite and specific shared ideal-typical qualities. By means of these regularities, analysts may give their representations some measure of discursive coherence. Of particular concern in economic decision-making are the physical–technical structures of production, the organizations of production and distribution, such as firms and corporations, and the economically oriented institutions of the state. It has been apparent that from all these perspectives, such matters warrant more detailed treatment than Weber allowed himself to pursue.

A third difficulty in Weber's ideas about which I have been concerned is the methodological principle of arguing explanations of individual phenomena by means of comparisons between the rational ideal and irrational reality. On his own terms, because of the inherent infinity of real world object characteristics, any claimed knowledge of the reality against which the comparison is to be made is necessarily itself already a selective conceptual construction. The result must be that these comparisons will be realized only as between one conceptual construction and another. Such an exercise cannot, therefore, provide any immediate empirical contact, or establish any confirmation or refutation, for the knowledge revealed by the ideal type in the manner that he suggested. As a consequence, Weber's objective of *Verstehen* involved him in espousing methodological principles that are necessarily tainted with relativism or conventionalism and that must fail any test of 'objectivity'.

Weber's investigations into the ontology of situated human agency and its methodological implications were seminal endeavours to found social–economic inquiry on bases that avoided the dilemmas of naturalism, formalism and historicism. He was determined to develop metatheoretical foundations for empirical understanding and explanation in the human sciences in a form that was consistent with the subjectivist and individualist ontology of their object phenomena. His pioneering work has been shown in my analysis to be replete with well-directed subjectivist insights. It remained the case, though, that the coverage and depth of intellectual penetration that he achieved was limited in certain crucial respects.

The final stage of my retrospective came in the critical assessment that Mises was able to make of the limited subjectivist legacies of Menger, Dilthey and Weber. Mises was one successor who took up their and other contributions with serious scholarly purpose. As I have suggested, whatever may be thought of the idiosyncratic nature of his ideas and ideals, he can be seen selectively and critically to have absorbed much more of the subjectivist philosophy that surrounded him than he is often given credit for. It will be appreciated from my study of his subjectivism that establishing the nature of the interface between epistemology and ontology, and the balance of antecedent influences that shaped his approach to them, is no straightforward matter. There exist in the literature a number of key alternative philosophical orientations that have been attributed to Mises. Most important were the Aristotelian and Mengerian milieu of his education and his critical study of the Neo-Kantians and Max Weber. Each of these we found to have left some traces of influence on his work, and there is ample textual evidence that this led to the philosophical ambivalence that dogged the formulation of his core concept of praxeology. I have drawn attention to the clear indications of the Kantian and neo-Kantian epistemological roots and orientations that are evident in his writings and to how these are situated alongside passages in which he emphasized the ontology of Aristotelian realism. My exegetical reading has left us with mixed results to apply in assessing Mises's most fundamental contributions to subjectivist economics. He was able to make quite clear the nature and point of praxeology as the existential foundation for understanding observed economic actions and phenomena. What was left with much less definitude was the ontological and epistemological status to be ascribed to its *a priori* logical arguments.

In this respect, there is no denying his ambivalence between the unreal conceptual forms of Neo-Kantianism and the demands of Aristotelian realism. Consciously or unconsciously, he left an incompatible mix of arguments in which the concepts of praxeology were sometimes

ontologically sterile and sometimes essentially real. I have argued that
a reasonable and defensible response to this epistemological dilemma
in Mises's work is to give priority to his realist inclinations. If we can
agree that maximum sense of his praxeology is made by reading it as
expressing a core rationality that active agents actually can and do
universally exercise, albeit always in some imperfect but purposeful
empirically manifested form, then the dilemma is resolved. This resolution is made insecure, though, by Mises himself insisting at times on
a vision of human agents that included facets that negate any realistic
ontology of rational action even at the most essential level.

Much of Mises's thought on the foundations for subjectivist economics remained a mixture of ontological claims about the nature of
human action and the epistemological positions that may be adopted in
the search for formal knowledge about such action and its phenomenal
results. From an ontological perspective, he gave clear and concise
attention to situated and conditioned, subjectively driven human agents
as the active generators of the objects of study in economics. The
variable and contingent origins of these phenomena in the deliberated
actions of individuals give them an appearance of impermanence and
disorder that apparently defies scientific generalization. Mises, as with
all subjectivists, refused to take the naive escape route of merely
imposing the required regularity to allow natural scientistic methodology to be applied. In his epistemological argument, he recognized
explicitly that the status of claims to knowledge must be consistent with
and shaped by the ontological nature of the science's objects. This
ontology for economics comprised most essentially human action as it
originates in the deliberated choices of situated human agents.

He approached this core theme on two levels: one was the pure thesis
of praxeology as an ontology of rational human action, and the other
was the study and explanation of observed economic phenomena. I
have argued that this distinction enables us, on balance, to read Mises
as ultimately establishing the meaning of the tenets of praxeology as
necessarily manifested within the reality of observed economic
phenomena. In attributing to agent rationality an ontologically *a priori*
status, he recognized that the idea is not readily defended once the
contingent realities of human agency situated in time are examined. It
is quite evident that he was aware of these temporal realities, but that
he chose not to link them to the rationality thesis upon which his
praxeology as an *a priori* principle depended. Although Mises
developed his subjectivist economics on this premiss as a purely general
science of human action, its rationale and utility could only be in its
application to the understanding and explanation of empirico-historical

phenomena. The conclusion that I have reached is that it is the immediately ontological interpretation of the axioms of human action, and the contingencies of such action thus exposed, that rendered indefensible Mises's own epistemological foundations for subjectivism. Contrary to what he expressly sought to do at a number of points in his writings, he was unable to provide rational action with a sustainable defence as an ontologically relevant axiom. As a consequence, he failed to give his praxeology a cogent realist grounding and left formulating its actual links to observed human action unresolved. The subjectivist metatheory for economics that comprises his legacy is largely a compendium of observations concerning the problematic at issue. Beyond that, he left much to be done to provide a complete and cogent alternative to the established foundations of orthodox economics.

In this sense Mises's work was one piece in the subjectivist and individualist metatheoretical jigsaw that has been assembled in the foregoing chapters. In assembling the pieces, I have indicated the ambiguities and limitations that remained for those who were later to align themselves with the Austrian heritage and take up subjectivism as the foundation for their economics research programme. It was to be in the foundations of neo-Austrian economics that the unresolved problems remaining as an integral part of Mises's legacy in particular surfaced in the period of its revival during the early 1970s. The ambiguous nature and status of subjectivism has plagued Neo-Austrians since then and has contributed to the bifurcation of their efforts to bring some human dimension to economics. However, for all their limitations and disagreements, Neo-Austrians who have been reacting to the work of Mises are, most probably as a consequence, among the few who explicitly treat economics as primarily a science of human action and are prepared to give due recognition to the resulting distinctive metatheoretical implications and demands. They have been prepared to argue against the unjustified wholesale adoption of naive versions of positivism and instrumentalism as these have appeared in orthodox economics. And, they have done so on the well-reasoned basis of the need to preserve the ontological insight that all economic phenomena are the consequence of individual, but situationally conditioned and directed, subjective human actions. They have also, for the most part, demanded priority for realist ontological consistency of discursive representation over the demands of scientism and formalism. Whatever the endeavours of the neo-Austrian factions have turned out to lack with respect to the extended nature of subjectivism canvassed in my retrospective study, this should not be allowed to detract from the very real merit that they have taken such intractable and fundamental issues seriously. All this, however, is another story to be taken up at a future time (see Oakley, forthcoming 1998).

Bibliography

Addleson, M. (1984), 'Robbins's *Essay* in retrospect: on subjectivism and an "economics of choice" ', *Rivista Internazionale di Scienze Economiche e Commerciali*, 31.

Addleson, M. (1986), ' "Radical subjectivism" and the language of Austrian economics', in Kirzner (ed.)(1986).

Albert, H. (1988), 'Hermeneutics and economics: a criticism of hermeneutical thinking in the social sciences', *Kyklos*, 41.

Alter, M. (1982), 'Carl Menger and *homo oeconomicus*: some thoughts on Austrian theory and methodology', *Journal of Economic Issues*, 16 (1).

Alter, M. (1990a), *Carl Menger and the Origins of Austrian Economics*, Boulder: Westview Press.

Alter, M. (1990b), 'What do we know about Menger?', in Caldwell (ed.)(1990).

Betanzos, R.J. (1988), 'Wilhelm Dilthey: an introduction', in Dilthey (1988).

Birner, J. (1990), 'A roundabout solution to a fundamental problem in Menger's methodology and beyond', in Caldwell (ed.)(1990).

Blaug, M. (1980), *The Methodology of Economics: or How Economists Explain*, Cambridge: Cambridge University Press.

Bloch, H.-S. (1940), 'Carl Menger: the founder of the Austrian School', *Journal of Political Economy*, 48 (3).

Boettke, P.J. (ed.)(1994), *The Elgar Companion to Austrian Economics*, Aldershot: Edward Elgar.

Böhm, S. (1982), 'The ambiguous notion of subjectivism: comment on Lachmann', in Kirzner (ed.)(1982).

Böhm, S. (1985), 'The political economy of the Austrian School', in P. Roggi (ed.), *Gli economisti e la politica economica*, Napoli: Edizioni Scientifiche Italiane.

Böhm, S. (1989), 'Subjectivism and PostKeynesianism: towards a better understanding', in J. Pheby (ed.), *New Directions in PostKeynesian Economics*, Aldershot: Edward Elgar.

Böhm, S. (1990), 'The Austrian tradition: Schumpeter and Mises', in Hennings and Samuels (eds)(1990).

Böhm-Bawerk, E. von (1994), 'The historical versus the deductive method in political economy' [1891], in Kirzner (ed.)(1994), vol. I.

Bostaph, S. (1976), *Epistemological Foundations of Methodological Conflict in Economics: the Case of the Nineteenth Century Methodenstreit*, unpublished Doctoral Dissertation, Southern Illinois University, UMI Dissertation Services, Ann Arbor.

Bostaph, S. (1978), 'The methodological debate between Carl Menger and the German Historicists', *Atlantic Economic Journal*, VI (3).

Brentano, F. (1973), *Psychology from an Empirical Standpoint* [1874], edited by L.L. McAlister, translated by A.C. Rancurello, D.B. Terrell and L.L.McAlister, London: Routledge & Kegan Paul.

Brubaker, R. (1984), *The Limits of Rationality: an Essay on the Social and Moral Thought of Max Weber*, London: Allen & Unwin.

Buchanan, J.M. (1982), 'The domain of subjectivist economics: between predictive science and moral philosophy', in Kirzner (ed.)(1994), vol. I.

Bulhof, I.N. (1980), *Wilhelm Dilthey: a Hermeneutic Approach to the Study of History and Culture*, The Hague: Martinus Nijhoff.

Burger, T. (1976), *Max Weber's Theory of Concept Formation: History, Laws, and Ideal Types*, Durham, North Carolina: Duke University Press.

Cahnman, W.J. (1964), 'Max Weber and the methodological controversy in the social sciences', in W.J. Cahnman and A. Boskoff (eds), *Sociology and History: Theory and Research*, London: Free Press of Glencoe.

Caldwell, B.J. (1982), *Beyond Positivism: Economic Methodology in the Twentieth Century*, London: Allen & Unwin.

Caldwell, B.J. (1984), 'Praxeology and its critics: an appraisal', *History of Political Economy*, 16 (3).

Caldwell, B.J. (ed.)(1990), *Carl Menger and His Legacy in Economics*, Durham, North Carolina: Duke University Press.

Caldwell, B.J. (1991), 'Comment on Lavoie', in de Marchi and Blaug (eds) (1991).

Caldwell, B.J. and Böhm, S. (eds) (1992), *Austrian Economics: Tensions and New Directions*, Boston: Kluwer Academic.

Coats, A.W. (1983), 'The revival of subjectivism in economics', in J. Wiseman, (ed.), *Beyond Positive Economics?*, London: Macmillan.

Craver, E. (1986), 'The emigration of the Austrian economists', *History of Political Economy*, 18 (1).

Cubeddu, R. (1993), *The Philosophy of the Austrian School*, London: Routledge.

de Marchi, N. and Blaug, M. (eds) (1991), *Appraising Economic Theories: Studies in the Methodology of Research Programs*, Aldershot: Edward Elgar.

Dilthey, W. (1914 –), *Gesammelte Schriften*, 19 vols, Stuttgart, Leipzig & Berlin: Verlag von B.G. Teubner; Göttingen: Vandenhoeck & Ruprecht.

Dilthey, W. (1961), *Meaning in History: W. Dilthey's Thoughts on History and Society*, edited and translated by H.P. Rickman, London: Allen & Unwin.

Dilthey, W. (1976), *W. Dilthey: Selected Writings*, edited and translated by H.P. Rickman, Cambridge: Cambridge University Press.

Dilthey, W. (1977), *Descriptive Psychology and Historical Understanding*, translated by R.M. Zaner and K.L. Heiges, The Hague: Martinus Nijhoff.

Dilthey, W. (1988), *Introduction to the Human Sciences: an Attempt to Lay a Foundation for the Study of Society and History*, [1883], translated by R.J. Betanzos, London: Harvester Wheatsheaf.

Dolan, E.G. (ed.) (1976), *The Foundations of Modern Austrian Economics*, Kansas City: Sheed & Ward.

Droysen, J.G. (1967), *Outline of the Principles of History*, [1867] 3rd edition [1881], translated by E.B. Andrews [1892], New York: Howard Fertig.

Earl, P.E. (1992), 'Shearmur on subjectivism: discussion', in Caldwell and Böhm (eds) (1992).

Ebeling, R.M. (1981), 'Mises' influence on modern economic thought', *Wirtschaftspolitische Blätter*, 28 (4).

Ebeling, R.M. (1987), 'The roots of Austrian economics', *Market Process*, 5 (2).

Ebeling, R.M. (1988), 'Expectations and expectations formation in Mises's theory of the market process', *Market Process*, 6 (1).

Ebeling, R.M. (1990a), 'Introduction', in Mises (1990).

Ebeling, R.M. (1990b), 'What is a price? Explanation and understanding (with apologies to Paul Ricoeur)', in D. Lavoie (ed.), *Economics and Hermeneutics*, London: Routledge.

Endres, A.M. (1984), 'Institutional elements in Carl Menger's theory of demand: a comment', *Journal of Economic Issues*, 18 (3).

Ermarth, M. (1978), *Wilhelm Dilthey: the Critique of Historical Reason*, Chicago: University of Chicago Press.

Fabian, R. and Simons, P.M. (1986), 'The second Austrian school of value theory', in Grassl and Smith (eds) (1986).

Fling, F.M. (1903), 'Historical synthesis', *American Historical Review*, IX (1).

Giddens, A. (1987), 'Weber and Durkheim: coincidence and divergence', in Mommsen and Osterhammel (eds) (1987).

Gordon, D. (1993), 'Ludwig von Mises and the philosophy of history', in Herbener (ed.) (1993).

Graber, E. (1981), 'Translator's introduction to Max Weber's essay on some categories of interpretive sociology', *Sociological Quarterly*, 22.

Grassl, W. (1986), 'Markets and morality: Austrian perspectives on the economic approach to human behaviour', in Grassl and Smith (eds) (1986).

Grassl, W. and Smith, B. (eds) (1986), *Austrian Economics: Historical and Philosophical Background*, London: Croom Helm.

Gunning, J.P. (1989), 'Professor Caldwell on Ludwig von Mises' methodology', *Review of Austrian Economics*, 3.

Haberler, G. (1981), 'Mises's private seminar', *Wirtschaftspolitische Blätter*, 28. Jahrgang (4).

Hayek, F.A. von (1955), *The Counter-Revolution of Science: Studies in the Abuse of Reason*, New York: Free Press of Glencoe.

Hayek, F.A. von (1973), 'The place of Menger's *Grundsätze* in the history of economic thought', in Hicks and Weber (eds) (1973).

Hayek, F.A. von (1981), 'Introduction', in Menger (1981).

Hekman, S.J. (1983), *Max Weber and Contemporary Social Theory*, Notre Dame, Indiana: University of Notre Dame Press.

Hennings, K. and Samuels W.J. (eds) (1990), *Neoclassical Economic Theory 1870 to 1930*, Boston: Kluwer Academic.

Hennis, W. (1987), 'A science of man: Max Weber and the political economy of the German historical school', in Mommsen and Osterhammel (eds) (1987).

Herbener, J.M. (ed.) (1993), *The Meaning of Ludwig von Mises: Contributions in Economics, Epistemology, Sociology, and Political Philosophy*, Norwell, Massachusetts: Kluwer Academic.

Hicks, J.R. and Weber, W. (eds) (1973), *Carl Menger and the Austrian School of Economics*, Oxford: Clarendon Press.

Hirsch, A. (1986), 'Caldwell on praxeology and its critics: a reappraisal', *History of Political Economy*, 18 (4).

Hodges, H.A. (1944), *Wilhelm Dilthey: an Introduction*, London: Routledge & Kegan Paul.

Hodges, H.A. (1952), *The Philosophy of Wilhelm Dilthey*, London: Routledge & Kegan Paul.

Hopper, H.-H. (1993), 'On praxeology and the praxeological foundations of epistemology and ethics', in Herbener (ed.) (1993).

Howey, R.S. (1960), *The Rise of the Marginal Utility School 1870–1889*, Lawrence, Kansas: University of Kansas Press.

Hutchison, T.W. (1973), 'Some themes from *Investigations into Method*', in Hicks and Weber (eds) (1973).

Hutchison, T.W. (1981), *The Politics and Philosophy of Economics: Marxians, Keynesians and Austrians*, Oxford: Basil Blackwell.

Hutchison, T.W. (1994), *The Uses and Abuses of Economics: Contentious Essays on History and Method*, London: Routledge.

Jaffé, W. (ed.) (1965a), *Correspondence of Léon Walras and Related Papers*, vol. I: 1857–1883, Amsterdam: North-Holland.

Jaffé, W. (ed.) (1965b), *Correspondence of Léon Walras and Related Papers*, vol. II: 1884–1897, Amsterdam: North-Holland.

Jaffé, W. (1976), 'Menger, Jevons and Walras de-homogenized', *Economic Inquiry*, XIV.

Johnston, W.M. (1972), *The Austrian Mind: an Intellectual and Social History 1848–1938*, Berkeley: University of California Press.

Kalberg, S. (1994), *Max Weber's Comparative Social History*, Cambridge: Polity Press.

Kauder, E. (1957), 'Intellectual and political roots of the older Austrian School', *Zeitshcrift für Nationalökonomie*, XVII (4).

Kauder, E. (1965), *A History of Marginal Utility Theory*, Princeton: Princeton University Press.

Kirzner, I.M. (1976), 'On the method of Austrian economics', in Dolan (ed.) (1976).

Kirzner, I.M. (ed.) (1982), *Method, Process, and Austrian Economics: Essays in Honor of Ludwig von Mises*, Lexington, Massachusetts: Lexington Books.

Kirzner, I.M. (ed.) (1986), *Subjectivism, Intelligibility and Economic Understanding: Essays in Honour of Ludwig M. Lachmann on his Eightieth Birthday*, London: Macmillan.

Kirzner, I M. (1990a), 'Mises and the renaissance of Austrian economics' [1981], in Littlechild (ed.) (1990) vol. I.

Kirzner, I.M. (1990b), 'Menger, classical liberalism, and the Austrian school of economics,' in Caldwell (ed.) (1990).

Kirzner, I.M. (1992), *The Meaning of Market Process: Essays in the Development of Austrian Economics*, London: Routledge.

Kirzner, I.M. (ed.) (1994), *Classics in Austrian Economics: a Sampling in the History of a Tradition*, 3 volumes, London: William Pickering.

Kirzner, I.M. (1994a), 'Introduction', in Kirzner (ed.), (1994) vol. I.

Kirzner, I.M. (1994b), 'Introduction', in Kirzner (ed.), (1994) vol. II.

Kirzner, I.M. (1994c), 'Introduction', in Kirzner (ed.), (1994) vol. III.

Knight, F.H. (1950), 'Introduction', in Menger (1950).

Krausser, P. (1968–69), 'Dilthey's revolution in the theory of the structure of scientific inquiry and rational behavior', *The Review of Metaphysics*, 22 (2).

Lachmann, L.M. (1970), *The Legacy of Max Weber*, London: Heinemann.

Lachmann, L.M. (1976), 'From Mises to Shackle: an essay on Austrian economics and the kaleidic society', *Journal of Economic Literature*, XIV (1).

Lachmann, L.M. (1977), *Capital, Expectations, and the Market Process; Essays on the Theory of the Market Economy*, Kansas City: Sheed Andrews & McMeel.

Lachmann, L.M. (1978a), 'Carl Menger and the incomplete revolution of subjectivism', *Atlantic Economic Journal*, VI (3).

Lachmann, L.M. (1978b), 'An Austrian stocktaking: unsettled questions and tentative answers', in Spadaro (ed.) (1978).

Lachmann, L.M. (1982a), 'Ludwig von Mises and the extension of subjectivism', in Kirzner (ed.) (1982).

Lachmann, L.M. (1982b), 'The salvage of ideas: problems of the revival of Austrian economic thought', *Zeitshrift für die gesamte Staatswissenschaft*, 138.

Latsis, S.J. (1972), 'Situational determinism in economics', *British Journal for the Philosophy of Science*, 23.

Latsis, S.J. (1983), 'The role and status of the rationality principle in the social sciences', in R. Cohen and M. Wartofsky (eds), *Epistemology, Methodology, and the Social Sciences*, Boston: D. Reidel.

Lavoie, D. (1986), 'Euclideanism versus hermeneutics: a reinterpretation of Misesian apriorism', in Kirzner (ed.) (1986).

Lavoie, D. (1991), 'The progress of subjectivism', in de Marchi and Blaug (eds) (1991).

Littlechild, S.C. (ed.) (1990), *Austrian Economics*, 3 volumes, Aldershot: Edward Elgar.

Mäki, U. (1990), 'Mengerian economics in realist perspective', in Caldwell (ed.) (1990).

Makkreel, R.A. (1969), 'Wilhelm Dilthey and the neo-Kantians: the distinction of the *Geisteswissenschaften* and the *Kulturwissenschaften*', *Journal of the History of Philosophy*, 7.

Makkreel, R.A. (1975), *Dilthey: Philosopher of the Human Studies*, Princeton: Princeton University Press.

Menger, Carl (1871), *Grundsätze der Volkswirtschaftslehre*, in *Gesammelte Werke*, Band I, Tübingen: J.C.B. Mohr (Paul Siebeck), 1968; translated as Menger (1950 [1981]).

Menger, Carl (1883), *Untersuchungen über die Methode der Socialwissenschaften und der politischen Oekonomie insbesondere*, in *Gesammelte Werke*, Band II, Tübingen: J.C.B. Mohr (Paul Siebeck), 1969; translated as Menger (1963).

Menger, Carl (1884), 'Irrthürmer des Historismus in der deutschen National-ökonomie', in Menger (1935); partially translated in Small (1924).

Menger, Carl (1887), 'Zur Kritik der politischen Oekonomie', in Menger (1935).

Menger, Carl (1889), 'Grundzüge einer Klassifikation der Wirtschaftswissen-schaften', in Menger (1935); translated as Menger (1960).

Menger, Carl (1891), 'Die Sozialtheorien der klassischen Nationalökonomie und die moderne Wirthschaftspolitik', in Menger (1935).

Menger, Carl (1892), 'On the origin of Money', in Kirzner (ed.) (1994).

Menger, Carl (1894), 'Wilhelm Roscher', in Menger (1935).

Menger, Carl (1906), 'John Stuart Mill', in Menger (1935).

Menger, Carl (1923), *Grundsätze der Volkswirtschaftslehre*, 2. Ausgabe, aus dem Nachlaß herausgegeben von Karl Menger, Wien: Hoelder-Pichler-Tempsky.

Menger, Carl (1935), *The Collected Works of Carl Menger: Kleinere Schriften zur Methode und Geschichte der Volkswirtschaftslehre*, volume III, No. 19 in Series of Reprints of Scarce Tracts in Economics and Political Science, London: London School of Economics and Political Science.

Menger, Carl (1950), *Principles of Economics*, translated and edited by James

Dingwall and Bert F. Hoselitz, Introduction by F.H. Knight, Glencoe, Illinois: The Free Press.

Menger, Carl (1960), 'Toward a systematic classification of the economic sciences' [1889], in L. Sommer (ed.), *Essays in European Economic Thought*, Princeton: D. van Nostrand.

Menger, Carl (1963), *Problems of Economics and Sociology* [1883], edited by L. Schneider, translated by F.J. Nock, Urbana: University of Illinois Press.

Menger, Carl (1981), *Principles of Economics*, translated and edited by James Dingwall and Bert F. Hoselitz, Introduction by F.A. von Hayek [1934], New York: New York University Press.

Menger, Carl (1985 [1963]), *Investigations into the Method of the Social Sciences with Special Reference to Economics* [1883], edited by L. Schneider, translated by F.J. Nock, new Introduction by L.H. White, New York: New York University Press.

Meyer, W. (1981), 'Ludwig von Mises und das subjektivistische Erkenntnisprogramm', *Wirtschaftspolitische Blätter*, 29 (4).

Milford, K. (1989), *Zu den Lösungsversuchen des Induktionsproblems und des Abgrenzungsproblems bei Carl Menger*, Wien: Verlag der österreichischen Akadamie der Wissenschaften.

Milford, K. (1990), 'Menger's methodology', in Caldwell (ed.) (1990).

Milford, K. (1992a), 'Nationalism, *Volksgeist*, and the methods of economics: a note on Ranke, Roscher and Menger', *History of European Ideas*, 15.

Milford, K. (1992b), 'Carl Menger and the standard-statement positions in economics', mimeograph.

Milford, K. (1995a), 'Roscher's epistemological and methodological position and its importance for the *Methodenstreit*', *Journal of Economic Studies*, 22.

Milford, K. (1995b), 'A note on Hayek's analysis of scientism', in S.F. Frowen (ed.), *Hayek the Economist and Social Philosopher: a Critical Retrospective*, London: Macmillan.

Milford, K. (1995c), 'Hufeland als Vorläufer von Menger und Hayek', mimeograph.

Mises, L. von (1958), *Theory and History* [1957], London: Jonathan Cape.

Mises, L. von (1960), *Epistemological Problems of Economics* [1933], translated by G. Reisman, Princeton: D. van Nostrand.

Mises, L. von (1962), *The Ultimate Foundation of economic science: an Essay on Method*, Princeton: D. van Nostrand.

Mises, L. von (1966), *Human Action: a Treatise on Economics* [1949], 3rd revised edition, Chicago: Henery Regnery.

Mises, L. von (1969), *The Historical Setting of the Austrian School of Economics*, New Rochelle, New York: Arlington House.

Mises, L. von (1978), *Notes and Recollections*, translated by H.F. Sennholz, South Holland, Illinois: Libertarian Press.

Mises, L. von (1990), *Money, Method, and the Market Process: Essays by Ludwig von Mises*, Edited with an Introduction by Richard M. Ebeling, Norwell, Massachusetts: Kluwer Academic.

Mommsen, W.J. and Osterhammel, J. (eds) (1987), *Max Weber and his Contemporaries*, London: Unwin Hyman.

Neudeck, W. (1981), 'Der Einfluß von Ludwig von Mises auf die österreichische akademische Tradition gestern und heute', *Wirtschaftspolitische Blätter*, 28 (4).

Nozick, R. (1977), 'On Austrian methodology', *Synthese*, 36.

Oakes, G. (1975), 'Introductory essay', in Weber (1975a).

Oakes, G. (1977a), 'The Verstehen thesis and the foundations of Max Weber's methodology', *History and Theory*, 16.

Oakes, G. (1977b), 'Introductory essay', in Weber (1977).

Oakes, G. (1982), 'Methodological ambivalence: the case of Max Weber', *Social Research*, 49.

Oakes, G. (1986), 'Introduction: Rickert's theory of historical knowledge', in Rickert (1986).

Oakes, G. (1987), 'Weber and the southwest German school: the genesis of the concept of the historical individual', in Mommsen and Osterhammel (eds) (1987).

Oakes, G. (1988), *Weber and Rickert: Concept Formation in the Cultural Sciences*, Cambridge, Massachusetts: MIT Press.

Oakley, A.C. (forthcoming 1998), *The Revival of Modern Austrian Economics: A Critical Assessment and Reconstruction of Subjectivism*, Aldershot: Edward Elgar.

O'Sullivan, P.J. (1987), *Economic Methodology and Freedom to Choose*, London: Allen & Unwin.

Osterhammel, J. (1987), 'Varieties of social economics: Joseph A. Schumpeter and Max Weber', in Mommsen and Osterhammel (eds) (1987).

Parsons, S. (1990), 'The philosophical roots of modern Austrian economics: past problems and future prospects', *History of Political Economy*, 22 (2).

Philippovich, E. von (1912), 'The infusion of socio-political ideas into the literature of German economics', *American Journal of Sociology*, XVIII (2).

Plantinga, T. (1980), *Historical Understanding in the Thought of Wilhelm Dilthey*, Toronto: University of Toronto Press.

Rickert, H. (1962), *Science and History: a Critique of Positivist Epistemology*, 7th edition [1926], translated by G. Reisman, Princeton: D. van Nostrand.

Rickert, H. (1986), *The Limits of Concept Formation in Natural Science*, [1902] 5th edition [1929], edited and translated by G. Oakes, Cambridge: Cambridge University Press.

Rickman, H.P. (ed.) (1961), *Wilhelm Dilthey: Pattern and Meaning in History – Thoughts on History and Society*, New York: Harper & Row.

Rickman, H.P. (1967), *Understanding and the Human Studies*, London: Heinemann.

Rickman, H.P. (1976), 'Introduction' in Dilthey.

Rickman, H.P. (1979), *Wilhelm Dilthey: Pioneer of the Human Studies*, London: Paul Elek.

Rickman, H.P. (1988), *Dilthey Today: a Critical Appraisal of the Contemporary Relevance of his Work*, Westport, Connecticut: Greenwood Press.

Riha, T. (1985), 'German political economy: a history of an alternative economics', *International Journal of Social Economics*, 12.

Robbins, L. (1932), *The Nature and Significance of Economic Science*, second edition 1935, London: Macmillan.

Roscher, W. (1972), *Principles of Political Economy*, [1854] thirteenth edition [1877], translated by J.J. Lalor, New York: Arno Press.

Rosner, P. (1990), 'To what extent was the Austrian school subjectivist? A Note on Carl Menger', PPE-Lectures, Lecture 3, Department of Economics, University of Vienna, April.

Rothbard, M.N. (1973), 'Praxeology as the method of economics', in Natanson, M. (ed.), *Phenomenology and the Social Sciences*, vol. 2, Evanston: Northwestern University Press.

Rothbard, M.N. (1976a), 'Praxeology: the methodology of Austrian economics', in Dolan (ed.) (1976).

Rothbard, M.N. (1976b) 'New light on the prehistory of the Austrian School', in Dolan (ed.) (1976).

Rothbard, M.N. (1989), 'The hermeneutical invasion of philosophy and economics', *Review of Austrian Economics*, 3.

Rotwein, E. (1986), 'Flirting with apriorism: Caldwell on Mises', *History of Political Economy*, 18:4.

Runciman, W.G. (1972), *A Critique of Max Weber's Philosophy of Social Science*, Cambridge: Cambridge University Press.

Runde, J.H. (1988), 'Subjectivism, psychology, and the modern Austrians', in P.E. Earl (ed.), *Psychological Economics: Development. Tensions, Prospects*, Boston: Kluwer Academic.

Sadri, M. (1982), 'Reconstruction of Max Weber's notion of rationality: an immanent model', *Social Research*, 49.

Scaff, L.A. (1984), 'Weber before Weberian sociology', *British Journal of Sociology*, 35 (2).

Schefold, B. (ed.) (1994), *Wilhelm Roscher und seine 'Ansichten der Volkswirtschaft aus dem geschichtlichen Standpunkte'*, Düsseldorf: Verlag Wirtschaft und Finanzen.

Schmoller, G. von (1883), 'Die Schriften von K. Menger und W. Dilthey zur Methodologie der Staats-und Sozialwissenschaften', in Schmoller (1968); partial translation in Small (1924).

Schmoller, G. von (1952), 'Schmoller on Roscher', in H.W. Spiegel (ed.), *The Development of Economic Thought: Great Economists in Perspective*, New York: John Wiley.

Schmoller, G. von (1968), *Zur Literaturgeschichte der Staats- und Sozialwissenschaften* [1888], New York: Burt Franklin.

Schnädelbach, H. (1984), *Philosophy in Germany 1831–1933*, translated by Eric Matthews, Cambridge: Cambridge University Press.

Schön, M. (1987), 'Gustav Schmoller and Max Weber', in Mommsen and Osterhammel (eds) (1987).

Schumpeter, J.A. (1910), *Das Wesen und der Hauptinhalt der theoretischen Nationalökonomie*, Leipzig: Duncker & Humblot.

Schumpeter, J.A. (1954a), *Economic Doctrine and Method* [1912], translated by R. Aris, London: Allen & Unwin.

Schumpeter, J.A. (1954b), *History of Economic Analysis*, London: Allen & Unwin.

Schweitzer, A. (1970), 'Typological method in economics: Max Weber's contribution', *History of Political Economy*, 2.

Shackle, G.L.S. (1980), 'Letter to Alex H. Shand concerning his monograph', in Shand (1980).

Shand, A.H. (1980), *Subjectivist Economics: the New Austrian School*, London: Pica Press.

Shearmur, J. (1992), 'Subjectivism, explanation and the Austrian tradition', in Caldwell and Böhm (eds) (1992).

Small, A. (1924), *The Origins of Sociology*, New York: Russell & Russell.

Smith, B. (1986a), 'Preface: Austrian economics from Menger to Hayek', in Grassl and Smith (eds) (1986).

Smith, B. (1986b), 'Austrian economics and Austrian philosophy', in Grassl and Smith (eds) (1986).

Smith, B. (1990a), 'Aristotle, Menger, Mises: an essay in the metaphysics of economics', in Caldwell (ed.) (1990).

Smith, B. (1990b), 'The question of apriorism', *Austrian Economics Newsletter*, 12 (1).

Smith, B. (1990c), 'On the Austrianness of Austrian economics', *Critical Review*, 4.

Smith, B. (1994), 'The philosophy of Austrian economics', *Review of Austrian Economics*, 7 (2).

Spadaro, L.M. (ed.) (1978), *New Directions in Austrian Economics*, Kansas City: Sheed Andrews and McMeel, Inc.

Streissler, E.W. (1969), 'Structural economic thought: on the significance of the Austrian School today', *Zeitshrift für Nationalökonomie*, 29.

Streissler, E.W. (1972), 'To what extent was the Austrian school marginalist?', *History of Political Economy*, 4.

Streissler, E.W. (1990a), 'Arma Virumque Cano: Friedrich von Wieser, the bard as economist' [1986], in Littlechild (ed.) (1990), vol. I.

Streissler, E.W. (1990b), 'The intellectual and political impact of the Austrian school of economics' [1988], in Littlechild (ed.) (1990), vol. I.

Streissler, E.W. (1990c), 'Menger, Böhm-Bawerk, and Wieser: the origins of the Austrian School', in Hennings and Samuels (eds) (1990).

Streissler, E.W. (1990d), 'The influence of German economics on the work of Menger and Marshall', in Caldwell (ed.) (1990).

Streissler, E.W. (1990e), 'Carl Menger and economic policy: the lectures to Crown Prince Rudolf', in Caldwell (ed.) (1990).

Streissler, E.W. (1994), 'Wilhelm Roscher als führender Wirtschaftstheoretiker', in Schefold (ed.) (1994).

Tenbruck, F.H. (1987), 'Max Weber and Eduard Meyer', in Mommsen and Osterhammel (eds) (1987).

Tribe, K. (1980), 'Introduction to Weber', *Economy and Society*, 9 (4).

Tuttle, H.N. (1969), *Wilhelm Dilthey's Philosophy of Historical Understanding: a Critical Analysis*, Leiden: E.J. Brill.

Vaughn, K.I. (1978), 'The reinterpretation of Carl Menger: some notes on recent scholarship', *Atlantic Economic Journal*, VI (3).

Vaughn, K.I. (1982), 'Subjectivism, predictability, and creativity: comment on Buchanan', in Kirzner (ed.) (1994).

Vaughn, K.I. (1990), 'The Mengerian roots of the Austrian revival', in Caldwell (ed.) (1990).

Vaughn, K.I. (1994), *Austrian Economics in America: The Migration of a Tradition*, Cambridge: Cambridge University Press.

Weber, Max (1949a), *The Methodology of the Social Sciences*, translated and edited by E.A. Shils and H.A. Finch, Glencoe, Illinois: Free Press.

Weber, Max (1949b), ' "Objectivity" in social science and social policy' [1904], in Weber (1949a).

Weber, Max (1949c), 'Critical studies in the logic of the cultural sciences: a critique of Eduard Meyer's methodological views' [1905], in Weber (1949a).

Weber, Max (1949d), 'The meaning of "ethical neutrality" in sociology and economics' [1917], in Weber (1949a).

Weber, Max (1964), *The Theory of Social and Economic Organization*, edited by T.Parsons [1947], translated by A.M. Henderson and T. Parsons, London: Free Press of Glencoe.

Weber, Max (1968), *Economy and Society* [1921], edited by G. Roth and C. Wittich, New York: Bedminster.

Weber, Max (1970), *Max Weber: the Interpretation of Social Reality*, edited by J.E.T. Eldridge, London: Michael Joseph.

Weber, Max (1973a), *Gesammelte Aufsätze zur Wissenschaftslehre*, Tübingen: J.C.B. Mohr (Paul Siebeck).

Weber, Max (1973b), 'Die Grenznutzlehre und das "psychophysische Grundgesetz"' [1908], in Weber (1973a).

Weber, Max (1973c), 'Über einige Kategorien der verstehenden Soziologie' [1913], in Weber (1973a).

Weber, Max (1975a), *Roscher and Knies: the Logical Problems of Historical Economics* [1903–1906], translated with an introduction by Guy Oakes, New York: Free Press.

Weber, Max (1975b), 'Marginal utility theory and "the fundamental law of psychophysics"' [1908], translated by L. Schneider, *Social Science Quarterly*, 56.

Weber, Max (1977), *Critique of Stammler* [1907], translated with an Introduction by G. Oakes, New York: Free Press.

Weber, Max (1980), 'The national state and economic policy (Freiburg address)' [1895], translated by B. Fowkes, *Economy and Society*, 9 (4).

Weber, Max (1981), 'Some categories of interpretive sociology' [1913], translated by E. Graber, *Sociological Quarterly*, 22.

Weber, W. and Streissler, E. (1973), 'The Menger tradition', in Hicks and Weber (eds) (1973).

White, L.H. (1990a), 'Methodology of the Austrian School' [1984], in Littlechild (ed.) (1990), vol. I.

White, L.H. (1990b), 'Restoring an "Altered" Menger', in Caldwell (ed.) (1990).

White, L.H. (1992), 'Afterword: appraising Austrian economics: contentions and misdirections', in Caldwell and Böhm (eds) (1992).

Wieser, F. von (1967), *Social Economics* [1914], translated by A.F. Hinrichs, New York: Augustus M. Kelley.

Wieser, F. von (1994a), 'The Austrian school and the theory of value' [1891], in Kirzner (ed.) (1994), vol. I.

Wieser, F. von (1994b), 'The nature and substance of theoretical economics' [1911], in Kirzner (ed.) (1994), vol. I.

Willey, T.E. (1978), *Back to Kant: the Revival of Kantianism in German Social and Historical Thought, 1860–1914*, Detroit: Wayne State University Press.

Windelband, W. (1901), *A History of Philosophy with Especial Reference to the Formation and Development of its Problems and Conceptions*, second edition, translated by J.H. Tufts, New York: Macmillan.

Windelband, W. (1980), 'History and natural science', [1894], translated by G. Oakes, *History and Theory*, 19.

Yagi, K. (1993), 'Carl Menger's *Grundsätze* in the making', *History of Political Economy*, 25 (4).

Yeager, L.B. (1987), 'Why subjectivism?', *Review of Austrian Economics*, 1.
Yeager, L.B. (1993), 'Mises and his critics on ethics, rights, and law', in Herbener (ed.) (1993).

Index

Addleson, M. 46
Alter, M. 35, 36, 38, 39, 40, 41, 43, 50, 51, 53, 55, 59
Aristotelian realism 32, 33, 34, 39, 41, 42, 44, 45, 57, 145, 157, 180, 183, 190–91, 228
Aristotle 57, 80, 178
  Nicomachaean Ethics 33
astronomy
  precision of calculations 94
Austrian economics 1, 3, 38
  and British economics 46
  and Marshallian analyses 46
  post-Mengerian decline of 46
  and scientism 46
  in Vienna 1920s and 1930s 46
  and Walrasian analyses 46–7
Austrianness 2
Austrian philosophy 1, 31–5, 176, 180, 188
  and Aristotelian heritage 32, 33, 34, 41, 176
  impositionist *a priori* 33, 179
  and Kantianism 32
  reflectionist *a priori* 33, 35, 179, 180, 187
Austrian thought 2, 9, 31, 39, 221
  and Aristotelian realism 9, 15, 31, 178, 228
  development of 2–3
  independent of German influence 19, 176, 228
  and scholastic tradition 9, 19, 31, 178, 228
  subjectivism in 9, 14, 18

Birner, J. 53
Blaug, M. 220–21
Böhm-Bawerk, E. von 3, 157, 179, 227
  and Aristotelian realism 44
  on exact method as 'isolating' method 44

and Historical School 44
and mantle of subjectivism 3
and Menger's subjectivism 44
and neoclassical simplifications 38
role of capital 43
as second generation Austrian 38
and subjectivist methodology and epistemology 43, 44, 45–6
and supply side 43
theory of production 43
value and price theory 44
Bostaph, S. 20, 23, 40
Brentano, F. 34
Brubaker, R. 159
Buchanan, J.M. 186
Buckle, H.T.
  The History of Civilization in England 25–7
Bulhof, I.N. 97, 100, 101, 102, 116
Burger, T. 136, 148, 169

Caldwell, B. 2, 3
chemistry 70
classical economics 20, 21, 23, 35, 39, 50, 51, 92, 156

determinism 8
Dilthey, W. 9, 12, 125, 127, 142, 143, 144, 174, 227, 230–31
  on agency and time 100–101, 102
  and classical economics 92
  on descriptive psychology 11, 96–102, 108, 112, 126
  on *die Geisteswissenschaften* 93, 126, 128
  and Droysen 10
  and 'hermeneutical circle' 117–18
  his hermeneutical orientation 96, 112–13, 116–17, 120, 231
  and Historicism 91, 92
  on human agents 92, 95, 96, 98–9,